Medicinal Wild
Plants of the Prairie

Medicinal Wild Plants of the Prairie

An Ethnobotanical Guide

Kelly Kindscher

Drawings by William S. Whitney

University Press of Kansas

© 1992 by the University Press of Kansas

Plant drawings © 1992 by William S. Whitney

Published by the University Press of Kansas (Lawrence, Kansas 66049), which was organized by the Kansas Board of Regents and is operated and funded by Emporia State University, Fort Hays State University, Kansas State University, Pittsburg State University, the University of Kansas, and Wichita State University

Printed in the United States of America

10 9 8 7 6 5 4

The paper used in this publication meets the minimum requirements of the American National Standard for Permanence of Paper for Printed Library Materials z39.48-1984.

Library of Congress Cataloging-in-Publication Data

Kindscher, Kelly.

    Medicinal wild plants of the prairie : an ethnobotanical guide / Kelly Kindscher ; drawings by William S. Whitney.

    p.   cm.

Includes bibliographical references and index.

ISBN 0-7006-0526-6 (alk. paper : hardcover)—ISBN 0-7006-0527-4 (paper)

    1. Indians of North America—Great Plains—Ethnobotany. 2. Indians of North America—Prairie Provinces—Ethnobotany. 3. Ethnobotany—Great Plains. 4. Ethnobotany—Prairie Provinces. I. Title.

E78.G73K56   1992

581.6'34'097–dc20   91-38471

British Library Cataloguing in Publication Data is available.

To
Daniel Bentley

Contents

Preface

The ecology and human use of our native prairie plants have been areas of great interest to me. With the completion of *Edible Wild Plants of the Prairie* in 1987, I had already begun to accumulate considerable information on medicinal prairie plants. I decided that investigating this area of knowledge would be a useful pursuit and a valuable contribution to the conservation of prairies and prairie plants.

Many people have provided assistance and support during the completion of this book. The project formally started as a master's thesis in the Department of Systematics and Ecology at the University of Kansas. I am thankful for help and guidance from my committee members: Jerry DeNoyelles, Bill Bloom, Jerry Stannard, and Craig Martin.

The following University of Kansas faculty and staff members were also helpful in providing information and feedback: Les Mitscher, Department of Medicinal Chemistry; Bud Hersh and Roy Gridley, English Department; Don Stull, Anthropology Department; and Ron McGregor of the McGregor Herbarium. The Kansas Biological Survey provided funding for background research at the beginning of this project, supervised by Ed Martinko and Ralph Brooks. The Interlibrary Loan Department of the Kansas University Library helped me track down many obscure plant references.

The project grew as I worked to transform the thesis into a book and to add more ethnobotanical and recent scientific information. For their help in this process, I want to thank William S. Whitney, whose illustrations capture the spirit of each plant; Travis J. Berkley for his precise work in making the plant distribution maps; Craig Freeman for his carefully crafted plant descriptions; Ted Barkley for his review of the manuscript and his constructive criticism; Steven Foster for providing a second helpful review and many useful follow-up references and suggestions; Rich Niebaum for his editing; Sandra Strand for her personal support; the staff at the University Press of Kansas; and Daniel Bentley, to whom the book is dedicated, for his inspiration and his willingness to share medicinal plant information, observations, interests, and esoterica over the last fifteen years.

Many people have provided other information and help. I would like to acknowledge: Florentine Blue Thunder, Carolyn Coleman, Caryn Goldberg, Katherine Greene, Linda Gwaltney, Ken Lassman, Chris Lauver, Alex and Marj Lunderman, Laurie Mackey, Chuck and Joey Magerl, Fred Scheutz, Alice Steuerwald, Dave Van Hee, Bill Ward, and Julie Waters. I am also grateful to my parents, the members of the Kansas Areas Watershed (KAW) Council, and my friends for their unfailing support and encouragement.

Introduction

To develop a way of life in greater harmony with the environment, we need to know our place in the world. One important way to do this is to study the plants around us. My goals in writing this book are twofold: to promote a greater understanding of prairie plants and their uses and to encourage the conservation, protection, and reestablishment of prairie plants and prairies throughout the region. There is a great need to preserve the biodiversity of the prairie because of the loss of prairies to the plow, to development, and through overgrazing.

First the homeland of the Indians, whose impact was noticeable but small, the North American prairie has been transformed by travelers and emigrants crossing it, by cattlemen's stock heavily grazing it, by pioneers and farmers extensively plowing it, and by developers building on it. Today the inherent value of the remaining native prairie is beginning to be recognized. Some prairies are managed properly for grazing or as hay meadows; others are now preserved and protected for their beauty, history, ecological richness, and future uses for all beings. It is my hope that the information that follows on the medicinal use of prairie plants will nurture the seeds of conservation and increase appreciation of this resource.

Generally people relate more strongly to individual species, such as the panda, the bald eagle, or a rare orchid, than to biological communities, such as wetlands or the tallgrass prairie. The developing awareness of and affection for wild creatures is demonstrated by public support for the Endangered Species Act enacted in 1973, and the recent growth of local, national, and global environmental organizations.

I also hope that by highlighting the history, ecology, and pharmacology of medicinal prairie plants, I can contribute to making this information part of the current folklore of these plants and help establish their value as a potential source of future medicines. It may then become easier to protect and preserve remnants of native prairies in areas where such plant communities have been almost totally destroyed—primarily in suburban areas, but also in areas where agriculture has converted most of the landscape to crop production. In addition, many of these plants have horticultural value and can be planted in wildlife areas, along roadsides, on farms, and especially in flower beds and for landscaping.

For all these reasons, it is important to educate people about specific prairie plants. Public understanding of the relationship between people and plants is an essential factor in preserving biodiversity, because this knowledge gives us a reason to safeguard this relationship. When we learn to recognize individual species, such as the purple coneflower, butterfly milkweed, and leadplant; when

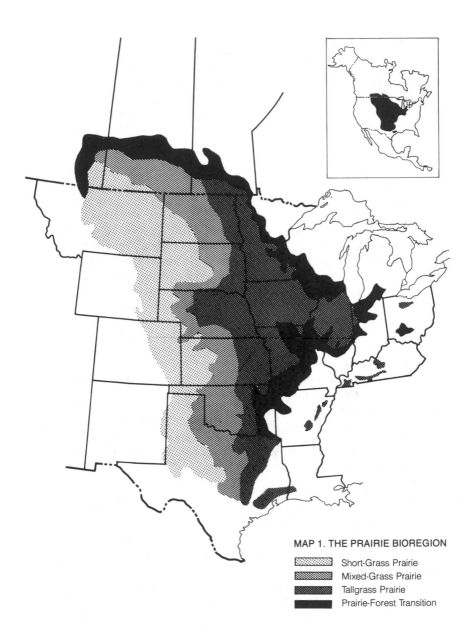

MAP 1. THE PRAIRIE BIOREGION

░░░ Short-Grass Prairie
▨▨▨ Mixed-Grass Prairie
▦▦▦ Tallgrass Prairie
■■■ Prairie-Forest Transition

we understand their historical importance and their potential uses, then we can tell their stories to others, and in this way communicate their importance.

The intended audience for this book is broad, encompassing readers whose interest in prairie plants has arisen from a variety of perspectives: those who are interested in the prairie plants themselves, Indian uses of plants, potential human uses, herbal medicine, the history of medicine, medicinal chemistry and pharmacology, horticulture, and the history and geography of the Prairie Bioregion.

This book is neither an herbal nor a medical guide. It is primarily a history of the traditions and beliefs that have surrounded the medicinal use of native prairie plants. While many of these plants do have medicinal value, this book provides only limited information on their medical uses. It should not be interpreted as promoting experimental use of these plants. This book contains descriptions, not prescriptions.

The geographical setting for this study is the North American prairie, referred to here as the Prairie Bioregion (see Map 1). Bioregions are geographical areas whose "soft" boundaries are determined by nature, in contrast to the "hard" boundaries of politically defined areas, such as states. The Prairie Bioregion is distinguished from the neighboring Rocky Mountain and Ozark bioregions by characteristic plants, animals, water relations, climate, and geology. For a discussion of the concept of bioregions, see Kirkpatrick Sale's *Dwellers in the Land: The Bioregional Vision* (1985) and J. J. Parsons "On 'Bioregionalism' and 'Watershed Consciousness'" (1985).

The Prairie Bioregion is immense, covering over 3 million square kilometers (1 million square miles). It stretches from Texas north to Saskatchewan and from the Rocky Mountains (from New Mexico to Montana) in the west to the deciduous forests of Missouri, Indiana, and Wisconsin in the east. It is a region of few trees, but it contains a rich variety of grasses and wildflowers that are drought tolerant and require full sunlight. Before intervention by European settlers, fires started by Indians or by lightning prevented shrubs and trees from becoming established, except in moist soils and protected areas (Wells, 1970, pp. 1,574–82). Drought and the grazing of buffalo, antelope, and elk also helped keep trees out of the area.

The Prairie Bioregion can be divided into three north-south zones: the tallgrass prairie in the east; the mixed-grass prairie in the center; and short-grass prairie in the west. These last two areas are often defined as the Great Plains. The tallgrass prairie is dominated by big bluestem, *Andropogon gerardii*; Indian grass, *Sorghastrum nutans*; switch grass,

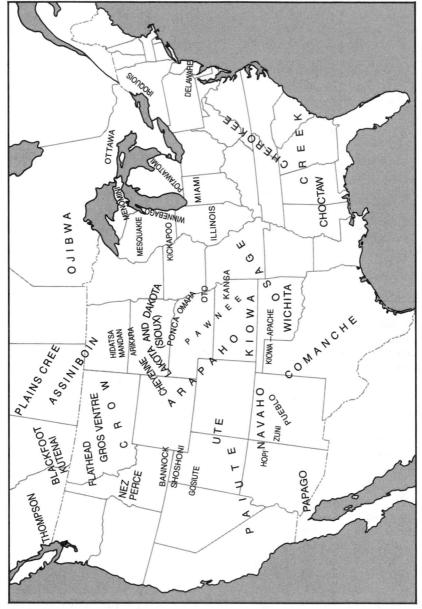

MAP 2. Indian tribes mentioned in this book that used prairie plants for medicinal purposes (locations c. A.D. 1700, before white settlement).

4

Panicum virgatum; and little blue-stem, *Andropogon scoparius.* The soil of the tallgrass prairie is rich and fertile, and rainfall is adequate for row crops. As a result, much of the area has been plowed for agriculture.

The short-grass prairie features buffalo grass, *Buchloë dactyloides,* and blue grama and hairy grama grasses, *Bouteloua gracilis* and *B. hirsuta.* Here large herds of buffalo once roamed. Because of its dry climate, the short-grass prairie is best suited for grazing, although drought-tolerant and irrigated crops are now grown here. For a further discussion of the entire region, see *The Prairie World* by David Costello (1981) and the Introduction to *Flora of the Great Plains* (Great Plains Flora Association, 1986).

As the name implies, the mixed-grass prairie contains a mixture of species from the other two zones. The proportions of various plants change over the years, depending on rainfall cycles. Overall, the flora of the Prairie Bioregion is quite varied. There are more species of forbs and woody plants than grasses, and many of these species have been used as medicine.

The European woodland per-spective associated with our domi-nant historical roots, a perspective that maintains "woods are best," still colors perceptions of the Prai-rie Bioregion and its use. Public parks throughout the region are rarely prairies; most often they are planted with nonnative grass species, such as fescue, and shade trees. When people think of wild-flowers or medicinal plants, they seldom think of prairie species, even if they live in the Prairie Bio-region or near a prairie remnant. To most people, wilderness means virgin forest rather than virgin prairie. It is not surprising, then, that at the time this is written, the prairie is still not represented in our national park system. Its uniqueness has been little appreci-ated.

This study documents the use of 203 native prairie plant species used as medicine by Indians, settlers, and doctors. This informa-tion is primarily historical, since the Indians of the region made the greatest use of these plants (Indians used 172 of these species). Many of these plants were also used by doctors from the time of first settlement (the 1830s in the earliest areas) until the 1930s. Only a few have been studied more recently to determine the bio-logically active compounds they contain.

Ethnobotanical reports and his-torical accounts provide informa-tion on uses of medicinal prairie plants by the following twenty-five Indian tribes that have lived in the region (see Map 2): Arapahos, Arikaras, Assiniboins, Blackfeet, Cheyennes, Comanches, Crows, Dakotas, Gros Ventres, Hidatsas, Illinois, Kansas, Kiowas, Kiowa-Apaches, Lakotas, Mandans,

5

Omahas, Osages, Otoes, Pawnees, Poncas, Sioux (both Lakotas and Dakotas), Plains Crees, Wichitas, and Winnebagos. There is more ethnobotanical information on the Sioux than on any other Indian tribe of the region, so I have divided it to present information on the two groups within the Sioux tribe, the Lakotas and Dakotas.

Because there was trading and communication between tribes, I have also included information from tribes outside the region on the prairie plants whose geographical ranges extend into their native homelands. These tribes include the Cherokees, Chippewas, Choctaws, Creeks, Delawares, Flatheads, Gosiutes, Hopis, Iroquois, Kickapoos, Kutenais, Mesquakies (sometimes called the Meskakis or Fox), Miamis, Navahos, Objibwas, Ottawas, Paiutes, Papagos, Potawatomis, Shoshones, Tewas, Thompsons, Utes, and Zunis. It is probable that information concerning medicinal uses of plants was shared between tribes and that in at least some cases, these plants were used similarly.

I have made three visits to the Rosebud Sioux Reservation in South Dakota to learn about the use of medicinal plants by the Lakotas. During my visits I saw that some medicine men and traditional Lakotas still use a variety of plants in their healing practices. However, they use plants for spiritual healing, not because they contain medicinal substances.

They believe that the spirit heals rather than the plant. Through my visits, I have come to respect this perspective on healing and have greatly appreciated the wisdom that has been shared with me.

This situation created a dilemma for me. The traditional Lakotas believe in an oral tradition—that learning comes through experience, discipline, and rituals. From their perspective, it is not appropriate for some "white guy" like me to drive up for a few days, ask questions about medicinal plants, then go home and publish his field notes.

I respect this perspective because it tells me how they view truth. For them, truth is deeper than just facts or observations. I am a student of that deeper truth, and I believe that what I have learned so far are only observations. For that reason, I have grounded this book on the historical information I uncovered rather than the wisdom of the traditional Lakotas I met while conducting my research. Beyond the information I have provided here is the truth about the use of plants for healing.

Most Indian tribes had hierarchies of medicinal plants, with certain plants commonly used for a wide variety of purposes. Ales Hrdlicka, a medical doctor and physical anthropologist at the Smithsonian Institution, emphasized this when he stated in 1932:

*In every tribe the older women
and men knew scores of herbs
and various mechanical or other
means, which they employed
exactly as did many of our country grandmothers and grand-
fathers, simply, rationally, and
often with marked success. They
knew poisons, emetics, cathartics,
antifebriles, tonics, narcotics, and
hemostatics, cleansing solutions,
healing gums and powders. They
had antidotes. They employed
massage, pressure, scarification,
cauterization, bandaging, splints,
sucking, enemas, cutting, scrap-
ing, and suturing.*

*But whenever the cause of a
complaint was obscure, or when
the complaint was proving dangerous and all ordinary aid had
failed, particularly if this was in a
hitherto healthy adult—then their
minds turned to the supernatural
(Hrdlicka, 1932, pp. 1661–66).*

There were both medicine men
and medicine women in the Plains
Indian tribes (Denig, 1930, p. 422;
and Grinnell, 1905, p. 37). Frederick Hodge stated in his *Handbook of American Indians North
of Mexico*: "These shaman healers
as a rule were shrewd . . . ; some
were sincere, noble characters,
worthy of respect; others were
charlatans to a greater or less degree" (Hodge, 1959, p. 838). As
part of their healing ceremonies,
they used ritual, songs, drumming,
prayer, and medicinal plants.

The Indians did not separate the
use of these various methodologies
in their healing practices. For the
purpose of this study, however, I
have examined one component in
isolation—their use of medicinal
plants.

Medicinal plants have played
a major role in the health and
healing system of the Indians.
This system is not static, but
has changed to meet new needs.
Diseases that were apparently
brought to North America from
Europe, such as venereal disease
and smallpox, have in some cases
been treated with native prairie
plants (Camazine and Bye, 1980,
pp. 381–83).

The Indians of the region also
used moxa. For this they burned a
piece of a plant (such as the stem
of lead plant, *Amorpha canescens*) on top of an injury. The
burn was believed to counteract
the injury underneath it. Moxa is
used in Asia today to stimulate
an acupuncture point or serve as a
counterirritant. The use of moxa
shows a link in healing methodologies between native peoples of
Asia and North America. Plants
used as moxa by the Plains Indians include: lead plant, *Amorpha
canescens*; asters, *Aster* species;
white sage, *Artemisia ludoviciana*; nine-anther prairie clover,
Dalea enneandra; round head
lespedeza, *Lespedeza capitata*;
prickly pear, *Opuntia* species;
prairie ground cherry, *Physalis
pumila heterophylla*; and wild
alfalfa, *Psoralea tenuiflora*.

There are also examples in
Indian medicine of what in Europe

7

was known as the Doctrine of Signatures, or belief in signs. According to this doctrine, the distinctive characteristics of a plant revealed its medical uses. For example, both the green milkweed, *Asclepias viridiflora*, and snow-on-the-mountain, *Euphorbia marginata*, have milky sap, which was taken as a sign or signature that these plants were good medicines for nursing mothers who needed to produce more breast milk.

The Indians' tremendous knowledge of prairie plants is evident throughout the book. Probably all native plants had Indian names, and in some cases the Indians recognized a greater number of species or varieties than we do. For example, Beebalm, *Monarda fistulosa*, is recognized today to have two distinct varieties in the Great Plains (Great Plains Flora Association, 1986, p. 725; and Gilmore, 1977, p. 59). The Pawnees had four names to distinguish the four varieties they recognized and used.

At least two plants, yarrow, *Achillea millefolium*, and sage, *Artemisia* species, were used almost identically by Indians in North America and folk practitioners in Europe before the two cultures had contact. Concerning *Artemisia*, the botanist William Chase Stevens stated:

In the New World, as in the Old, the lives of the natives were intimately and vitally related to the plant population, and it need not surprise us that our Indians put the indigenous Artemisias to much the same medicinal uses as the early Europeans and Asiatics did theirs; but that our Indians should have, as they did, the same kind of superstitions about the Artemisias and use them in similar rites and ceremonies, with confidence in their magic powers is amazing (Stevenson, 1915, p. 422).

In addition, there were some highly specialized uses of plants that today are considered to be dangerous. For example, yucca, *Yucca glauca*, and puccoon, *Lithospermum* species, were known to be birth control substances, and locoweed, *Oxytropis* species, was used for sore throat, asthma, sores, ear troubles, and to increase the flow of breast milk (Johnston, 1970, p. 314; Hellson, 1974, p. 73; and Hart, 1981, p. 29). These species contain poisonous substances, so successful use indicates considerable knowledge.

Many of the Indians' remedies can be explained by the presence of pharmacologically active substances in the plants. Twenty-eight of the 203 plants included in this study have been listed at some time in the *U.S. Pharmacopoeia*. However, the majority have ranges that extend into the more wooded eastern United States. There was only one species listed in the *U.S. Pharmacopoeia*, the purple coneflower, *Echinacea angustifolia*, that had a range confined to the Prairie Bioregion. This does not indicate that the prairie has fewer plants with biologically active substances, but rather, that prairie plants have not been sufficiently studied. It has been estimated that only 5 to 15 percent of the world's 250,000 to 750,000 existing species of higher plants have been surveyed for biologically active compounds, and many of those have been analyzed for only one type of compound, such as antitumor agents (Croom, 1983, p. 23).

There is a growing recognition of the value of plants for medicines. The World Health Organization concluded "that to meet the minimum health needs of developing countries by the year 2000, traditional medicine must be utilized" (ibid.).

There is also a growing interest in plant medicines in the more developed countries. In Germany, a country with liberal regulations on herbal preparations based on a strong tradition of natural drug usage, a survey found that 76 percent of women interviewed drank herbal teas for their beneficial effects, and about 52 percent turned to herbal remedies for the initial treatment of minor illnesses (Tyler, 1986, p. 281). It is remarkable that the greatest interest in the purple coneflower today comes from Germany, where most of the research on its immunostimulatory properties is being conducted. This plant, native only to North America, was also the medicinal plant most widely used by the Indians of the Prairie Bioregion.

In the United States, public interest in herbs and medicinal plants has spawned a booming industry that is expected to gain momentum. Varro Tyler, a medicinal chemist, stated that "a government that underwrites a program for engineers to send people to the moon will probably be forced to provide some support to biological scientists to investigate plant drugs to cure human disease." He predicts that the government will "therefore ease somewhat the unnecessarily rigid standards for marketing new drugs, particularly drugs from plants long in use as folk remedies, and thus stimulate more producers to begin research and development of them" (ibid.).

Many plants have been used for medicinal purposes in the United States. An 1849 study by the American Medical Association showed that there were more than a thousand species of plants in the United States "reputed to possess medicinal qualities of value in the treatment of disease" (Davis, 1849, p. 663). In 1950, the American drug trade was using about 900 plant species, but only 350 of them were native, naturalized, or cultivated. Although no exact figures are available, it is estimated that 40 percent of the prescription drugs now sold in the United States contain at least one ingredient derived from nature. Up to 25 percent of our prescription drugs contain an ingredient derived from higher (flowering) plants (Foster and Duke, 1990, p. vii). Although further study of native prairie plants in the laboratory probably will not find a cure for cancer or AIDS, antitumor agents and substances that stimulate the human immune system have been discovered in some of these plants.

The medicinal constituents and ethnobotanical uses of the plants of the Prairie Bioregion have not been adequately studied. The most comprehensive study to date is Melvin Gilmore's ethnobotanical work on the Indians of the Prairie Bioregion, *Uses of Plants by the Indians of the Missouri River Region*, first published in 1919 (Gilmore, 1977). In this work, Gilmore recounted the use of plants by the Omahas, Poncas, Dakotas and Lakotas, Pawnees, and Winnebagos. He reported the ethnobotanical use of over 150 species, either for food or for medicinal purposes.

I have identified 203 species of native prairie plants that were used medicinally by Indians of the Prairie Bioregion. The medicinal use of these plants was probably as important, if not more important, than their use as food. A previous study showed that only 123 species of prairie plants were used for food (Kindscher, 1987, p. 4). Many plants were used for both food and medicine, but medicine was usually made with more potent parts of the plant and with different preparation techniques, and higher dosages were given. A few well-known medicinal species (peyote, *Lophophora williamsii*;

jimsonweed, *Datura innoxia*; and tobacco, *Nicotiana rustica*) were excluded from this study because they are not native to the Prairie Bioregion. Their use in this region is probably a relatively recent development.

Paul Vestal and Richard Schultes of the Harvard Botanical Museum concluded in 1939 that "the economic botany of no group of Indians in North America is probably so inadequately known as is that of the Plains tribes" (Vestal and Schultes, 1939, p. 83). Since then, there have been few studies of specific Plains tribes. This is the first study of the medicinal plants of the entire Prairie Bioregion.

In examining both the ethnobotanical and historical literature on the Prairie Bioregion, I found little recorded use of tree species or aquatic species. This supports the conclusions of historians and plant ecologists that the region had few trees before white settlers arrived. It also indicates that tribes like the Mesquakies of present-day Iowa, who used primarily prairie plants for their medicines, are people of the prairie rather than the woodland. Their affinities remain with the original and predominant vegetation type of their native homelands, the prairies.

In addition to studying the Indian use of these plants, I investigated their use by pioneers and settlers in Anglo folk medicine and by medical practitioners. I also reviewed recent scientific research involving native prairie plants. It is significant that all prairie plants that were used by medical practitioners had been used previously by the Indians of the region.

By the time the region was being settled, many of the Indians had been displaced and removed to reservations. What little contact there was between the remaining Indians and white settlers was generally not conducive to the sharing of information. This lack of positive interaction may explain why the medicinal use of native prairie plants by pioneers and settlers on the Oregon, California, and Santa Fe trails was almost nonexistent (Olch, 1985, pp. 196–212). In addition, the fundamentally different spiritual worldviews that underlay the health systems of the two groups effectively prevented the exchange of information on plants or health.

A study of Kansas folklore listed 1,017 folk customs concerning "The Prevention and Cure of Illnesses and Injuries" (Koch, 1980). This was the largest number of customs in any of the twelve areas of Kansas folklore studied, indicating that health and healing were primary concerns. Nevertheless, only a handful of plants native to the region were used for treatments (prickly pear was listed three times, cedar trees were listed twice, and ragweed, ironweed, sagebrush, and milkweed were each listed only once). Plants from outside the region (sassafras listed nine times) and cultivated plants (tobacco listed eight times) were more frequently used. Nonplant remedies were the most common of all. Not only did settlers overlook the medicinal uses of native prairie plants, they also overlooked their potential as food (Kindscher, 1987, p. 5). In sum, since the time of settlement by pioneers, the use of plants by humans in the Prairie Bioregion has received little attention from either specialists or nonspecialists. The time is ripe for the discovery of the plants around us.

The prairie plant species covered in the study are arranged in alphabetical order by scientific name. I divided the information on the forty-three plants that have had the widest use into subcategories: Indian use, Anglo folk use, medical history, and recent scientific research. Plants of secondary use are covered more briefly in a section called Other Medicinal Plant Species. Species in the same genus are covered together because they often had similar uses. Differences in use between related species are noted.

For the major medicinal plants, a list of common names is provided. These aid in recognition of the plant and provide added information about the plant's use or characteristics. The first name listed is from the *Flora of the Great Plains*, unless it is confusing with other names. Other names were gleaned from a number of sources: Stevenson, 1915; Steyermark, 1981;

Bailey and Bailey, 1976; Bolyard et al., 1981; Erichsen-Brown, 1979; Henkel, 1906; and the Nebraska Statewide Arboretum.

Indian names and their translations offer clues to the use of a plant or a tribe's perception of it. Some tribal names, however, can be translated only to English common names. Others are meaningless to us today, because we no longer know the context in which the name originated. Even the names that don't have translations have been included to encourage future communication with native peoples concerning the uses of these plants. I have found it very helpful in my work to be able to point to a printed name of a plant in another language as part of the communication about it.

Scientific names are based on *Flora of the Great Plains* (Great Plains Flora Association, 1986). Derivation and meaning of the scientific names came from several sources (Stevens, 1961; Bare, 1979; and Bailey, 1962). For the most important species of a genus, descriptions, habitats, and geographical ranges are provided. These are condensed, primarily from *Flora of the Great Plains* and the *Atlas of the Flora of the Great Plains* (Great Plains Flora Association, 1977). The sections on Indian use, Anglo folk use, medical history, and recent scientific research constitute the main portion of each entry and are fully referenced. Information on listings in the *U.S. Pharmacopoeia* and the *National Formulary*

is from Virgil Vogel's *American Indian Medicine* (Vogel, 1970) and several editions of the *Pharmacopoeia of the United States* (1882, 1905, 1926, 1965).

The section on cultivation is included to promote the propagation of prairie plants because some are rare and many are locally uncommon. Many are attractive ornamentals suitable for wildflower gardens. A number of these plants have been harvested for the pharmaceutical trade, and harvesting methods are described in this section. Information in the cultivation section came from several sources and from personal research and observations: Art, 1986; Bailey and Bailey, 1976; Barr, 1983; Rock, 1977; Steyermark, 1981; Stevens, 1961; and Salac et al., 1978.

To help in the identification of plants discussed in this book, Bill Whitney of the Prairie/Plains Resource Institute illustrated each major species. His beautiful line drawings not only provide technical details, but also impart the essence and grace of each plant.

Maps are included to show the approximate geographical distribution of these plants. They were drawn from distributions listed in several sources: Great Plains Flora Association, 1986; Great Plains Flora Association, 1977; Steyermark, 1981; and Kindscher, 1987. Some plants will occasionally be found outside the ranges shown on these maps; others will be hard to find in portions of their ranges.

In conclusion, the Prairie Bioregion is an area with a unique array of fascinating plants. Some of the species have medicinal properties and have an interesting history of use by Indians, Anglos, and doctors. Many of these medicinal prairie plants have also been studied recently by scientists in their effort to find novel chemical substances. I hope that the stories of these plants and their uses will increase appreciation of and interest in prairie plants and ultimately lead to a greater understanding of the prairie.

Medicinal Wild
Plants of the Prairie

Achillea millefolium
Yarrow

COMMON NAMES

Yarrow, milfoil, thousandleaf, wild tansy, nosebleed, old-man's pepper, sneezewort, knight's milfoil, herbe militaris, staunchweed, bloodwort, and soldier's woundwort. The last five names refer to its use in the military to heal wounds.

INDIAN NAMES

The Cheyenne name for the plant is "i ha i se e yo" (cough medicine) (Grinnell, 1962, 2: 189). The Osage name is "wetsaoindse egon" (rattlesnake's tail-like) (Munson, 1981, p. 231). The Lakota names are "xante canxlogan" (cedar weed) and "taopi pexuta" (wound medicine) (ibid.). The Winnebago name is "hank-sintsh" (woodchuck tail), in reference to the appearance of the leaf (Gilmore, 1977, p. 82).

SCIENTIFIC NAME

Achillea millefolium L. is a member of the Asteraceae (Sunflower Family). *Achillea* refers to the Greek hero Achilles, who supposedly used this plant to heal a soldier's wounds. The species name, *millefolium*, means "thousand leaf" in reference to the many fine dissections of the leaf.

DESCRIPTION

Faintly aromatic perennial herbs 2–6 dm (¾–2 ft) tall; stems erect, woolly, few-branched above.

Leaves alternate, gradually reduced upward, 3–15 cm (1³⁄₁₆–6 in) long, 0.5–3 cm (³⁄₁₆–1³⁄₁₆ in) wide, highly dissected, with a fernlike appearance. Flower heads in domed or flat-topped clusters at ends of branches, from May to Oct; ray flowers 5, less than 3 mm (⅛ in) long, white or rarely pink; disk flowers white. Fruits dry, smooth, flattened achenes.

HABITAT

Yarrow is found on all northern continents, in prairies, meadows, open woods, and especially in areas of mild disturbance.

PARTS USED

All parts, but especially the flower tops and leaves.

INDIAN USE

Yarrow has been used in a wide variety of medicinal treatments by at least 58 different Indian tribes

17

(Chandler et al., 1982, pp. 203–23; Duke, 1986, p. 3; Shemluck, 1982, pp. 307–9; and references cited below). Many of its uses were identical to those in Europe. The most common were to treat coughing and throat irritations and to stop bleeding.

The Cheyennes used the fresh or dried plant to make a tea for these three purposes and also for colds and slight nausea (Grinnell, 1962, 2:189; Hart, 1981, p. 17). The tea stimulated sweating, to break a fever and alleviate cold symptoms, and was also drunk after a sweat bath to encourage further sweating. They also made a tea from the above-ground portions of the plant to treat respiratory diseases like tuberculosis and for heart trouble and chest pains. In addition, they chewed the leaves and also rubbed them on the body to soothe unspecified afflictions.

The Blackfeet made a tea that was taken as a diuretic in the belief that the sickness would pass with the urine. This tea was also rubbed on the affected part (Hellson, 1974, p. 69). The Osages used some unspecified part of the plant for a toothache medicine and used the flowers as a perfume (Munson, 1981, p. 231). The Lakotas used the plant to treat wounds. The entire plant was dried and then chewed and placed on the wound. A tea of the leaves was also used to treat coughing, whooping cough, and fainting (Buechel, 1983, p. 172). The Crows made a

tea that was held in the mouth to soothe toothache and sore gums (Shemluck, 1982, p. 307). They also used the crushed plant (probably fresh) for burns and made a poultice from it for boils and open sores. They added goose fat to make a salve. The Assiniboins and Gros Ventres made a tea from the flowers to treat colds and stomach complaints. The Gros Ventres also made a poultice of the boiled flowers for hand wounds (ibid.). The Winnebagos made a yarrow tea for bathing swellings, and they alleviated earaches by placing a wad of the leaves (probably fresh) in the afflicted ear (Gilmore, 1977, p. 82).

John B. Dunbar, a Presbyterian missionary who lived with the Pawnees for many years on a reservation in Nebraska, observed the use of yarrow in cauterization or moxa. This method of treatment has long been used in China and Japan as a counterirritant, and its use in combination with acupuncture has recently been brought to the attention of the American public. Among the Pawnees, it was used to relieve pain. Its use "was not infrequent. It was done by inserting a bit of the stalk of the *achillea millefolium*, about an inch long, in the skin and setting fire to the exposed end, and allowing it to burn down into the flesh. Sometimes several pieces were inserted near each other at once" (Dunbar, 1880, p. 339).

ANGLO FOLK USE

Yarrow has been a popular medicinal plant in Europe throughout the ages. It was used by Achilles and Dioscorides and has been recommended in many herbals. The Gerarde herbal, printed in England in 1636, stated:

The leaves of Yarrow do close up wounds, and keepe them from inflammation, or fiery swellings: it staunches bloud in any part of the body, and it is likewise put into bathes for women to sit in: it stoppeth the laske, and being drunke it helpeth the bloudy flix.

Most men say that the leaves chewed, and especially greene, are a remedy for the tooth-ache.

The leaves being put into the nose, do cause it to bleed, and ease the paine of the megrim. . . .

One dram in pouder of the herbe given in wine prefently taketh away the paines of colicke. (Gerarde, 1636, p. 1073)

MEDICAL HISTORY

Constantine Rafinesque wrote in his 1830 *Medical Flora or Manual of Medical Botany of the United States:*

Yarrow, common to Europe and America. Whole plant used. Bitter . . . tonic, restringent, and vulnerary, but subnarcotic and inebriant. Used for hemorrhoids, dysentery, hemotysis, menstrual afflictions, wounds, hypochondria, and cancer. The infusion and extract are employed. The American plant is stronger than the European, and has lately been exported for use: this often happens with our plants, our warm summers rendering our medical plants more efficacious. (Rafinesque, 1830, p. 185).

In his *American Medicinal Plants* (1892) Charles Millspaugh gave directions for preparations of a tincture to be used for a variety of common ailments:

The whole fresh plant should be gathered when flowering begins, excluding all old and woody stems, and chopped and pounded to a pulp; then in a new piece of linen press out thoroughly all the juice and mix it by brisk succession with an equal part by weight of alcohol. Allow the mixture to stand eight days in a dark, cool place, then filter. The tincture thus prepared should be by transmitted light of a clear reddish-orange color; its odor peculiar, resembling that of malt yeast, pungent and agreeable, like the fresh plant; to the taste acrid and slightly bitter, and shows an acid reaction to test papers.

One other related use was reported by the botanist Linnaeus, who noted that the Swedes had used yarrow instead of hops to make beer and considered the beer thus brewed to be more intoxicating (ibid., p. 335).

The dried leaves and flowering tops of yarrow were officially listed in the *U.S. Pharmacopoeia* from 1863 to 1882. They were used as a tonic, stimulant, and emmenagogue. Yarrow is still listed in the pharmacopoeias of Austria, Hungary, Poland, and Switzerland (Chandler et al., 1982, p. 205).

SCIENTIFIC RESEARCH

Yarrow's chemical constituents have received considerable study, and over 120 compounds have been identified. Other chemicals have been isolated but not completely determined, and still others have only been detected. An extract from the flower head contains a blue volatile oil called azulene, azulenelike compounds, and a water-soluble glycoprotein (ibid., pp. 210–16). It is now generally agreed, however, that azulene is found only in the North American plants of *Achillea millefolium* var. *lanulosa*. Sesquiterpene lactones found in the volatile oil have been investigated because they have novel chemical structures and are precursors for the azulenes. These lactones exhibit many interesting biological effects, including antimicrobial, cytotoxic, and anticancer activities.

The flavonoids in yarrow exhibit considerable antispasmodic activity. The alkaloid achilleine has been found to be an active hemostatic. Other compounds that may have beneficial effects include the volatile oils (menthol and camphor), tannins, sterols, and triterpenes. Some of these substances could account for the plant's apparent effectiveness in treating skin diseases. Local analgesia could result from the salicylic acid derivatives, eugenol, menthol, or other compounds in the volatile oil. The antipyretic activity may be attributable to the presence of salicylic acid derivatives, chamazulene, or other substances. Thujone is a known abortifacient and may account for yarrow's use in the treatment of problems associated with the female reproductive system (ibid.).

Constituents of the volatile oil extracted from the plant apparently have expectorant, analgesic, and diaphoretic properties that may provide relief from some cold and influenza symptoms (ibid.).

The characteristic properties of the various chemicals don't tell the whole story. Concentrations of chemical substances can vary from plant to plant. The mere presence of a substance with known effects does not mean that it will cause those effects in combination with the many other chemicals found in the plant. Yarrow, for example, contains some substances that may counteract each other. It has both achilleine, with its hemostatic properties, and coumarin, which promotes bleeding.

Yarrow is considered to be nonpoisonous. Nonetheless, some people are reported to be allergic to it, being susceptible to dermatitis (ibid.; Lampe and McCann, 1985,

p. 198). Anyone allergic to any member of the Asteraceae (Sunflower Family), which includes ragweed, should be careful in using this plant. Large or frequent doses of yarrow may be harmful, and the plant does contain small quantities of thujone, which is considered toxic (Foster and Duke, 1990, p. 64).

The leaves and flowers of yarrow are harvested when they first begin flowering because there is great variation in content of the chemical constituents (specifically oil and azulene) based on season of collection, variety, age of the plant, parts used, and habitat of the plant. For example, the content of azulene is higher in sun-grown plants (Chandler et al., 1982, p. 213; Fluck, 1955, p. 369).

Yarrow is easy to grow, hardy, drought-resistant, and aromatic; it does well in full sun. It has both lacy-leaved foliage and attractive flower clusters. It seems to thrive under stress; it can tolerate overgrazing by cattle in pastures. It is propagated by division of the rootstock in spring or fall and sometimes by cuttings. Plants are most easily grown from seed and will bloom the second year. When planted, they should be spaced 20–25 cm (8–12 in) apart (Foster, 1985, p. 168). Clumps should be divided every three to four years to stimulate growth. There are numerous cultivars of yarrow, including the reddish-pink 'Rubra' and the light pink 'Rosea.' The yellow yarrows are another species, usually *Achillea filipendulina* Lam.

Acorus calamus
Calamus

Calamus, sweet flag, sweet cane, pine root, sweet rush, and sweet sedge.

INDIAN NAMES

The Omaha and Ponca name is "makan-ninida," the Winnebago name is "mankan-kereh," the Pawnee name is "kahtsha itu" (medicine lying in water), and the Dakota name is "sinkpe-ta-wote" (muskrat food) (Gilmore, 1977, pp. 17–18). This last name is used by the Lakotas, who also call the root "sunka ce" (dog penis) in reference to its shape (Munson, 1981, p. 231). The Osage name is "pexe boao'ka" (flat herb) (ibid.). The Cheyenne name is "wi' ukh is e' evo" (bitter medicine) (Grinnell, 1962, 2:171).

SCIENTIFIC NAME

Acorus calamus L. is a member of the Araceae (Arum Family). *Acorus* is a Latin word for "aromatic plant"; the species name, *calamus*, means "reed."

DESCRIPTION

Aromatic, grasslike perennial herbs 9–15 dm (3–5 ft) tall; flowering stems 3-angled. Leaves sword-shaped, erect, thick, 9–12 dm (3–4 ft) long, 4–10 cm (1½–4 in) wide. Flowers tiny, light brown or greenish-brown, in dense cylindrical spikes 4–9 cm (1½–3½ in) long, from May to Aug. Fruits

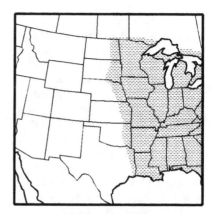

small, gelatinous, berrylike, each one containing few seeds.

HABITAT

Marshes, seepy areas, and wet ditches. Calamus is found throughout much of the world, especially in northern continents.

PARTS USED

Rhizomes, leaves, and entire plant.

INDIAN USE

Ethnobotanist Melvin Gilmore reported in 1919 on some Plains Indian uses of calamus:

All the tribes hold this plant in very high esteem. It was used as a carminative, a decoction was drunk for fever, and the rootstock was chewed as a cough remedy and as a remedy for toothache. For colic an infusion of the pounded root stock was drunk. As a remedy for colds the root-

stock was chewed or a decoction was drunk, or it was used in the smoke treatment. In fact, this part of the plant seems to have been regarded as a panacea. When a hunting party came to a place where the calamus grew the young men gathered the green blades and braided them into garlands, which they wore round the neck for their pleasant odor. It was one of the plants to which mystic powers were ascribed. The blades were used also ceremonially for garlands. In the mystery ceremonies of the Pawnee are songs about the calamus.

Among the Teton Dakota in old times warriors chewed the rootstock to a paste, which they rubbed on the face to prevent excitement and fear in the presence of the enemy (Gilmore, 1977, p. 18).

There is still some debate about whether this plant is native to the region or introduced. In either case, the Plains Indians probably established its westernmost distribution. Gilmore reported that

calamus is a plant which very seldom blooms, and I have never known it to produce seeds, so that it is not adapted to disseminate itself or invade new territory. But it is found in certain places all the way from Canada to Texas, all these places being at considerable distance from any other stations of the species.

There is a large field of Acorus calamus in the low ground in the great bend of the Mouse River in the northern part of North Dakota, not far from the village of Towner in that state. About five hundred miles away to the south, on Minichaduza River, near the south boundary of South Dakota, there is another patch of calamus. There are other patches farther to the south in the state of Nebraska on the Calamus River, on the branches of the Loup River, on the Platte and on the Republican River. In Kansas there are patches in places on the Republican, the Kansas, the Arkansas and other rivers. In Oklahoma also there are various patches on certain streams.

Acorus calamus is a plant very highly valued by Indians for medicinal and other uses. All the places which I have mentioned above as stations of this plant are well known to the people of the tribes in those regions. And all these stations are in localities formerly much frequented by them. They either are in the vicinity of old village sites, or are located near camping places on old Indian trails. My opinion is that every one of these patches had its origin by intentional planting long ago by Indian medicinemen (Gilmore, 1913a, pp. 90–91).

Further evidence that calamus was spread by Indians is contained in J. W. Blankenship's 1905 "Native Economic Plants of Montana." He wrote that calamus root is "still an object of barter among the various Indian tribes and said by the Ft. Peck Sioux to be used to cause abortion. . . . The plant is not found in Montana, but is obtained from the Indians eastward" (Blankenship, 1905, p. 5).

Calamus is still a popular remedy on the Rosebud Sioux Reservation in South Dakota. When I visited there in the summer of 1987, I brought dried and live calamus plants, which were welcomed as gifts. Several people told me that the plant did not grow on the reservation, but had been planted nearby, where it is still growing today.

The calamus root was also used by the Dakotas for the treatment of diabetes. When diabetics chewed the root regularly, they were reportedly cured within a few months. In the 1950s when Howard reported this use of calamus, he cited cases of Indian diabetics who had been "given up" by white doctors, but were later cured by calamus (Howard, 1953, pp. 608–9).

The Cheyennes obtained the plant from the Sioux (Grinnell, 1962, 2:171). They drank a tea from the root for pain in the bowels and chewed the root and rubbed it on the skin for any illness. A bit of root was tied on a child's necklace, dress, or blanket to keep away night spirits.

ANGLO FOLK USE

Calamus has an ancient history. It was used as a common remedy two thousand years ago in India and by the early Greeks (Lloyd, 1921b, p. 10). Moses was commanded by God to use calamus in an ointment he was to prepare in the Tabernacle (Exodus 30). Calamus also appeared in many European herbals as a folk remedy with a variety of uses.

MEDICAL HISTORY

Calamus was considered a carminative, a stimulant, and an aromatic bitter tonic as well as a flavoring agent. The unpeeled, dried rhizome was officially listed in the *U.S. Pharmacopoeia* from 1820 to 1916 and in the *National Formulary* from 1936 to 1950.

SCIENTIFIC RESEARCH

Because its piney-smelling essential oil was found to be carcinogenic in long-term feeding trials with rats, calamus is considered an unsafe herb by the Food and Drug Administration (Locock, 1987, p. 342). However, research conducted since the FDA proclamation has shown that only the variety of calamus native to India contains the carcinogenic beta-asarone (Keller and Stahl, 1983, p. 71). The American variety contains monoterpene hydrocarbons, sesquiterpene ketones and acorones. The beta-asarone-free oil from American calamus was found to be as effective as a standard antihistamine in its spasmolytic activity (Keller, Odenthal, and Leng-Peschlow, 1985, p. 6). Beta-asarone also seems to be a mild hallucinogen (Embroden, 1979, p. 82).

CULTIVATION

The sweet flag can be easily propagated by division of the rhizomes. Although they thrive along the edges of ponds, marshes, or other wet locations, I have successfully cultivated them in my northeast-Kansas garden, which I seldom water.

Allium canadense
Wild Onion

COMMON NAMES

Wild onion, wild garlic, prairie onion, meadow garlic, and Canada onion.

INDIAN NAMES

The Cheyenne names for wild onions are "kha-a'-mot-ot-ke-'wat" ("skunk testes" or, more derogatorily, "skunk nuts") and "kha-ohk-tsi-me-is'tse-hi" (skunk, it smells) (Grinnell, 1962, 2:171; Hart, 1981, p. 12). The Lakotas call wild onions "psin"; they specifically call *A. drummondii* Regel. "ps'in s'ica'mna" (bad-smelling onion) (Rogers, 1980, p. 25). The Osage name is "monzonxe" (earth, to bury) (Munson, 1981, p. 231). No translations were given for the following names: the Omaha and Ponca name is "manzhonka-mantanaha"; the Winnebago, "shinhop"; and the Pawnee, "osidiwa" (Gilmore, 1977, p. 19). The Blackfeet name is "pissats'e-mi-kim" (Johnston, 1970, p. 308).

SCIENTIFIC NAME

Allium canadense L. is a member of the Liliaceae (Lily Family). *Allium* is the ancient name for garlic, possibly derived from the Celtic "all," which means "pungent." The species name, *canadense*, means "of Canada."

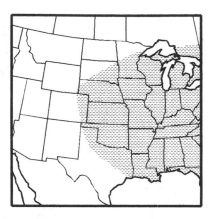

DESCRIPTION

Perennial herbs 2–9 dm (¾–3 ft) tall, growing from egg-shaped bulbs with a strong onion odor. Leaves 2 or more, basal, linear, 1–3 mm (¹⁄₁₆–⅛ in) wide, shorter than flowering stems. Flowers small, in round clusters at tops of erect stems, from Mar to Jul; petals and sepals alike, 6, separate, 4–8 mm (³⁄₁₆–⁵⁄₁₆ in) long, white to pink or lilac, sometimes fragrant; flowers often replaced by bulblets. Fruits dry, small, round to oval, opening to release black seeds.

HABITAT

Prairies, roadsides, and open woods.

PARTS USED

Bulbs and leaves.

Wild onions were widely used as a food source (Kindscher, 1987, pp. 12–17) and for a variety of medicinal purposes. It seems likely that the different species were used interchangeably. The Blackfeet made a tea of wild onion bulbs to control coughs and vomiting (Hellson, 1974, pp. 65, 70, 69, 75, and 79). Nursing mothers drank the tea in order to pass its medicinal properties to their children through their milk. It was also drunk for an unnamed disease that causes a swollen penis and severe constipation. An infusion of the bulb was used as an eyewash and for ear infections. When combined with bee balm (*Monarda* species), it was applied to swellings and sores to produce a cooling sensation. The Blackfeet treated colds, headache, and sinus trouble by having the patient inhale the smoke of a smudge made from the bulb. They also used snuff made from the dry bulb to open the sinuses.

The Cheyennes made a poultice from the ground roots and stems of the wild onion, *A. brevistylum* S. Wats., to treat opened and unopened carbuncles (Grinnell, 1962, 2:171). After the carbuncle was opened, a tea of boiled plant parts was poured into the cavity to loosen and clear out the pus.

The Dakotas and Winnebagos used the bruised wild onion to treat the sting of bees and wasps, according to F. Andros, a medical doctor who lived on or near Indian reservations much of his adult life. This treatment, he wrote, "almost instantly relieves the pain" (Andros, 1883, p. 117).

ANGLO FOLK USE

During both the Stephen Long expedition to the Rocky Mountains (1819–1920) and the expedition of Prince Maximilian of the German kingdom of Wied, which explored the Missouri River region from 1832 to 1834, the wild onion was eaten to cure an illness thought to be scurvy, which is caused by a vitamin C deficiency (Thwaites, 1905, 14:282–83). Prince Maximilian reported in his journal:

At the beginning of April I was still in hopeless condition, and so very ill that the people who visited me did not think that my life would be prolonged beyond three or, at the most, four days. The cook of the fort, a negro from St. Louis, one day expressed his opinion that my illness must be scurvy, for he had once witnessed the great mortality among the garrison of the fort at Council Bluffs, when several hundred soldiers were carried off in a short time; of this there is an account in Major Long's expedition to the Rocky Mountains. He said that the symptoms were in both cases nearly similar; that, on that occasion, at the beginning of spring, they had gathered the green herbs in the prairie, especially the small white flowering Allium reticula-

tum [probably A. canadense], with which they had soon cured the sick. I was advised to make trial of this recipe, and the [Omaha] Indian children accordingly furnished me with an abundance of this plant and its bulbs: these were cut up small, like spinage, and I ate a quantity of them. On the fourth day the swelling of my leg had considerably subsided, and I gained strength daily. The evident prospect of speedy recovery quite reanimated me, and we carried on with pleasure the preparations for our departure, though I was not yet able to leave my bed (ibid., 24:81–82).

MEDICAL HISTORY

Constantine Rafinesque reported in his 1830 Medical Flora of the United States that the Cherokees used several species of wild garlic in their cookery and made a tincture, usually from A. canadense, that was used "for the gravel" (Rafinesque, 1830, p. 187).

In folk medicine, croup, pneumonia, and chest colds have been treated with onion poultices (Vogel, 1970, pp. 306–7). Bulbs have been used as stimulants, diuretics, expectorants, diaphoretics, anthelmintics, antiscorbutics, antiseptics, and laxatives (Burlage, 1968, p. 111; Smythe, 1901, p. 192).

The wild onion listed in the U.S. Pharmacopoeia, 1820–1905, and in the National Formulary, 1916–1936, was the bulb of the European species, A. sativum L. However, according to Dr. A. Clapp, a prominent nineteenth-century medical doctor, the bulbs of A. canadense were equal to the official onion in medicinal use and a good substitute for it (Vogel, 1970, pp. 306–7).

SCIENTIFIC RESEARCH

Controlled studies in India revealed that individuals consuming more than 600 grams (21 ounces) per week of domestic onions had significantly lower serum triglycerides, beta lipoproteins, phospholipids, and plasma-fibrinogen levels than those who had never eaten onions. Consuming a moderate amount of onions (7 ounces per week) or an even smaller amount of domesticated garlic appeared to reduce the blood levels of phospholipids and plasma-fibrinogen. It also had a protective effect on important factors that prevent arteriosclerosis (Tyler, 1981, p. 102). The greatest health benefits seem to come from eating onions raw.

Eaten in quantity, all parts of the wild onion and the cultivated onion have poisonous properties that can cause gastroenteritis, especially in young children. Although most of the active chemicals in onions remain unknown, the toxins are N-propyl sulfide, methyl disulfide, and allyl disulfide (Lampe and McCann, 1985, p. 28).

HARVESTING AND CULTIVATION

Wild onions can be easily transplanted from the wild in the spring or fall. They can also be started from seed that has been stratified, but it is best to start them in a flat and then transplant them when they are large enough to compete with weeds. The springtime flowers of the varieties that bloom rather than produce bulbils have attractive vertical leaves and white-to-pink flowers.

Ambrosia artemisiifolia
Ragweed

Ragweed, common ragweed, short ragweed, hogwort, and stammer-wort.

INDIAN NAMES

The Lakotas have three names for ragweed (Rogers, 1980, p. 35): "canhlogan wastemna" (sweet-smelling weed); "canhlogan onzi-pakinte" (weed to wipe the rear); and "poipiye" (to doctor swellings with). The Dakotas call this plant "pexhuta pa" (bitter medicine) (Gilmore, 1913b, p. 369). The Cheyenne name for western ragweed, *A. psilostachya* DC., is "mohk tah' wanotst" (black medicine) (Grinnell, 1962, 2:188). The Kiowa names for the plant are " 'ko-'khad-la, tzan-go-pan-ya" (horse worm plant) and "a 'sahe" (green plant) (Vestal and Shultes, 1939, p. 55). Several of these names refer to the plant's bitter taste.

SCIENTIFIC NAME

Ambrosia artemisiifolia L. is a member of the Asteraceae (Sunflower Family). *Ambrosia* comes from the Greek "ambrotos," which means "immortal," in reference to several plants believed to have special properties. The species name, *artemisiifolia*, means "Artemisia leaf," denoting the similarity of its leaf shape to wormwood or mugwort.

DESCRIPTION

Annual herbs 3–10 dm (1–3 ¼ ft) tall, with a strong ragweed odor when bruised; stems rough-hairy, erect, branched upward. Leaves on lower stem opposite, becoming alternate above, reduced upward, 4–10 cm (1.5–4 cm) long, up to 7 cm (2 ¾ in) wide, once or twice deeply divided, the segments linear. Flower heads from Jul through Oct; male heads in spikelike groups at ends of branches, female heads in small clusters at bases of leaves; flowers tiny and green. Fruits dry, egg-shaped achenes with a short beak and 5–7 stubby spines at the top.

HABITAT

Pastures, roadsides, stream banks, and disturbed sites.

PARTS USED

Leaves, top, root, and entire plant.

The Lakotas applied a tea made from the leaves of the common ragweed to swellings (Buechel, 1983, p. 117). The Dakotas made a tea from the leaves and small tops of the plant to cure bloody flux and stop vomiting (Gilmore, 1913b, p. 369). White Horse, an Omaha medicine man, reported that common ragweed was an Oto remedy for nausea (Gilmore, 1977, p. 80). For this treatment, the surface of the patient's abdomen was scarified, and a dressing of the bruised leaves was placed on it.

The Cheyennes drank a tea made from a pinch of finely ground leaves and stems of the western ragweed, *A. psilostachya*, to treat bowel cramps, bloody stools, and colds. A Cheyenne named White Man reported that this tea was also drunk for constipation (Grinnell, 1962, 2:188; Hart, 1981, p. 18). The Kiowas boiled small pieces of the western ragweed to make a medicine that was rubbed on sores. (Vestal and Shultes, 1939, p. 55). The same tea was a remedy for "worm holes," a skin disease of horses, and for sores that were slow in healing. The Zunis had several uses for the annual bursage, *A. acanthicarpa* Hook., that were recorded by Matilda Stevenson in 1915: "The entire plant is made into tea, which is drunk warm for obstructed menstruation. The tea is also rubbed over the abdomen while it is massaged. The Zuni claim that the tea taken

sufficiently strong will produce abortion. While this vice exists in Zuni, cases are very rare. The ground root is placed in a hollow tooth to relieve toothache" (Stevenson, 1915, p. 52).

The seeds of the giant ragweed, *A. trifida* L., have been found in large quantities at several archaeological sites. Archaeologists originally believed that the seeds were used for medicine, but they now recognize that giant ragweed was a food source and was even cultivated (Wedel, 1955, p. 145; Kindscher, 1987, pp. 25–26).

ANGLO FOLK USE

Charles F. Millspaugh in his 1892 *American Medicinal Plants* wrote:

The former uses of this plant were but slight, its principal use being as an antiseptic emollient fomentation; its bitterness caused its use in Maryland as a substitute for quinine, but not successfully. J. A. Zabriskie, of Closter, N.J., claims it to be a successful application to the poisonous effects of Rhus [poison ivy] if rubbed upon the inflamed parts until they are discolored by its juice. Being very astringent, it has also been used to check discharges from mucous surfaces, such as mercurial ptyalism, leucorrhoea, gonorrhoea, and especially septic forms of diarrhoea, dysentery, and enteritis. It lays some claim also to be a stimulant and tonic and is recognized in the Mexican

Pharmacopoeia as an emmena-gogue, febrifuge, and anthelmintic (Millspaugh, 1974, p. 326).

SCIENTIFIC RESEARCH

There is no historical evidence that ragweed was used by physicians. The essential oil of ragweed, *A. artemisiifolia*, contains p-cymene, a small amount of limonene, alpha-pinene, and alicyclic ketone (Dominguez et al., 1970, p. 52). Ragweed may cause dermatitis and is widely known as a major source of pollen. It may be responsible for up to 90 percent of the pollen-induced allergies in the United States (Foster & Duke, 1990, p. 218).

CULTIVATION

Ragweeds are not recommended for cultivation. They are weedy, they lack showy flowers, and they produce large quantities of allergy-causing pollen.

Anemone patens
Pasque Flower

COMMON NAMES

Pasque flower, prairie crocus, pulsatilla, twin flower, blue tulip, windflower, prairie smoke, lion's beard (these last two names refer to the hairy plumes of the seed-like fruits), Easter flower (referring to the flowering date in some locations), hartshorn plant (referring to its peculiar effect upon one's nose and eyes when the plant is crushed between the fingers and smelled; it is similar to smelling hartshorn or ammonia water), and goslin weed (this name apparently originated with children in South Dakota because of the silky, hairy or ghostly appearance of the leaves and flower buds) (last two names from Leiberg, 1884 in Millspaugh, 1974, p. 3).

INDIAN NAMES

The Dakotas call the pasque flower "hokshi-chekpa wahcha" (twin flower) because each plant usually has only two flowering stalks (Gilmore, 1977, p. 28). The Lakota name, "hoksi' cekpa" (child's navel), refers to the flower bud, which is similar in color and form to a baby's navel in the healing process (Rogers, 1980, p. 55). The Blackfeet name, "Napi" (old man), reflects the similarity of the grayish, silky seedheads to the heads of old men (Murphey, 1959, p. 43).

The Blackfeet names for the windflower, *Anemone multifida* Poir., are "a-sa-po-pinats" (looks-like-a-plume) and a name (un-known) that translates as "crooked stem" (McClintock, 1923, p. 320; Hellson, 1974, p. 60). The Omaha and Ponca name for meadow anemone, *A. canadensis* L., is "te-zhinga-makan" (little buffalo medicine) (Gilmore, 1977, p. 30), and the Mesquakie names for this plant are "wapaski'paskone'wiki" (very bitter root) and "wasa'wusk" (yellow weed) (Smith, 1928, p. 238).

SCIENTIFIC NAME

Anemone patens L. is a member of the Ranunculaceae (Buttercup Family). *Anemone* comes from the Greek "anemos" (wind). Pliny says the name was given because the flowers open only when the wind blows. On the other hand, *Anemone* may be a corruption of the Semitic word "na'man" (Adonis), from whose blood the crimson-flowered *Anemone* of the orient is said to have sprung.

Perennial herbs 5–45 cm (2–18 in) tall, with stout rootstocks; stems densely hairy, gray-green. Leaves numerous at base of plant, stalked, broader than long, kidney-shaped in outline, 3- to 7-lobed, each lobe further divided into linear segments. Flowers showy, 4–8 cm (1 ½–3 ⅛ in) across, solitary at ends of stalks that project above the leaves, from Apr to Jun; sepals petal-like, blue to lavender or white. Fruiting heads spherical, with numerous densely woolly achenes, each one tipped with a long, featherlike plume.

HABITAT

Open prairie, often in rocky soil, in northern latitudes (also in Eurasia).

PARTS USED

All parts.

INDIAN USE

The pasque flower is a familiar wildflower in northern states and Canadian provinces and was used as medicine by many tribes. Blackfeet women boiled the plant and drank the tea to speed delivery in childbirth. The Blackfeet also bound the crushed pasque flower leaves, which contain a vesicant, on some injuries as a counterirritant (Hellson, 1974, p. 60; Johnston, 1970, p. 312).

An Omaha informant told ethnobotanist Melvin Gilmore that the crushed leaves of the pasque flower were applied externally as a counterirritant for rheumatism, neuralgia, and similar diseases. However, the Omaha recognized this medicine as dangerous if taken internally. The Dakotas believed that "each species has its own particular song which is the expression of its life or soul." Melvin Gilmore recorded their reverence and affection for all plants, including the twin-flower or pasque flower, in the following poem and account, "The Song of the Twin-flower," translated from the Dakota language by Dr. A. McG. Beede (Gilmore, 1977, pp. 28–30):

I wish to encourage the children
Of other flower nations now
*   appearing*
All over the face of the earth;
So while they awaken from
*   sleeping*
And come up from the heart of
*   the earth*
I am standing here old and
*   gray-headed.*

When an old Dakota first finds
one of these flowers in the spring-
time it reminds him of his child-
hood, when he wandered over the
prairie hills at play, as free from
care and sorrow as the flowers and
the birds. He sits down near the
flower on the lap of Mother Earth,
takes out his pipe and fills it with
tobacco. Then he reverently holds
the pipe toward the earth, then

*toward the sky, then toward the
north, the east, the south, and
the west. After this act of silent
invocation he smokes. While he
smokes he meditates upon all the
changing scenes of his lifetime, his
joys and sorrows, his hopes, his
accomplishments, his disappoint-
ments, and the guidance which
unseen powers have given him in
bringing him thus far on the way,
and he is encouraged to believe
that he will be guided to the end.
After finishing his pipe he rises
and plucks the flower and carries
it home to show his grandchildren,
singing as he goes, The Song of the
Twin-flower, which he learned as
a child, and which he now in turn
teaches his grandchildren.*

Several other species of windflower (*Anemone*) have been used
as medicine. The root of the windflower, *A. canadensis*, was a highly
esteemed medicine of the Omahas
and Poncas. It was applied externally and taken internally, especially for wounds, but for many
types of illness as well. It was also
used as a wash for sores, including
those affecting the eyes. The right
to use this plant belonged to the
medicine men of the "Te-sinde"
gens (a patrilineal clan); since
touching a buffalo calf was taboo
in this gens, they called it "little
buffalo medicine." Amos Walker,
an Omaha informant and member of this gens, reported "that
the plant is male and female, and
that the flower of the male plant is
white and that of the female red"

(ibid.). The windflower was used
by the Mesquakies as a remedy
to correct crossed eyes (Smith,
1928, p. 238). They also made a
root tea to wash the eyes when
they twitched and when an eye
was "poisoned."

The Blackfeet used the windflower, *A. multifida* Poir., to induce an abortion (method not
given) (Hellson, 1974, p. 60). As
reported by Walter McClintock,
this species "is adapted for a windy
place and is found growing on
hillsides where the wind strikes
it, either on the plains, or in the
mountains. In midsummer the
flower turns into cotton, which
the Blackfeet burn on a hot coal
for headache" (McClintock, 1923,
p. 320). Apparently they inhaled
the fumes for relief.

MEDICAL HISTORY

In 1933 ethnobotanist Huron
Smith reported that the Eclectic
practitioners, a group of college-
trained physicians whose practices
were based on a wide variety of
techniques, used most species of
the *Anemone* interchangeably for
many ailments. "Included in these
ailments are: cataract, paralysis,
rheumatism, melancholia, syphilis, dysmenorrhea, and many other
morbid conditions." Smith, however, had previously questioned its
effectiveness (Smith, 1933, p. 383;
Smith, 1928, p. 238).

The pasque flower, along with
two European *Anemone* species,
was officially listed in the *U.S.*

Pharmacopoeia from 1882 to 1905 and in the *National Formulary*, along with two European *Anemone* species, from 1916 to 1947.

SCIENTIFIC RESEARCH

Species of *Anemone* contain ranunculin, a glycoside. On hydrolysis it produces protoanemonin, which is responsible for the vesicant action of these plants (Trease and Evans, 1973, p. 396). Protoanemonin is considered a toxin (Lampe and McCann, 1985, p. 32). Numerous negative side effects of ingestion are reported by Millspaugh (1892, pp. 3–4). This genus also contains the glycosides ranunculetin and flavescetin as well as saponins.

HARVESTING AND CULTIVATION

The pasque flower, the state flower of South Dakota, is the first wildflower of spring from the northern part of the Prairie Bioregion into the tundra. It is best propagated from seed planted in flats, as it does not compete well with other vegetation. Seeds benefit from a short period of stratification (two to three weeks), but will germinate without treatment. Ideally, seedlings should be grown in nursery conditions the first year and then transplanted in the late fall or early spring to a permanent location in full or nearly full sun and well-drained soil. The pasque flower can also be propagated by division or by cuttings of the roots made early in the spring or late fall. Root segments should be several inches long, planted 2.5 cm (1 in) deep and kept moist until established.

The windflower, *A. canadensis*, has bright white flowers in mid-spring and is also one of the easiest wildflowers to grow. It is propagated by division of the rhizomes when the plants are dormant. This plant can be quite aggressive and will take over a flower bed; it may be necessary to install borders to contain it. It grows well in sun or partial shade and tolerates various soil conditions.

Apocynum cannabinum
Dogbane

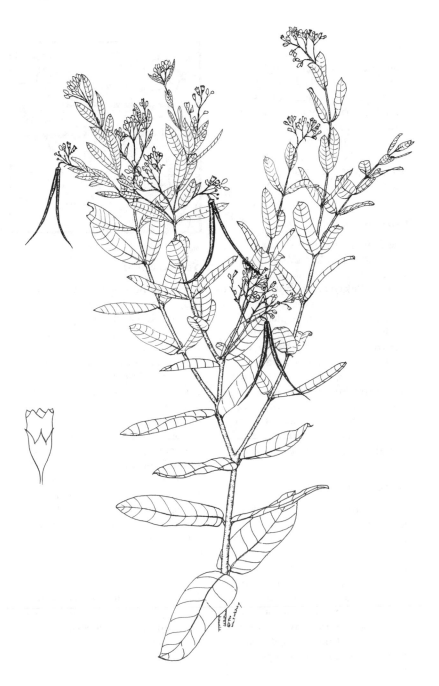

Dogbane, Indian hemp dogbane, prairie dogbane, black Indian hemp, Canadian hemp, dropsy weed, American hemp, Amy-root, Bowman's root, bitter root, Indian-physic, rheumatism-weed, milk-weed, wild cotton, Choctaw-root, hairy dogbane, glabrous hemp, Coctaw-root, and silkweed.

INDIAN NAMES

The Blackfeet name is "nuxa-pist" (little blanket) (McClintock, 1909, p. 276). The Lakota name is "nape'oi'lekiyapi" (to burn it in the hand), referring to the fact that the fluffy seeds can be placed in the hand, lit, and burned without hurting the hand (Rogers, 1980, p. 34). The Mesquakie names are "mukoseki' ashikiki" (like a milk weed) and "mukosaka'sakuk" (sharp podded weed) (Smith, 1928, p. 201). The Kiowa name is " 'gho-la" (no translation given) (Vestal and Shultes, 1939, p. 47).

SCIENTIFIC NAME

Apocynum cannabinum L. is a member of the Apocynaceae (Dog-bane Family). Dioscorides, a Greek medical writer of the first century, named the plant *apokynon*, which refers to a plant with milky juice. The species name, *cannabinum*, means "of *cannabis*" or "of hemp," referring to the woody outer fibers in the stem. Like hemp, dogbane makes good cordage or rope.

DESCRIPTION

Perennial herb 2–10 dm (¾–3 ¼ ft) tall, with milky sap and often forming loose colonies; stems erect, smooth to hairy, often waxy, branched above, arising from creeping rhizomes. Leaves opposite, simple, lance-shaped to egg-shaped, 1.5–14 cm (¾–5 ½ in) long, 0.3–4.5 cm (⅛–1¾ in) wide. Flowers in loose to dense clusters at ends of branches, from Jun to Sep; petals white to pinkish, bell-shaped, with flaring lobes. Fruits slender, tapering, cylindrical pods to 20 cm (8 in) long, occurring in pairs, splitting to release abundant seeds, each with a tuft of long, whitish hairs at the tip.

HABITAT

Prairies, open and wooded water-ways, lakeshores, disturbed road-sides and fields, and sparsely wooded slopes.

Roots.

The Blackfeet boiled dogbane roots in water to make a tea that they drank as a laxative (McClintock, 1909, p. 276). They also used it as a wash to prevent hair loss. The Mesquakies used the root for dropsy, ague, and as a universal remedy (Smith, 1928, p. 200). They also used the bast fibers of the stem as a fine thread for sewing. The Kiowas made chewing gum by allowing the milky latex of the sap to harden a few hours or overnight (Vestal and Shultes, 1939, p. 47). The botanist Constantine Rafinesque reported in 1828:

The root when chewed has an intensely bitter and unpleasant taste perceptible in the whole plant in a lesser degree except the flowers, and arising from the bitter milk it contains. . . . This is a very active plant, highly valued by the Southern Indians. It is tonic, emetic, alterative and antisyphilitic. The root is the most powerful part; but it must be used fresh, since time diminishes or destroys its power. At the dose of thirty grains of the fresh powdered root, it acts as an emetic, equal to Ipecacuana; in smaller doses, it is a tonic, useful in dyspepsias and fevers. The Chickasaw and Choctaw Nations employ it in syphilis and consider it a specific, they use the fresh root chewed, swallowing

only the juice. This later use has been introduced into Tennessee and Kentucky as a great secret (Rafinesque, 1828, pp. 51–52).

It has also been reported that some North American Indians (no tribal designation given) made a tea from the boiled root for use as an oral contraceptive (De Laszlo and Henshaw, 1954, p. 627). It was drunk once a week and thought to cause temporary sterility.

Dogbane was used extensively in folk medicine. John Uri Lloyd recounted its history in his *Origin and History of all the Pharmacopeial Drugs, Chemicals and Preparations*:

Since the days of the earliest settlers, who learned its qualities from the Indians, the root of apocynum has been used in decoction as an active hydragogue cathartic and also as a diuretic. As a remedy in "dropsy" it was extensively employed in home medication, and was thus introduced to physicians concerned in remedial agents of American origin. Its favor with physicians engaged in general practice, led finally to its introduction to the pages of the Pharmacopoeia (Lloyd, 1921a, pp. 17–18).

Although early settlers in Montana used dogbane root as a tonic, a febrifuge, and a purgative, they recognized large doses as poisonous (Blankenship, 1905, p. 6). It is still used in Appalachia as a tonic and a home remedy for migraine headaches, colds, pleurisy, and constipation; when mixed with other plants, it is used for liver, stomach, and lung ailments, rheumatism, bursitis, and arthritis (Bolyard et al., 1981, p. 33). A root decoction is used to cause abortion in South Carolina.

MEDICAL HISTORY

Dogbane was popular with early doctors. Dr. Finley Ellingwood, in *A Systematic Treatise on Materia Medica and Therapeutics*, stated:

> The most direct action of this remedy is upon an enlarged heart, where there is functional weakness. It lessens the force of the heart's action, controlling violence and irritability. It overcomes dyspnoea of these cases, the vertigo and general sense of weakness, with other reflex symptoms.
>
> In bronchitis, asthma, dyspnoea, and in jaundice or dropsy, all of cardiac origin, it is said to be one of our best agents, in some cases acting magically. Galen used it in rheumatic affections. The agent has not received the attention it is said to deserve (Ellingwood, 1902, p. 268).

The root of dogbane was officially listed in the *U.S. Pharmacopoeia* from 1831 to 1916 and in the *National Formulary* from 1916 to 1960. It was regarded as a cardiac stimulant. The root of the closely related spreading dogbane, *A. androsaemifolium* L., was also officially listed as a diuretic, cathartic, diaphoretic, emetic, and expectorant.

SCIENTIFIC RESEARCH

Cymarin has been determined to be the major medicinal constituent of dogbane. Cymarin and apocannoside are found throughout the entire plant. They are cardiac glycosides, both of which have shown antitumor activity on human carcinomas (Kupchan, Hemingway, and Doskotch, 1964, pp. 803–4). Dogbane also contains the cardiac glycosides, K-strophanthin, cynocannoside, and genin strophanthidin (Lee, Carew, and Rosazza, 1972, p. 150), which can have specific effects on the heart. In addition, dogbane contains tannins, resin, fatty oil, alpha-amyrin, lupeol, oleanolic acid, P-oxyacetophenone, saponins, androsterol, homoandrosterol, and harmalol (Duke, 1985, p. 50).

Dogbane is apparently poisonous to humans. Although the toxicity of several of the glycosides and resins has been established in the laboratory, "cases of poisoning in humans are unknown" (Hardin and Arena, 1974, cited in Duke, 1985, p. 50). The cymarin in dogbane is also toxic to grazing animals, but because they find it distasteful, cases of poisoning are rare.

Earlier in this century, when the root of dogbane was more extensively harvested for medicinal use, it was recommended that it be collected in the fall (Henkel, 1907, p. 56). Dogbane can be propagated by seed. In one experiment, a 60 percent germination rate was reported (Lee et al., 1972, p. 153). The seeds do not need stratification.

However, division of the rootstock while the plant is dormant is an even easier method of propagation. In fact, the root system of this plant is so vigorous that during the spring when I mow mature plants in the orchard behind my house, the horizontal roots (4–8 m [12–25 ft long]) seem to retaliate by sending up dozens of new shoots along their entire length.

Artemisia ludoviciana
White Sage

White sage, wild sage, prairie
sage, wormwood, white mugwort,
western mugwort, Louisiana sagewort, darkleaf mugwort, Mexican
sagewort, Chihuahua sagewort,
Garfield tea, and lobed cudweed.

INDIAN NAMES

The Omaha and Ponca name for
the wild sage is "pezhe-hota" (gray
herb), the (Dakota) Sioux name is
"pezhihota blaska" (flat medicine),
the Winnebago name is "hanwin-
ska" (white herb), and the Pawnee
name is "kiwaut" (no translation
given) (Gilmore, 1977, pp. 82–83).
The Lakotas used the wild sages
extensively and have names for
seven different species as well
as two names for the white sage.
A. ludoviciana var. *gnaphalodes* is
called "peji' ho'ta ape' blaska'ska"
(gray herb with a flat leaf) and
A. ludoviciana var. *ludoviciana*
is called "peji' ho'ta" (gray herb),
which is the Lakota's generic name
for sage (Rogers, 1980, p. 36). The
Cheyenne name for white sage is
"hetane'-vano ?estse" (man sage)
(Hart, 1981, p. 18). The Comanche
name for white sage is "pehebiv"
(no translation given) (Rogers,
1980, p. 36). The Kiowa-Apache
name translates as "burning stick,
easy breaking," in reference to its
use as incense (Jordan, 1965, p. 99).
The Mesquakie names for the
white sage are "wapu'skwi" (white)
and "sokimeuskwi" (mosquitoes)
(Smith, 1928, p. 211).

The Blackfeet name for the
sage, *A. frigida* Willd., is "kaksa-
mis" (she sage) (McClintock, 1923,
p. 321). The Arapaho name for the
same plant is "Na-ko-ha-sait" (no
translation given) (Murphey, 1959,
p. 12).

SCIENTIFIC NAME

Artemisia ludoviciana Nutt. is a
member of the Asteraceae (Sunflower Family). *Artemisia* is Latin
for mugwort. Pliny explained
that this name honors Artemisia,
wife of Mausolus, King of Caria
(a province in Asia Minor). After
the king's death in about 350 B.C.,
Artemisia built the renowned
Mausoleum, one of the Seven
Wonders of the World. The species
name, *ludoviciana*, means "of
Louisiana," but refers to the vast
Louisiana Territory rather than to
the state.

White-woolly perennial herbs 3–7 dm (1–2 ¼ ft) tall, with a strong odor of sagebrush; stems erect, often clustered from creeping rhizomes. Leaves alternate, entire to irregularly toothed or lobed, 3–11 cm (1 ¼–4 ½ in) long, up to 1.5 cm (⁹⁄₁₆ in) wide. Flower heads small, greenish, in tight clusters among leaves near the ends of stems, from Aug through Sep. Fruits dry, smooth, broadly cylindrical achenes.

HABITAT

Prairies and semidisturbed sites.

PARTS USED

Leaves and stems, infrequently the root or seeds.

INDIAN USE

All species of wild sage were probably used as medicine by the Indians. The Dakotas and other tribes used white sage tea for stomach troubles and many other ailments (Gilmore, 1977, p. 83). They also used it for cleansing the body in some purification rites; any person who had unwittingly broken a taboo or touched a sacred object had to bathe in *Artemisia*. Short Bull, a well-known Brule (Lakota) chief, reported that the men used the white sage and the women used the dwarf sagebrush, *Artemisia cana* Pursh, for protection against evil influences (ibid.; Gilmore, 1913b, p. 369). The essence of the plant served as a "protection against maleficient powers; therefore it was always proper to begin any ceremonial by using *Artemisia* in order to drive away any evil influences." (Gilmore, 1977, p. 83). This was done either by burning the sage or by drinking a ceremonial tea. The Lakotas also made bracelets for the Sun Dance from white sage (Rogers, 1980, p. 36).

Both Lakotas and Dakotas used the sagebrush, *Artemisia campestris* L. subsp. *caudata* (Michx.) Hall & Clem., for medicine. The Lakotas made a tea from the roots to remedy constipation, inability to urinate, and difficulty in childbirth (Munson, 1981, pp. 231–32). Women also used the sage, *A. frigida*, to correct menstrual irregularity (Hart, 1976, p. 45).

Hart reported extensive ceremonial use of the white sage or man sage by the Cheyennes:

'Man sage' was perhaps the most important ceremonial plant of the Cheyennes. It was spread along the borders in almost every ceremonial lodge, the tops of the stems pointing to the fire. The leaves were burned as incense which was believed to have the power to drive away bad spirits, evil influences, and ominous and persistent dreams of sick persons. A small pinch of Actea rubra *was often mixed with it for this purpose. Its use for purification was wide-*

spread: the leaves were burned as incense to purify implements, utensils, or people in various ceremonies; or in a bundle employed to wipe a person guilty of breaking a taboo. Cheyenne Contrary Warriors found this sage especially beneficial for purification. When they left a lodge, they passed the plant over the ground to purify the soil; if their lances (which protected them from Thunder) happened to touch anyone, then they rubbed sage on that person; if these same lances touched their horses (usually the case when riding), they wiped their horses with sage before turning them loose to pasture; and after eating from a dish, they wiped it, too, with purifying sage. Nowadays, hunters rub their rifles with sage (Hart, 1981, pp. 18–19).

The Cheyennes also used the white sage in their Sun Dance and Standing Against Thunder ceremonies (ibid.; Hart, 1976, pp. 44–45). They used the crushed leaves as snuff for sinus attacks, nosebleed, and headache.

The Crows made a salve for use on sores by mixing white sage with neck-muscle fat (probably from buffalo) (Hart, 1976, p. 45). They used a strong tea as an astringent for eczema and as a deodorant and an antiperspirant for underarms and feet. The Kiowas made a bitter drink from white sage, which they used to reduce phlegm and to relieve a variety of lung and stomach complaints (Vestal and

Shultes, 1939, p. 56). Usually, though, they simply rolled up the leaves and stem, chewed them, and swallowed the juice.

The Kiowa-Apaches also used a thin, sharp-pointed section of the stem, about 0.6–1.2 cm (¼–½ in) long, as a moxa to relieve headaches or other pain (Jordan, 1965, p. 103). It was inserted into the skin at the painful spot, touched with a live coal, and allowed to smolder down to the skin. It was then pinched off just as it began to burn the skin.

The Mesquakies used the leaves as a poultice to "cure sores of long standing" (Smith, 1928, p. 211). They also made a tea of the leaves to treat tonsillitis and sore throat and a smudge of the leaves to drive away mosquitoes.

One of the clan names of the men of the Omaha "Te-sinde" gens is "Pezhe-hota" (white sage) (Gilmore, 1977, p. 83). In addition to their ceremonial use of the plant, the Omahas used the leaves (apparently fresh) in a tea for bathing, and then used the dried, powdered leaves for nosebleed by inhaling them into the nostrils (Gilmore, 1913a, p. 335).

Pawnee women drank an *Artemisia* tea "at certain periods" (probably associated with menstruation) (Dunbar, 1880, p. 341). During the four-day periods when Arikara women lived away from their lodges in a menstrual hut, they drank the bitter tea made from the leaves of the white sage, *A. ludoviciana*, or the root of the sage, *A. frigida* (Gilmore, 1930, p. 80).

The Blackfeet used the white sage in sweat-lodge rituals and as an ingredient in a steam vapor inhaled for respiratory problems. They also applied the white sage for its cooling effect on blisters and boils that had burst (Hellson, 1974, pp. 60, 66, 71, 75, and 78). They chewed the fresh leaves of the sagebrush, *A. campestris*, for stomach trouble and also applied the chewed leaves to rheumatic joints and sore eyes. A tea of fresh sagebrush leaves was drunk to abort difficult pregnancies. The Blackfeet stored the dried leaves for use in a tea that was drunk to relieve coughs and applied externally to relieve eczema.

The Blackfeet chewed the leaves of the sage, *A. frigida*, for heartburn (McClintock, 1923, p. 321; Hellson, 1974, p. 83) and applied the leaves to wounds to reduce swelling. It was also used to treat nosebleed by stuffing the nose with the soft leaves. The roots or tops were boiled and drunk as a tea for "mountain fever."

Other tribes who used these species of sage include the Arapahos, Comanches, Gros Ventres, Crees, Navahos, Tewas, and Utes (Nickerson, 1966, p. 50; Carlson and Jones, 1939, p. 520; Hart, 1976, p. 45; Thwaites, 1905, 23: 140; Denig, 1855, p. 317; Elmore, 1944, pp. 96–98; Robbins, Harrington, and Freire-Marreco, 1916, p. 53; Chamberlin, 1909, p. 32). An extensive listing of medicinal uses of all *Artemisia* species is found in Melvin Shemluck's 1982 "Medicinal and Other Uses of the *Compositae* by Indians in the United States and Canada."

ANGLO FOLK USE

In discussing the European species, *A. vulgaris* L., the 1636 Gerarde herbal gave the history of its use beginning in Rome in the first century.

Pliny *saith, That Mugwort doth properly cure womens diseases.*

Dioscorides *writeth, That it bringeth downe the termes, the birth, and the after-birth.*

And that in like manner it helpeth the mother, and the paine of the matrix, to bee boyled as baths for women to sit in; and that being put up with myrrh, it is of like force that the bath is of. And that the tender tops are boyled and drunke for the same infirmities; and that they are applied in manner of pultesse to the share, to bring downe the monethly course.

Pliney *saith, that the traveler or wayfaring man that hath the herbe tied about him feeleth no wearisomnesse at all; and that he who hath it about him can be hurt by no poysonsome medicines, nor by any wilde beast, neither by the Sun it selfe; and also that it is drunke against* Opium, *or the juyce of blacke Poppy. Many other fantastical devices invented by Poets are to be seene in the Works of the ancient Writers, tending to* witchcraft and sorcerie, and the great dishonour of God; wherefore I do of purpose omit them, as things unworthie of my recording, or your reviewing.

Mugwort pound with oyle of sweet almonds, and laid to the stomacke as a plaister, cureth all the paines and griefes of the same. It cureth the shakings of the joynts, inclining to palsie, and helpeth the contractions or drawing together of the nerves and sinews (Gerarde, 1636, pp. 1104–5).

There are many similarities between American and European uses of Artemisia species. William Chase Stevens wrote in Kansas Wild Flowers:

In the New World, as in the Old, the lives of the natives were intimately and vitally related to the plant population, and it need not surprise us that our Indians put the indigenous Artemisias to much the same medicinal uses as the early Europeans and Asiatics did theirs; but that our Indians should have, as they did, the same kind of superstitions about the Artemisias and use them in similar rites and ceremonies, with confidence in their magic powers is amazing (Stevens, 1961, p. 422).

MEDICAL HISTORY

Constantine Rafinesque in his 1830 Medical Flora of the United States reported:

Artemisia vulgaris, L. Mugwort. common to both continents. . . . Antiseptic, detergent, deobstruant, laxative, diuretic, diaphoretic, menagogue, corroborant, antispasmodic and vermifuge. Useful in hysterics, spasms, palpitations of the heart, worms, obstructions, &c. in tea, infusion or powder. The leaves, tops and seeds are used, these last and their oil equal to Santomic seeds as vermifuge. Warm fomentations of the leaves are an excellent discutient and antiseptic. Many equivalent species grow in the West. . . . All species make the milk of cows bitter when grazed upon. Moxa made with them (Rafinesque, 1830, p. 196).

Although the native species of Artemisia have never been listed as official drugs in the U.S. Pharmacopoeia, A. frigida is listed as a source of camphor.

SCIENTIFIC RESEARCH

The lactone glycosides, santonin and artemisin, are probably found in all Artemisia species and account for their anthelmintic properties (Moore, 1979, p. 162). Thujone, a terpene-like ketone and essential oil, is also found in the plant and may be responsible for some of its medicinal effects. However, it is poisonous in large doses. Thujone is found in larger quantities in the European wormwood, A. absinthium, used in the now illegal liqueur absinthe. The Food and Drug Administration classifies *Artemisia* as an unsafe herb containing "a volatile oil which is an active narcotic poison" (Duke, 1985, p. 67).

HARVESTING AND CULTIVATION

Most of the wild sages are abundant in their natural habitats. White sage and other *Artemisia* species can be propagated by seeds, by division of the rootstock, or by cuttings taken in the early summer.

Asclepias tuberosa
Butterfly Milkweed

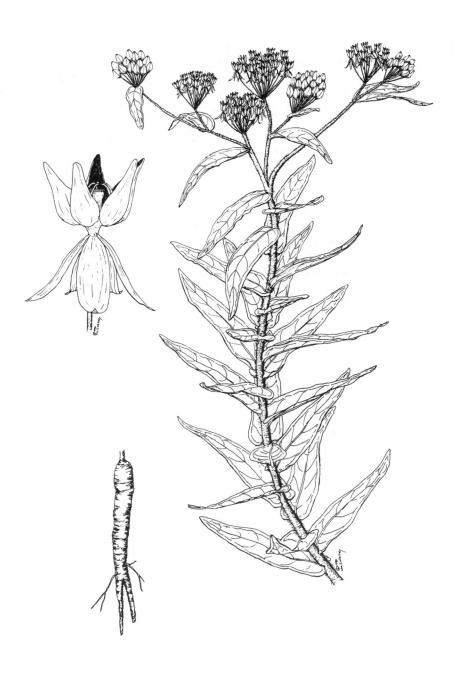

Butterfly milkweed, butterfly
weed, pleurisy root, Canada root,
orange milkweed, orangeroot,
orange swallow-wort, orange
apocynum, chigger flower, flux-
root, Indian nosy, rubber root,
silkweed, swallow-wort, tuber
root, white root, and wind root.

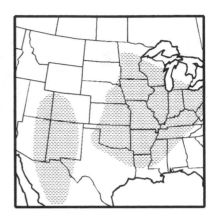

The Omaha and Ponca names
for the butterfly milkweed are
"makan saka" (raw medicine) and
"kiu makan" (wound medicine)
(Gilmore, 1977, p. 57). The Mesquakie name is "atiste'i" (knob
on roots) (Smith, 1928, p. 205).
The butterfly milkweed does not
grow on the Rosebud Sioux Reservation in South Dakota, but the
Lakotas have ten names for six
other species of Asclepias (Rogers,
1980, p. 34). The Gros Ventre
name for the root of an Asclepias
species they used as medicine
is "ahaan tjiinican" (wood-like)
(Kroeber, 1908, p. 225). There are
also numerous Indian names for
the common milkweed, A. syriaca, and the showy milkweed,
A. speciosa (Kindscher, 1987,
p. 55).

Asclepias tuberosa L. is a member
of the Asclepiadaceae (Milkweed
Family). Asclepias comes from the
name of the Greek god of medicine, Asklepios. The species name,
tuberosa, means "full of swellings
or knobs," referring to the enlarged
root system.

Perennial herb 3–9 dm (1–3 ft)
tall, with woody rootstocks;
stems erect, long-hairy, numerous, mostly unbranched, containing watery sap. Leaves alternate,
simple, crowded, lance-shaped, 5–
10 cm (2–4 in) long, 0.7–2.5 cm
($\frac{5}{16}$–1 in) wide, shiny green and
mostly smooth above, velvety beneath. Flowers in showy, rounded
to flat-topped groups near ends
of branches, from May to Aug;
petals 5, bent downward, orange to
red or sometimes yellow, topped
by a crown of 5 erect hoods, each
one containing a short horn. Fruits
hairy, spindle-shaped pods 8–
15 cm (3 ⅛–6 in) long, opening to
release numerous seeds, each with
a tuft of long white hairs at the tip.

HABITAT

Sandy, loamy, or rocky limestone soils of prairies, open woodlands, roadsides, and disturbed areas.

PARTS USED

The root.

INDIAN USE

The Omahas and Poncas ate the raw root of the butterfly milkweed for bronchial and pulmonary troubles. It was also chewed and placed on wounds, or dried, pulverized, and blown into wounds, especially old, obstinate sores. The ethnobotanist Melvin Gilmore reported on the ceremonial uses of butterfly milkweed:

In the Omaha tribe this medicine and its rites belonged to the Shell Society. A certain member of the society was the authorized guardian or keeper of this medicine. It was his prerogative to dig the root and distribute bundles of it to the members of the society. The ceremonials connected with digging, preparation, consecration, and distribution occupied four days. In this connection it may not be out of place to note that four is the dominant number in all ritual and in all orientation in space and time among the Plains tribes, just as the number seven is dominant with some other peoples. Whether four or seven be the dominant number depends on whether the four cardinal points of the horizon are given preeminence or whether equal place is given also to the three remaining points, the Zenith, the Nadir, and the Here (Gilmore, 1977, p. 57).

Dr. F. Andros reported in 1883 that the Dakotas used the butterfly milkweed as an emetic (Andros, 1883, p. 118). In the Great Lakes Bioregion, the Menominis considered the butterfly milkweed, which they called the "deceiver," one of their most important medicines. In his "Ethnobotany of the Menomini" Huron Smith described how it was used:

The root is pulverized and used for cuts, wounds and bruises. It is also used in mixing with other roots for other remedies. One of the most important of these compounds consists of this root, ginseng, man-in-the-ground [Echinocystis lobata], and sweet flag. This is considered by the Menomini to represent four Indians in power. The "deceiver" is half boiled, then pounded to strings, to get out the substance, in this case. When a Menomini cuts his foot with an axe, this is the first remedy that comes to his mind (Smith, 1928, p. 25).

The Lakota name for the swamp milkweed, A. incarnata L., is "wahinheya ipi'ye" ("medicine used to doctor gopher," i.e., swollen glands) (Rogers, 1980, pp. 27, 34). Probably the root was pulverized

55

made into a salve, and rubbed on scrofulous swellings. Lakota children were told to stay away from gopher mounds or they would get swellings in their necks similar to the cheek pouches of pocket gophers. The Lakota names for the plains or dwarf milkweed, *A. pumila* (A. Gray) Vail., are: "ces'los'lo peju'ta" (diarrhea medicine), "hante'iye'ceca" (it is like juniper), and "peji'swu'la cik'ala" (small fine herb). Like juniper or cedar tea, a tea made from plains milkweed was used as a diarrhea medicine, especially for children. The Lakota name for the narrow-leaved milkweed, *A. stenophylla* A. Gray, is "tin'psila pejuta" (prairie turnip medicine). The root was given to children who refused to eat to help them regain their appetite for the prairie turnip, *Psoralea esculenta* Pursh, a food staple, and other foods (ibid.; Kindscher, 1987, pp. 183–89). The Lakota name for the green milkweed, *A. viridiflora* Raf., is "hu cinska" (spoon-shaped stem), which describes the shape of the leaf. The pulverized roots of the green milkweed were also given to children with diarrhea. A tea of the whole plant was drunk by mothers unable to produce milk (Rogers, 1980, p. 34). This use is probably an example of the Doctrine of Signatures, the belief that certain characteristics of a plant signify its uses. In this case, the milky sap was thought to signify that the milkweed would promote the production of milk. The whorled milkweed, *A. verticillata*

L., was also used by the Lakotas for this purpose.

The Cheyennes made a medicine for snowblindness and other forms of blindness from the showy milkweed, *A. speciosa* Torr. (Hart, 1981, p. 15). They prepared it by making a tea from the top part of the plant, straining it, and applying the liquid to the eyes with a clean cloth. The Blackfeet chewed the root of the green milkweed, *A. viridiflora*, to relieve sore throat (Hellson, 1974, p. 71). They also applied the chewed root to swellings and rashes. It was particularly effective for diarrhea rash and for a nursing baby's sore gums.

The Mesquakies used the root of the swamp milkweed, *A. incarnata*, as a medicine to expel tapeworms (Smith, 1928, p. 205). The Gros Ventres used some *Asclepias* species for colic (Kroeber, 1908, p. 224). Both common milkweed, *A. syriaca*, and jack-in-the-pulpit, *Arisaema triphyllum*, are reported to act as contraceptives (Erichsen-Brown, 1979, p. 434; De Laszlo and Henshaw, 1954, p. 627). A Mohawk antifertility concoction was prepared by boiling a fistful of dried, pulverized milkweed and three jack-in-the-pulpit rhizomes in a pint of water for 20 minutes. The infusion was drunk, a cupful an hour, to induce temporary sterility.

In the Southeast, the Choctaws valued a strong tea made from the whorled milkweed, *A. verticillata*, as a remedy for snakebite (Campbell, 1951, p. 287). While the tea was applied to the snakebite wound, the victim also chewed the root and swallowed the saliva.

ANGLO FOLK USE

The butterfly milkweed, *A. tuberosa*, is also called pleurisy root because it was used to relieve inflammation of the lining of the lungs and thorax, and probably relieved the "muscular rheumatism of the walls of the chest" (Gaertner, 1979, pp. 119–23).

The current folk uses of the showy milkweed, *A. speciosa*, butterfly milkweed, and other species are described by Michael Moore in *Medicinal Plants of the Mountain West*:

> Stimulates both urine and perspiration, softens bronchial mucous, dilates bronchials, and encourages expectoration. For a diuretic, Milkweed acts to increase the volume and solids of the urine and will aid in chronic kidney weakness typified by a slight nonspecific ache in the middle back, most noticeable in the morning or after drinking alcohol. A tablespoon boiled in a pint of water, one-half cup drunk four times a day. For the lungs, a teaspoon boiled in a cup, drunk hot. Excess can cause nausea; the same physiological mechanism that will cause expectoration will also cause nausea and vomiting. Other Milkweeds with broad leaves can be used similarly, particularly Pleurisy Root, . . . It is a stimulant

> to the vagus nerve, producing perspiration, expectoration, bronchial dilation, and the like. As its name signifies, it is useful for pleurisy and mild pulmonary edema, increasing fluid circulation, cilia function, and lymphatic drainage. An average dose is a scant teaspoon of the chopped root, boiled in water, one or two cups drunk in a day. Amounts of a table spoon or more of the root can cause nausea or vomiting (Moore, 1979, pp. 106–7, 130).

MEDICAL HISTORY

In 1892 Charles Millspaugh recorded the early medical history of the butterfly milkweed:

> The pleurisy-root has received more attention as a medicine than any other species of this genus. . . . Schoepf first brought it before the medical profession, followed by Drs. Barton, Chapman, Eberle, and Parker, each of who found it often reliable, especially in cases where an expectorant or diaphoretic seemed requisite. . . . Other and more recent writers as usual have looked with doubt upon all its given qualities, except mayhap its utility as an expectorant and diaphoretic. The provings however, point to it as a valuable remedy in certain forms of dry coryza, indigestion, colic, diarrhoea, dry coughs, pleurisy, general rheumatic pains, and certain skin affections (Millspaugh, 1974, p. 540).

The root of the butterfly milk-weed, *A. tuberosa*, was officially listed in the *U. S. Pharmacopoeia* from 1820 to 1905 and in the *National Formulary* from 1916 to 1936. The common milkweed, *A. syriaca*, and the swamp milk-weed, *A. incarnata*, were also officially listed in the *U. S. Phar-macopoeia* from 1820 to 1863 and 1873 to 1882 (Vogel, 1970, pp. 288, 337).

SCIENTIFIC RESEARCH

Milkweed species as a group are known to contain cardiac glyco-sides that are poisonous both to livestock and to humans, as well as other substances that may account for their medicinal effects. Resinoids, glycosides, and a small amount of alkaloids are present in all parts of the plant (Stephens, 1980, p. 86). Symptoms of poi-soning by the cardiac glycosides include dullness, weakness, bloat-ing, inability to stand or walk, high body temperature, rapid and weak pulse, difficult breathing, dilated pupils, spasms, and coma.

Butterfly milkweed contains several cardiac glycosides of the 5-a series, including two, uzari-genin and syriogenin, that are known to be toxic to humans (Westbrooks and Preacher, 1986, p. 143; Bolyard et al., 1981, p. 47). Coraglaucigenin, frugoside, gluco-frugoside, and uzarin have been isolated from the root. A water extract of the root shows uter-ine stimulant activity in rabbits,

guinea pigs, cats, and rats, as well as antibiotic activity on *Myo-bacterium tuberculosis* cultures. The glycoside amplexoside was extracted from the milkweed *A. amplexicaulis* Sm. and has been shown to inhibit cell growth of human cancer (Piatak et al., 1985, p. 470).

The cardiac glycoside in milk-weeds has also been useful as a chemical defense for Monarch butterflies *Danaus plexippus*. Their relationship to the Viceroy butterfly, *Limenitis archippus*, is considered to be a classic example of Batesian mimicry and the co-evolution of two butterfly species (Brower et al., 1972, pp. 426–29). Monarch butterflies, in their cater-pillar phase, eat milkweeds almost exclusively and are able to store the toxic alkaloids in their cells without any apparent harm. After their metamorphosis into butter-flies, they are poisonous to birds because of the continued presence of alkaloids. It was experimen-tally determined that these cardiac alkaloids made blue jays and other birds vomit; they soon learned not to eat the Monarch butterflies. The poisonous glycoside not only gives the Monarch butterfly pro-tection from bird predators, but also indirectly the Viceroy butter-fly, which has apparently evolved to mimic the Monarch butter-fly in appearance. This mimicry gives the Viceroy similar protec-tion, even though it does not eat milkweeds and is not poisonous.

58

The butterfly milkweed is one of the most strikingly beautiful wildflowers. Its bright yellow-to-red-orange flowers are familiar accents on the prairie, along a roadside, or in a woodland opening. It is well suited to a sunny location in any flower garden and attracts Monarch and other butterflies. It is easily propagated from seed, which should be cold-treated for three months, although some seeds will germinate without cold treatment. Propagation by cuttings of the tuberous rhizome is also easy and reliable. The cuttings should be made when the plant is dormant. Each piece of the rhizome should have at least one bud (they are about two inches apart). Both seedlings and cuttings will usually bloom in their second year, although cuttings will occasionally bloom during their first year. Seeds and plants of selected cultivars are available from many nurseries. When the roots of the butterfly milkweed were more commonly harvested for their medicinal use, the plants were dug when dormant in the late fall.

Other milkweed species can be propagated similarly. The endangered Meade's milkweed, *A. meadii* Torr., should not be propagated from the wild as it is protected by federal law, difficult to propagate, and not very vigorous (Rock, 1977, p. 21).

Aster novae-angliae
New England Aster

New England aster, aster, Michael-
mas daisy, starwort, and frost
flower.

INDIAN NAMES

The Blackfeet name for the aster,
A. falcatus Lindl., is "Sik-a-pis-
chis" (white flower) (Johnston,
1970, p. 320). The Mesquakie name
for the smooth blue aster, *A. laevis*
L., is "no'sowini" (sweat smoke-
reviver) (Smith, 1928, p. 211). The
Cheyenne name for the aster,
Aster foliaceus Lindl., is "sto'
wahts is se' e yo" (ear medicine)
(Grinnell, 1962, 2:187).

SCIENTIFIC NAME

Aster novae-angliae L. is a member of the Asteraceae (Sunflower
Family). The genus name, *Aster*,
means "star" in both Greek and
Latin and refers to the radiating
ray flowers. The species name,
novae-angliae, means "of New
England."

DESCRIPTION

Perennial herbs 5–12 dm (1½–
4 ft) tall; stems erect, glandular-
hairy, especially toward the top,
often clustered. Leaves alternate,
simple, entire, lance-shaped to
egg-shaped, clasping at the base,
2–10 cm (¾–4 in) long, 1–2 cm
(⅜–¾ in) wide, the lowermost
typically absent at blooming,
the uppermost greatly reduced.

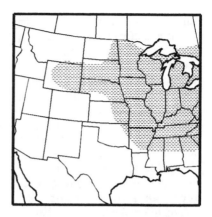

Flower heads clustered near ends
of branches, from Sep to Oct; ray
flowers 50–100, up to 2 cm (¾ in)
long, bluish-purple; disk flowers
yellow. Fruits dry, silky-hairy
achenes less than 2 mm (1/16 in)
long, with numerous tiny bristles
at the tip.

HABITAT

Prairies, thickets, stream banks,
and roadsides, often in sandy areas.

PARTS USED

Stems, leaves, or entire plant.

INDIAN USE

The Blackfeet used a tea made
from an unidentified aster as an
enema for babies with gas pains or
intestinal trouble (Hellson, 1974,
p. 66). It was administered by being
blown through a greased eagle
wing bone. The Cheyennes used
the aster, *A. foliaceus*, to relieve

earache by making a tea of the dry stems and dropping some into the ear (Grinnell, 1962, 2:187). The Pawnees claimed that an aster (unidentified) was the best material for moxa. Its stems were reduced to charcoal, then pieces a few millimeters in length were placed on the skin over a painful area and burned (Gilmore, 1977, p. 81).

The Mesquakies burned the smooth blue aster, *A. laevis*, and the white aster, *A. ericoides* L., to create smoke in a sweat bath. To revive an unconscious person, they forced this smoke up his or her nostrils (Smith, 1928, pp. 211–12). The Mesquakies used the white woodland aster, *A. lateriflorus* (L.) Britt., in a steam bath and also used the blossoms as a smudge to cure mental illness. The Potawatomis used the aster, *A. furcatus* Burgess, to cure severe headaches by steeping the leaves, then rubbing the solution on the head (Smith, 1933, pp. 49–50). In addition, they brewed a medicinal tea from the flowering tops of the aster, *A. shortii* Lindl., and like the Mesquakies, they used the New England aster, *A. novae-angliae* L., as a reviving smoke treatment.

The Zunis crushed the foliage of the panicled aster, *A. hesperius* A. Gray, sprinkled it on live coals, and inhaled the smoke to treat nosebleed (Stevenson, 1915, p. 43). They also had special uses of this plant. One of them involved a treatment for bullet or arrow wounds performed by members of the Priesthood of the Bow. This use was reported by Matilda Stevenson in 1915:

A tea is made by boiling the entire plant. If practicable, the missile is removed by squeezing. The wound is washed out with a bit of twisted cloth dipped into the warm tea. When possible the cloth is passed through the cavity of the wound; a slender twig wrapped with raw cotton is then dipped into the tea and the wound is again washed until thoroughly cleansed. Piñyon gum, softened by chewing, is made into a pencil, rolled in powdered root, and inserted into the wound. After withdrawing the gum pencil a quantity of the root powder is sprinkled into the wound; then a pinch of finely ground piñyon moistened with spittle is put on the wound, and bandaged in place. This treatment is repeated in the morning and at sunset. Previous to the dressing of the wound each time, if the missile has not been removed the medicine-man endeavors to extract it by pressure. The younger-brother Bow Priest informed the writer that usually not more than two days were required for the extraction of the bullet or arrow by means of this process; but should it not be removed in this way, resort was had to the knife (ibid.).

MEDICAL HISTORY

Constantine Rafinesque described the use of asters in 1830:

Aster, Starwort . . . Never before introduced in Materia Medica. I am indebted to Dr. Lawrence, of New Lebanon, for the following indications. The Aster novae angliae *is employed in decoction internally, with a strong decoction externally, in many eruptive diseases of the skin; it removes also the poisonous state of the skin caused by Rhus or Shumac [poison ivy or poison oak]. The* A. cordifolius *is an excellent aromatic nervine in many cases preferable to Valerian. Many other species must be equally good, such as* A. puniceus *and those with a strong scent; they ought to be tried as equivalents of Valerian in epilepsy, spasms, hysterics, &c (Rafinesque, 1830, p. 198).*

The 1916 *National Standard Dispensatory* states that the flowers of *A. shortii* have been used as an expectorant, emmenagogue, and also a cure for croup (Smith, 1933, p. 50).

SCIENTIFIC RESEARCH

Some asters are known to accumulate toxic amounts of selenium (Stephens, 1980, p. 154).

CULTIVATION

The numerous *Aster* species can be propagated either by seed or by root division. Stratification of the seeds increases the germination rate threefold, and seedlings started in the fall or early in the spring may bloom the first year (Art, 1986, p. 82). Most asters require full-to-partial sun. The best time for propagation by division is in the late fall. There are many cultivars of asters with purple, pink, or white flowers, and many of them are varieties of *A. novae-angliae*. In a garden, pruning asters back during the early summer will encourage a bushier form, and may be necessary to keep the plants from falling over when heavily laden with flowers in the fall. In my garden, I have encouraged a commercial variety of New England aster to bloom twice per season by growing it next to my greenhouse, which may warm its soil and cause it to bloom earlier than normal (in July). Then I cut back the plant to four inches, and it adds new growth and sends out a few more flowers in October. Once established, asters may self-sow their seeds if bare soil is available.

Astragalus canadensis
Canada Milkvetch

COMMON NAMES

Canada milkvetch, milkvetch
(some of the poisonous species are
referred to as poison milkvetch or
loco weed).

INDIAN NAMES

The Omaha and Ponca name
for the Canada milkvetch is
"gansatho" (rattle), in reference to
its seeds, which rattle in the pods
when dry (Gilmore, 1977, p. 39).
The Blackfeet name for Canada
milkvetch is "kach-a-tan" (tender root) (Johnston, 1970, p. 314).
The Lakota names for Canada
milkvetch are "peju'ta ska hu"
(white stem medicine) and "sunko'
wasa'kala" (yellow root). The
Lakotas call the slender milkvetch,
A. gracilis, "peju'ta skuya" (sweet
medicine). They have two names
for the alkali milkvetch, *A. racemosus* Pursh: "sunkle'ja hu" (horse
urine stem), referring to its pungent odor, probably caused by the
poisonous levels of selenium it
accumulates; and "peju'ta ska hu"
(white stem medicine) (Rogers,
1980, pp. 45–46). The Cheyenne
name for the standing milkvetch,
A. adsurgens Pall. var. *robustior*
Hook., is "mahkha' nowas" (poison weed medicine) (Grinnell,
1962, 2:40).

SCIENTIFIC NAME

Astragalus canadensis L. is a
member of the Fabaceae (Bean
Family). *Astragalus* is derived

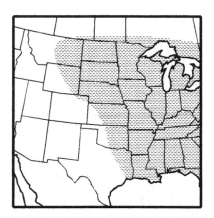

from the Greek "astragalos," an
ancient name of a plant in the
pea family. The species name,
canadensis, means "of Canada."

DESCRIPTION

Perennial herbs 3–12 dm (1–4 ft)
tall; stems erect, often branched,
1 to many from rhizomes. Leaves
alternate, pinnately compound;
leaflets 15–35, elliptic. Flowers
in dense, elongate groups among
upper leaves, from May to Aug;
petals 5, upper 1 larger and erect, 2
lower ones boat-shaped, 2 wings at
sides, greenish-white to pinkish-
white. Fruits cylindrical, beaked,
10–15 mm (⅜–⅝ in) long; seeds
about 2 mm (approximately 1/16 in)
long, smooth, brown.

HABITAT

Moist prairies, stream banks, and
open wooded hillsides, frequently
in sandy soils.

Roots, stems, and leaves.

INDIAN USE

A tea of the root of the Canada milkvetch was used by the Dakotas as a febrifuge for children (Gilmore, 1977, p. 39). The Lakotas pulverized the roots of Canada milkvetch and the alkali milkvetch, *A. racemosus*, and chewed them for pains of the chest and back (Rogers, 1980, p. 45; Buechel, 1983, p. 440). Apparently the roots of either plant could be eaten to relieve coughing. Canada milkvetch roots were used for treating loss of appetite. They could also be combined with roots of wild licorice, *Glycyrrhiza lepidota* Pursh, to arrest the spitting of blood. Lakota mothers with no breast milk chewed the roots of the slender milkvetch, *A. gracilis*, to promote milk production. The Lakotas used unidentified species of *Astragalus* to make a tea for treating heart trouble and stomach pains.

The Blackfeet treated patients who were spitting blood by having them chew the root of Canada milkvetch; a tea was made from the root for the same symptoms. Also, the vapor from the boiling roots was used to bathe the chest for these symptoms or to treat a child's aching chest, and the chewed root was applied to cuts before they were bandaged (Hellson, 1974, pp. 71, 83).

The Cheyennes used the stand-ing milkvetch, *A. adsurgens* Pall. var. *robustior* Hook., for cases of poison ivy and other cases of plant dermatitis (Grinnell, 1962, 2:40). They ground the leaves and stems of the plant into a powder and sprinkled it on the afflicted areas when the inflamed skin had a watery appearance.

The Arikaras apparently used some species of *Astragalus* as medicine. When the explorer John Bradbury visited the Arikara village along the Missouri River in present-day South Dakota on June 12, 1809, an Arikara medicine man showed Bradbury his "medicine bag." It contained two species of *Astragalus* that were new to Bradbury (Thwaites, 1905, 5:133).

SCIENTIFIC RESEARCH

Although at least one species, the ground plum milkvetch, *A. crassicarpus* Nutt., is edible (Kindscher, 1987, pp. 60–63), many others contain toxic substances. These include the poison milkvetches and locoweeds (*A. racemonsus, A. bisulcatus, A. adsurgens,* and *A. mollissimus*) and the related *Oxytropis lambertii* and *O. sericea*, which are similar in appearance. These locoweeds either produce a toxic alkaloid substance or accumulate selenium when growing on selenium-bearing soils, or both. Poisoning by these plants has been known to make cattle and horses "loco." In selenium poisoning, livestock become lethargic and suffer diarrhea, loss of hair, breakage at the base of the hoof, excessive urination, difficult breathing, rapid and weak pulse, and coma. Death results from the failure of the lungs and heart. In poisonings by the woolly locoweed, *A. mollissimus*, there is lack of coordination, vision trouble, trembling, listlessness, abortion, inability to eat or drink, and paralysis of the legs (Stephens, 1980, pp. 46–47). The poisonous substance in woolly locoweed has been identified as lococine (Bare, 1979, p. 165).

CULTIVATION

Because the milkvetches have attractive flowers and distinctive seed pods, they are interesting specimen plants for rock gardens. Many have specific soil requirements and will not tolerate wet conditions. The Canada milkvetch is easily established by planting stratified seed in the spring. Division of this milkvetch's rootstock is difficult, but cuttings are sometimes successful. Many other *Astragalus* species can be exceptional rock garden specimens in dry climates. For a thorough discussion of them, see Claude Barr's *Jewels of the Plains* (Barr, 1983, pp. 35–41).

Baptisia bracteata
Yellow Wild Indigo

Yellow wild indigo, wild indigo, plains wild indigo, false indigo, bastard indigo, and rattlepod.

INDIAN NAMES

The Omaha and Ponca name for the yellow wild indigo is "gasatho" (rattle), referring to the seeds that rattle in their seed pods (Gilmore, 1977, p. 38). Young Indian boys used the pods as rattles when they pretended to take part in ceremonial dances. The Omahas and Poncas also refer to the plant as "tdika shande nuga" (male ground plum milkvetch [*Astragalus crassicarpus* L.]) because it is similar to ground plum milkvetch, but much more robust (male). The Pawnee name for the yellow wild indigo is "pira-kari" (many children), apparently also referring to the seeds that rattle in their pods (ibid.). The Osage name for an unknown *Baptisia* species is "keugoe hi" (no translation given) (Munson, 1981, p. 232). The Mesquakie name for the white wild indigo, *Baptisia lactea* (Raf.) Thieret, is "takakwo'on" (shade for ground squirrels) (Smith, 1928, p. 228).

SCIENTIFIC NAME

Baptisia bracteata Muhl. ex Ell. is a member of the Fabaceae (Bean Family). The name *Baptisia* comes from the Greek "baptisis" (a dipping). Since this plant turns black upon injury or death, it was ap-

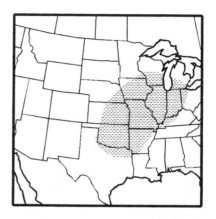

parently used as a weak dye. The species name, *bracteata*, refers to the plant's leaf-like appendages called bracts.

DESCRIPTION

Perennial herbs 2–6 dm (8–24 in) tall; stems soft, hairy, much-branched above. Leaves alternate, stalkless, compound; leaflets usually 3, lance-shaped to elliptic, 2.5–10 cm (1–4 in) long. Flowers in showy, drooping or spreading groups, from Apr to Jun; petals 5, upper 1 larger and erect, 2 lower ones boat-shaped, 2 wings at sides, pale yellow to dark yellow. Fruits inflated, egg-shaped, beaked, 3–5 cm (1 3/16–2 in) long, turning black with age or when damaged; seeds about 4 mm (3/16 in) long, brown.

HABITAT

Prairies and plains.

All parts.

The Pawnees ground yellow wild indigo seeds, mixed them with buffalo fat, and applied them as an ointment for colic by rubbing them on the abdomen (Gilmore, 1977, p. 38). The Osages made an eyewash from an unspecified part of a wild indigo, *Baptisia* species (Munson, 1981, p. 232).

The Mesquakies used the white wild indigo, *B. lactea*, to promote vomiting and to treat eczema. They also boiled it and applied it to sores of long-standing and to inflammed mucous membrane of the nose produced by catarrh. John McIntosh, a Mesquakie medicine man, used it as one of many ingredients in an internal medicine. The Mesquakies also mixed the stems and twigs of the white wild indigo with the bark of the sycamore, *Platanus occidentalis* L., for use on knife or ax wounds. They called this medicine "papikwaski" (hollow stem), referring to the hollow stem of the white wild indigo (Smith, 1928, pp. 228, 335).

The ethnobotanist Huron Smith reported in 1928 that the root and herbage of the white wild indigo were used in Iowa as an emeto-cathartic and intestinal stimulant and in the treatment of typhus, scarlet fever, and epidemic dysentery. He reported that moderate doses increased respiration and reflex action, while lethal doses produce death by respiratory paralysis (ibid.).

Professor B. B. Smythe of the Kansas Medical College reported in 1901 that the wild indigos, *B. bracteata, B. lactea,* and *B. australis* (L.) R. Br. var. *minor,* were "alterative, antipyretic, antiseptic, astringent, cathartic, emetic, and tonic" (Smythe, 1901, p. 194). The related wild indigo, *B. tinctoria* (L.) R. Br., found in the eastern United States, was officially listed in the *U.S. Pharmacopoeia* from 1831 to 1842 and in the *National Formulary* from 1916 to 1936.

Recent German research indicates that extracts from *Baptisia* species are potential stimulants to the immune system (Bodinet, Buescher, and Kopanski, 1989, p. 659; Beuscher and Kopanski, 1985, pp. 381–84). Yellow wild indigo contains the alkaloid anagyrine, while white wild indigo contains the alkaloids baptisin and cytisine. The wild blue indigo, *B. australis,* contains several alkaloids, including cystisine (probably the most common), N-methylcytisine, sparteine, anagyrine, rhombifoline, tinctorine, and lupaninne (Wink et al., 1983, p. 254). Not only are these alkaloids regarded as herbivore repellants, they are also thought to be active in allelopathic (plant versus plant) interactions. Most of these alkaloids are found in all parts of the plant, and most are toxic. No human poisonings from this plant have been reported (Lampe and McCann, 1985, p. 38). However, these plants should not be considered safe to use.

CULTIVATION

The wild indigos are spectacular in flower. If they were easier to propagate, they would be more commonly grown as ornamentals. One of the early observations of the yellow wild indigo was written by Thomas Nuttall, who described a colorful prairie in Arkansas: "The whole plain was, in places, enlivened with the *Sisyrinchium*

anceps [probably blue-eyed grass], producing flowers of an uncommon magnitude; amidst this assemblage it was not easy to lose sight of the azure larkspur, whose flowers are of the brightest ultramarine; in the depressions also grew the ochroleucous *Baptisia*, loaded with papilionaceous flowers, nearly as large as those of the garden pea" (Thwaites, 1905, 13:202).

Wild indigo seeds must be stratified for several weeks or scarified with a file to break the hard seed coat. Seeds gathered in the wild are often infested with weevils and should be frozen or refrigerated until planted. Unfortunately, seedlings are weak and often die, and division of the rootstock is difficult because of the extensive root system. Because of the low success rate, division should only be attempted with young, cultivated plants.

Croton texensis
Texas Croton

COMMON NAMES

Texas croton, croton, skunkweed (referring to its smell), and barbasco.

INDIAN NAMES

The Lakota name for Texas croton is "waxpe xca xca" (flower leaf) (Munson, 1981, p. 233). The Kiowa name is "tai-me" (Sun dance weed) (Vestal and Shultes, 1939, p. 36).

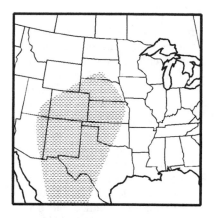

SCIENTIFIC NAME

Croton texensis (Kl.) Muell. Arg. is a member of the Euphorbiaceae (Spurge Family). *Croton* comes from the Greek "kroton" (tick), the ancient name for the castor bean plant. Its seeds resemble ticks, as do the seeds of the type species of the genus, *Croton tiglium* L. The species name, *texensis*, means "of Texas."

DESCRIPTION

Silvery annual herbs 2.3–7.5 dm (¾–2 ½ ft) tall; stems erect, single, branched above, covered with tiny star-shaped hairs. Leaves alternate, simple, stalked, lance-shaped to elliptic, 2–7 cm (¾–2 ¾ in) long, 0.6–2 cm (¼–¾ in) wide, margins entire. Flowers in small clusters near ends of branches, from May through Oct; male and female flowers on separate plants, without petals. Fruits rounded, hairy, 3-lobed capsules containing 3 seeds.

HABITAT

Sandhills and sandy soils.

PARTS USED

Leaves, entire plant.

INDIAN USE

The Lakotas made a tea from the leaves of Texas croton for stomach pains (Buechel, 1983, p. 520). The Pawnees used the leaf tea to bathe young babies when they were sick (Gilmore, 1977, p. 47). The Kiowas apparently learned of the Texas croton in 1765 from their allies, the Crows, but no specific use by the Kiowas was reported (Mooney, 1898, in Vestal and Shultes, 1939, p. 36).

In the Southwest, the Zunis made a tea of the entire plant that they used as a purgative; they also drank it to relieve stomach pains, to stimulate action of the kidneys, and to cure snakebite (Stevenson, 1915, p. 45; Camazine and Bye,

73

1980, pp. 381–83). The Zunis commonly used Texas croton and the yellow-spined thistle, *Cirsium ochrocentrum* A. Gray., for venereal disease by drinking a quantity of tea made from the plants. This treatment must be fairly recent, since gonorrhea and syphilis were probably unknown in North America before European contact. In this unusual and apparently successful treatment, the patient drinks the tea, runs rapidly for about a mile to induce sweating, then is bundled in blankets. Research has shown that raising the body temperature above its normal level may be effective in treating venereal disease. One study demonstrated that the syphilis-causing organism, *Treponema pallidum*, is immobilized by a temperature of 105.6°F sustained for two hours. Another study demonstrated that 104°F for two hours sufficed to kill the syphilis organism in the external lesions of primary and secondary syphilis (Stokes et al., in Camazine and Bye, 1980, p. 383; Carpenter et al., 1933, pp. 981–90). There is also substantial evidence that the organism responsible for gonorrhea is similarly sensitive to elevated temperatures.

MEDICAL HISTORY

Dr. B. B. Smythe, a Professor of Medical Botany at the Kansas Medical College, reported that several species of *Croton*, including the Texas croton, had the following general uses in 1901: "aperient, cathartic, diaphoretic, stimulant, and vesicant" (Smythe, 1901, p. 186). Texas croton and croton oil were rarely used in medicine in the United States, but croton oil was used medicinally in Europe.

SCIENTIFIC RESEARCH

The active chemical compound in the Texas croton is believed to be croton oil, which is obtained commercially from a small tree, *Croton tiglium* (Camazine and Bye, 1980, p. 382). Croton oil contains croton-resin, a mixture of croton-globulin and croton-albumin that is comparable with ricin from castor beans. The oil also contains "diesters of the tetracyclic diterpene, phorbol; acids involved are acetic as short-chain acid, and capric, lauric and palmitic as long-chain acids" (Trease and Evans, 1973, p. 473). Croton oil has been reported to be a co-carcinogen. It can cause skin dermatitis and is no longer used in Europe (where it was once widely used) because of its great toxicity. Twenty drops are lethal (Frohne and Pfander, 1984, p. 113).

CULTIVATION

Texas croton is a weedy annual plant, and its cultivation is not recommended.

Cucurbita foetidissima
Buffalo Gourd

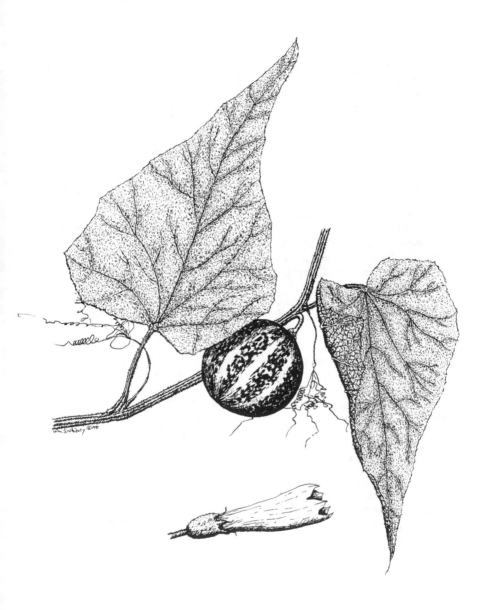

Buffalo gourd, coyote gourd, Missouri gourd, wild gourd, fetid gourd, fetid wild pumpkin, wild pumpkin, chili coyote, and calabezella.

INDIAN NAMES

The Osage names for the buffalo gourd are "monkon tonga" (big medicine) and "monkon nikasinga" (human being medicine) (Munson, 1981, p. 223). The Dakotas call it "wagamun pezhuta" (pumpkin medicine) (Gilmore, 1977, p. 64). The Omahas and Poncas call it "niashiga makan" (human being medicine), and they distinguish between male and female plant forms (ibid.). All of these names refer to both the mystical and medicinal powers of the plant. The Kiowa name is "ko-konbaw" (no translation given) (Vestal and Shultes, 1939, p. 53).

SCIENTIFIC NAME

Cucurbita foetidissima H.B.K. is a member of the Cucurbitaceae (Cucumber Family). *Cucurbita* means "gourd" in Latin. The name *foetidissima* means "ill-smelling," which describes the rank odor of the leaves and the inside of the gourd.

DESCRIPTION

Coarse perennial herbs; stems trailing on ground, to 3 m (10 ft)

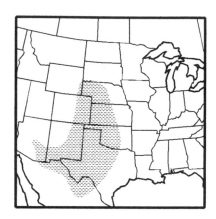

long. Leaves alternate, simple, gray-green, triangular to egg-shaped, 1–2 dm (4–8 in) long, upper surfaces rough, lower surfaces hairy, margins irregularly toothed. Flowers trumpetlike, solitary among leaves, from Jun to Aug; petals 5–12 cm (2–5 in) long, united into a tube below, separating into 5 lobes above, yellow-orange. Fruits fleshy, spherical, 5–10 cm (2–4 in) in diameter, green and white striped; seeds egg-shaped, flattened, and cream colored.

HABITAT

Prairies (in dry soil), railroad track right-of-ways, and disturbed areas.

PARTS USED

Roots, flowers, and seeds.

In 1919, the ethnobotanist Melvin Gilmore described the importance of the buffalo gourd to the Omahas, Poncas, and Dakotas:

This is one of the plants considered to possess special mystic properties. People were afraid to dig it or handle it unauthorized. The properly constituted authorities might dig it, being careful to make the prescribed offering of tobacco to the spirit of the plant, accompanied by the proper prayers, and using extreme care not to wound the root in removing it from the earth. A man of my acquaintance in the Omaha tribe essayed to take up a root of this plant and in doing so cut the side of the root. Not long afterward one of his children fell, injuring its side so that death ensued, which was ascribed by the tribe to the wounding of the root by the father (Gilmore, 1977, p. 64).

These tribes encouraged outsiders like Melvin Gilmore to harvest the root for them. He wrote: "When I have exhibited specimens of the root seeking information, the Indians have asked for it. While they fear to dig it themselves, after I have assumed the risk of so doing they are willing to profit by my temerity; or it may be that the white man is not held to account by the Higher Powers of the Indian's world" (ibid.).

The buffalo gourd was believed by these tribes to have male and female forms. An ailment (often a pain) was treated by using the corresponding portion of the almost human-sized root, thus following the Doctrine of Signatures.

The Omahas pulverized the portion of the root to be used in a treatment with water and drank it (Fletcher and La Flesche, 1911, p. 585). They used the root to speed protracted labor in childbirth. When mixed with gayfeather (*Liatris aspera* Michx.) and the bark of the Kentucky coffee tree, *Gymnocladus dioica* (L.) K. Koch, it was used as an appetizer and tonic (ibid.; Gilmore, 1913a, p. 335).

The Osages used the buffalo gourd as a mystical medicine for long life (Munson, 1981, p. 233). They believed that the medicine was revealed to them by the buffalo bull as recounted in the following legend:

Mon-kon' Ni-ka-shi-ga, *Man Medicine (*Cucurbita foetidissima*)*

In the presence of the Mon-kon'
Ni-ka-shi-ga, Man Medicine,
They came and stood,
Saying: Shall this plant be a
medicine to the little ones.
The grandfather replied: When the
little ones use this plant as
medicine
They live to see old age.
When the people use this plant
also for medicine,
They shall enable themselves to
see old age
(La Flesche, 1932, p. 367).

The Kiowas made a tea from the peeled, boiled roots to induce vomiting (Vestal and Shultes, 1939, p. 54). The Cheyenne use of "seotse'-ma'haono" (ghost melon), which has been identified as a *Cucurbita* species, may have been the buffalo gourd. If so, the Cheyennes living in Montana must have obtained it from the Cheyenne reservation in Oklahoma, since the buffalo gourd does not grow in Montana (Hart, 1981, p. 24). It was used for various medicinal treatments.

In the Southwest, the Zunis applied the powdered seeds and flowers, mixed with saliva, to swellings (Camazine and Bye, 1980, p. 375). The Tewas were reported to grind the roots to a powder, stir it in cold water, and drink it as a laxative (Robbins, Harrington, and Freire-Marreco, 1916, p. 63).

ANGLO FOLK USE

No Anglo folk use of buffalo gourd has been recorded. However, Chicanos in New Mexico have described the buffalo gourd (probably the root and the fruit) as a very strong, bitter laxative; overdoses they recognized as fatal. They also used the root, which contains saponin, as a soap substitute and a shampoo, although it can be irritating to the skin. They mixed fresh-baked fruits or ground roots with olive oil to treat rheumatism (Curtin, 1976, p. 46).

MEDICAL HISTORY

In B. B. Smythe's 1901 list of medicinal plants of Kansas, he reported that the buffalo gourd is "anthelmintic, astringent, and cathartic" (Smythe, 1901, p. 197).

SCIENTIFIC RESEARCH

Most scientific study of the buffalo gourd is related to its starch and oil production. It is being promoted as a cultivated plant for its root starch and seed oil content (Bemis et al., 1978, pp. 87–95; Hinman, 1984, p. 1447). The root, leaves, and fruits of the buffalo gourd contain the bitter glycosides called cucurbitacins that, along with the saponins, are probably responsible for some of the medicinal claims. These substances must be separated from the starch and oil before they can be used as human food.

CULTIVATION

Buffalo gourd has attractive, squashlike flowers and spherical gourds that turn from striped green to yellow-orange when mature. The gourds can be harvested for ornamental purposes in the fall. The buffalo gourd plant is extremely drought resistant because of its large root, which is literally human-sized. Plants can be propagated either by seed or by cuttings. However, its placement in the wild garden should be carefully considered, because it will quickly spread over all neighboring plants. One extremely large root of this plant weighed 178 pounds and had a maximum circumference of 4.7 feet and vines that averaged over 20 feet in length. Researchers estimated that it covered more than 1,200 square feet and had 15,720 leaves (Dittmer and Talley, 1964, p. 122).

Dalea candida
White Prairie Clover

Prairie clover, white prairie clover, and slender white prairie clover.

INDIAN NAMES

The Omaha and Ponca name for the prairie clovers is "makan skithe" (sweet medicine), a name they used for several medicinal plants. The Pawnees called the prairie clovers "kahts-pidipatski" (small medicine) and "kiha piliwus hawastat" (broom weed) because they used the tough stems to sweep their lodges (Gilmore, 1977, p. 42). The Lakota name for the purple prairie clover, *Dalea purpurea* Vent., is "toka'la tapejut'ta hu win'yula" (kit fox's medicine stem female), and their name for white prairie clover is its male equivalent, partly because it has coarser leaves (Rogers, 1980, p. 72). The Kiowa name for white prairie clover is "khaw-tan-ee" (Vestal and Shultes, 1939, p. 33).

The Mesquakie name for the purple prairie clover is "kepia'ekie'shikiki" (thimble top) (Smith, 1928, p. 229). Two Lakota names for the silky prairie clover, *Dalea villosa* (Nutt.) Spreng., are "casmu' huhloho'ta" (gray sand stem) and "wapta'ya huholho'ta" (gray weed stem) (Rogers, 1980, p. 47).

SCIENTIFIC NAME

Dalea candida Michx. ex Willd. is a member of the Fabaceae (Bean Family). *Dalea* is named in honor of Samuel Dale, an English botanist (1659–1739), and refers to the color of the flower; *candida* means "of dazzling white." Until recently, these plants were classified in the genus *Petalostemon*.

DESCRIPTION

Perennial herbs 3–10 dm (1–3 ¼ ft) tall, with thick taproots; stems 1 to several, ribbed, sometimes dotted with glands. Leaves alternate, pinnately compound, 1.5–6 cm (⅝–2 ⅜ in) long; leaflets 5–13, egg-shaped to elliptic or oblong, surfaces with minute dots. Flowers in oval to cylindrical spikes at ends of stems, from May to Sep; petals 5, white, upper 1 larger and erect, lower 2 boat-shaped, 2 wings at sides. Fruits oval, 2.6–4.5 mm (1/16–3/16 in) long, dotted with glands, sepals persisting around bases.

Prairies and rocky open woods.

PARTS USED

Mainly the root, also the flowers.

INDIAN USE

The white and purple prairie clovers were used for both food and medicine. The roots of both species were eaten and the leaves were made into a beverage (Kindscher, 1987, pp. 109–11).

The ethnobotanist Melvin Gilmore reported the ritualized use of the white and purple prairie clovers by the Plains Indians to ward off disease. The pulverized root was boiled, and after the sediment settled to the bottom, the liquid was drunk to prevent disease. "The sediment was collected in the drinking-shell and carried to a place prepared for it, where it was buried with respect" (Gilmore, 1977, p. 42).

The Lakotas used the purple prairie clover as medicine for unspecified ailments (Munson, 1981, p. 237). They also used the roots of the silky prairie clover, *Dalea villosa* (Nutt.) Spreng, as a purge, and the leaves and blossoms were eaten for a swollen throat (Buechel, 1983, p. 110). The Dakotas made a tea from the leaves of the nine-anther prairie clover, *Dalea enneandra* Nutt., to relieve cases of stomachache and dysentery (Gilmore, 1913b, p. 366). The

Kiowa-Apaches used short sections of the straight, brittle stems of the nine-anther prairie clover burned on the skin as a moxa for headache, rheumatism, and pneumonia (Jordan, 1965, p. 109).

The Mesquakies made a tea from the large taproot of the purple prairie clover as a cure for measles. To treat diarrhea they mixed the flowers with the bark of the white oak, *Quercus alba* L., and the root of wild cranesbill, *Geranium maculatum* L. They called this medicine "neswaiyagatwi" (of three different kinds) (Smith, 1928, p. 229). In the Southwest, the Navahos also used the white prairie clover in an unspecified manner to relieve abdominal pain (Elmore, 1944, p. 96).

SCIENTIFIC RESEARCH

The prairie clovers were apparently not used in any Anglo folk remedies or in modern medicine. The white and purple prairie clovers, which are very similar in appearance, are not known to have toxic properties. The woolly dalea, *D. lanata* Spreng., contains alkaloids (Burlage, 1968, p. 101).

CULTIVATION

The prairie clovers are attractive ornamental plants and important constituents of prairie restorations and native warm-season grass plantings. Their ability to fix atmospheric nitrogen gives them an important ecological role. The white and purple prairie clovers are easy to propagate by seed. Stratified seed, planted in the spring, will germinate and grow quickly the first year. For larger areas, such as prairie restorations, seeds can be sown in the fall. There are approximately 384,000 individual seeds in a pound of prairie clover seed; nine seeds per square foot is the recommended density for larger plantings (Salac et al., 1978, p. 4).

White and purple prairie clover grow rapidly after germination, reaching 15–22 cm (6–9 in) in height by midsummer. In my garden, I have observed some blossoms the first year after sowing and, unless there is an unusual drought, flowering will occur the second year. By midsummer of the first year, the taproot will be 14 to 22 inches deep. The roots of a mature white prairie clover extend 105–200 cm (3 ½–6 ft) downward (Weaver and Fitzpatrick, 1934, p. 223).

Echinacea angustifolia
Purple Coneflower

COMMON NAMES

Purple coneflower, echinacea, snakeroot, Kansas snakeroot, black sampson, narrow-leaved purple coneflower, scurvy root, Indian head, comb flower, black susans, and hedge hog. The last four names refer to the seed head, which is round, black, and spiny.

INDIAN NAMES

The numerous Indian names tell of the importance and uses of the purple coneflower. The Omahas and Poncas, who sometimes used the seed head to comb their hair, call it "mika-hi" (comb plant) (Gilmore, 1977, p. 74). They also call it "inshtogahte-hi," referring to their use of the plant as an eyewash ("inshta" means "eye"). The Pawnee name for purple coneflower, "ksapitahako" (hand, to whirl), refers "to its use by children in play when they take two stalks of it and whirl one round the other, the two stalks touching by the two heads." They also call it "saparidu hahts" (mushroom medicine) because its seed head is similar in shape to a mushroom (ibid). When they find it growing in the hills, the Lakota call it "ica'hpe hu" (something used to knock something down) (Rogers, 1980, p. 51). When they find it in lower places, it is called "on'glakcapi" (something to comb the hair with).

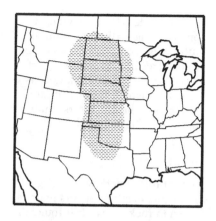

SCIENTIFIC NAME

Echinacea angustifolia DC. is a member of the Asteraceae (Sunflower Family). The eighteenth-century German botanist Conrad Moench named the genus *Echinacea*. This name, which comes from the Greek "echinos" (hedgehog), refers to the spiny, rounded seed head, similar in appearance to a hedgehog or sea urchin. The species name, *angustifolia*, means "narrow-leaved." In some of the older literature cited below, the names *Rudbeckia* and *Brauneria* were used for this genus instead of *Echinacea*.

DESCRIPTION

Perennial herbs 1.5–6 dm (½–2 ft) tall, with a woody taproot; stems 1 to several, mostly unbranched, rough-hairy. Leaves alternate, simple, narrowly lance-shaped to egg-shaped, 5–30 cm (2–12 in) long, 1.5–4 cm (½–1½ in) wide, margins entire. Flower heads 4–

7.5 cm wide (1½–3 in) wide, at ends of long stalks, from Jun to Jul; ray flowers 2–4 cm (¾–1½ in) long, spreading or drooping, light pink to pale purple; disk flowers 5-lobed, brownish-purple, situated among stiff bracts. Fruits small, dark, 4-angled achenes.

HABITAT

The purple coneflower, E. angustifolia, grows in dry upland prairies, often in rocky areas. It is found primarily in the Great Plains, east of the Rocky Mountains from Texas to Montana and Saskatchewan, to eastern Oklahoma, western Iowa, and western Minnesota. E. pallida occurs on rocky, open sites from northeast Texas to southwest Wisconsin (mainly on prairies east of the range of E. angustifolia). E. purpurea is found in rocky, open woods and prairies eastward from northeast Texas, Missouri, and Michigan.

PARTS USED

Primarily the root, but also the entire plant.

INDIAN USE

The purple coneflower, Echinacea angustifolia, was the most widely used medicinal plant of the Plains Indians. It was used as a painkiller and for a variety of ailments, including toothache, coughs, colds, sore throats, and snake bite.

In 1917 the ethnobotanist

Melvin Gilmore reported that the macerated root of the purple coneflower was used to treat snakebite as well as other venomous bites, stings, and poisonings by all the Indians of the Upper Missouri River region (Gilmore, 1977, p. 74). These Indians and others used the purple coneflower "for more ailments than any other plant" (Gilmore, 1913a, p. 333).

The Dakotas used the freshly scraped root as a remedy for hydrophobia and snakebite and applied it to wounds that had putrefied (Smith, 1928, p. 212). They applied the root (ground, probably) to inflamed areas to relieve the burning sensation with its "feeling of coolness" (Gilmore, 1913b, p. 368). The Lakotas ate the root and green fruit when they were thirsty or perspiring and as a painkiller for toothache, tonsillitis, stomachache, and pain in the bowels (Rogers, 1980, p. 37; Munson, 1981, p. 232). On a visit to the Rosebud Reservation in South Dakota during the summer of 1987, I learned that the purple coneflower is still widely harvested by the Lakotas for a variety of medicinal uses.

The Omahas recognized two kinds of purple coneflower: "nuga" ("male," larger and more masculine) and "miga" ("female," smaller and a more efficient medicine) (Gilmore, 1913a, pp. 323–33). They used some part of the plant for sore eyes. Omaha medicine men applied the macerated root as a local anesthetic so that they could remove pieces of meat from a boiling pot without flinching. A Winnebago medicine man also used it to make his mouth insensitive to heat so that he could take a live coal into his mouth to demonstrate his power (Gilmore, 1977, p. 79). Both of these feats helped create confidence in the ability of the medicine men to heal.

The Kiowas have used the purple coneflower root as a cough medicine since ancient times. In the 1930s, they still used the dried seed head as a comb and brush (Vestal and Shultes, 1939, p. 71). The Kiowas and the Cheyennes treated colds and sore throats by chewing a piece of the purple coneflower root and letting the saliva run down the throat (ibid.; Grinnell, 1962, 2:188).

The Cheyennes also made a tea from the leaves and roots of the purple coneflower that they used as a remedy for a sore mouth and gums. The same liquid was rubbed on a sore neck to relieve pain. Toothache caused by a large cavity was relieved by letting this liquid come in contact with it. The root was also chewed to stimulate the flow of saliva, which was especially useful for Sun Dance participants as a thirst preventative (Hart, 1981, p. 21). The Cheyennes also drank a purple coneflower tea for rheumatism, arthritis, mumps, and measles, and a salve was made for external treatment of these ailments. When the roots were mixed with blazing star, *Mentzelia laevicaulis*, and boiled, the resulting tea was drunk for smallpox. Purple

coneflower roots mixed with puffball (*Lycoperdon* species) spores and skunk oil were used in the treatment of boils.

The Mesquakies used the plant (probably *E. pallida* rather than *E. angustifolia*) as part of a medicine for stomach cramps, along with the roots of wild ginger, *Asarum canadense*, flowering spurge, *Euphorbia corollata*, and beebalm, *Monarda punctata* (Smith, 1928, p. 212).

Edwin Denig lived at Fort Union along the Missouri River in Montana for twenty-one years during the mid-1800s and came to know the Assiniboin people well. He reported that the purple coneflower was their most important medicinal plant:

The principal of these is the black root, called by them the comb root, from the pod on the top being composed of a stiff surface that can be used as a comb. It is called by the French racine noir, and grows everywhere in the prairie throughout the Indian country. It is chewed and applied in a raw state with a bandage to the part affected. We can bear witness to the efficacy of this root in the cure of the bite of the rattlesnake or in alleviating the pain and reducing the tension and inflammation of frozen parts, gunshot wounds, etc. It has a slightly pungent taste resembling black pepper, and produces a great deal of saliva while chewing it. Its virtues are known to all the tribes with which we are acquainted, and it is often used with success (Denig, 1930, pp. 425–26).

This passage also indicates that the French trappers and traders were probably aware of the medicinal qualities of the purple coneflower.

Other tribes who lived in the Prairie Bioregion (the Great Plains and the Tallgrass Prairie region to the east) and used the native purple coneflower medicinally were the Crows, Hidatsas, Comanches, and Pawnees. The Crows chewed the root for colds and drank a tea prepared from the root for colic (Hart, 1976, p. 38). Hidatsa warriors were known to chew small pieces of the root as a stimulant when traveling all night (Nickel, 1974, p. 63). The Comanches used the root for treating sore throat and toothache (Carlson and Jones, 1939, p. 521). Roots excavated from a Pawnee earthen lodge village (the Hill site, located near Guide Rock, Nebraska, and occupied around 1800) were identified as purple coneflower by Melvin Gilmore at the University of Michigan Ethnobotanical Laboratory (Wedel, 1936, p. 59).

An Indian from Mexico who served as a translator for Melvin Gilmore in 1912, when he was interviewing the Lakotas on the Pine Ridge Reservation in South Dakota, indicated that the purple coneflower was used by his people for snakebites (Gilmore, 1913b, p. 368). The native distribution of the purple coneflower does not extend into Mexico; thus its use in Mexico may indicate a history of trade for this root between tribes of the southern portion of the Prairie Bioregion and Mexico. Also, several tribes, including the Apaches, Kickapoos, and Potawatomis, retreated into Mexico in the nineteenth century and may have taken dried roots with them. On the other hand, the Mexican Indian may have been referring to *Iostephane heterophylla*, a closely related species found in Mexico.

ANGLO FOLK USE

The purple coneflower was the only native prairie plant popularized as a medicine by folk practitioners and doctors, and this did not happen quickly. During this process, the purple coneflower was used extensively as a folk remedy.

Dr. Ferdinand V. Hayden was one of the first physicians to mention the use of *Echinacea angustifolia*. In his 1859 "Botany Report to the Secretary of War" on the Upper Missouri River region, he stated that the root (incorrectly identified as *E. purpurea*) "is found abundantly throughout the country. It is very pungent and used very effectively by the traders and Indians for the cure of the bite of rattlesnake" (Hayden, 1859, p. 738).

Curtis Gates Lloyd of Lloyd Brothers Pharmacy, Inc. described the unique taste of *Echinacea angustifolia*: "Upon chewing the root of prime echinacea, a sweetish taste becomes first apparent, which on prolonged chewing is followed by an acrid, tingling sensation that remains long upon the tongue (Lloyd, 1921, p. 4).

In a 1914 issue of the *Gleaner*, Dr. J. S. Leachman reported the use of the purple coneflower root by early settlers in Oklahoma: "Old settlers all believe firmly in the virtues of Echinacea root, and use it as an aid in nearly every kind of sickness. If a cow or a horse does not eat well, the people administer Echinacea, cut up and put in the feed. I have noticed that puny stock treated in this manner soon begin to thrive" (ibid., p. 20).

MEDICAL HISTORY

H. C. F. Meyer, a patent medicine salesman from Pawnee City, Nebraska, discovered the usefulness of the purple coneflower, *E. angustifolia*, in 1871, probably learning about its medicinal qualities from Indians or early settlers (Lloyd, 1904, pp. 15–19). Meyer marketed a purple coneflower tincture as part of a secret remedy called "Meyer's Blood Purifier" and sent samples of his medicine along with the unknown western root to Dr. John King and John Uri Lloyd, both of Cincinnati, for identification and endorsement.

Dr. John King was a prominent medical practitioner and author of the 1852 *Eclectic Dispensatory of the United States of America*. John Uri Lloyd was a pharmacist and founder of Lloyd Brothers

Pharmacists, Inc., a firm that specialized in American medicinal plants (Foster, 1991, pp. 28–30). King was unwilling to endorse a secret formula that did not list its ingredients on the label; Lloyd informed Meyer that he would need the whole plant for identification, and that his company could only introduce a new drug under its botanical name.

Meyer sent the whole dried plant to Lloyd, and it was identified by Curtis Gates Lloyd as *Echinacea angustifolia* (Lloyd, 1917, p. 6). After its identification Meyer printed a new label for his patent medicine (ibid., p. 18):

ECHINACEA ANGUSTEFOLIA
This is a powerful drug as an alternative and Anti-septic in all tumorous and Syphilitic indications; old chronic wounds, such as fever sores, old ulcers, Carbuncles, Piles, eczema, wet or dry, can be cured quick and active; also Erysipelas. It will not fail in Gangrene. In fever it is a specific; typhoid can be adverted in two to three days; also in Malaria, Malignant, Remittent and Mountain fever it is a specific. It relieves pain, swelling and inflammation, by local use, internal and external. It has not and will not fail to cure Diphtheria quick. It cures bites from the bee to the rattlesnake, it is a Specific. Has been tested in more than fifty cases of mad dog bites in human and in every case it prevented hydrophobia. It has cured hydrophobia. It is

perfectly harmless, internal and
external. Dose.—One half to one
fluid-drachm 3 or 4 times a day.
Manufactured by H. C. F. Meyer,
M.D.
Patent   Pawnee City, Neb., U.S.A.

Meyer also claimed that his
medicine had produced prompt
cures in 613 cases of rattlesnake
bite in both humans and animals
(Meyer, 1887, p. 210). Lloyd wrote
that Meyer offered to "come to
Cincinnati and in the presence of a
committee selected by ourselves,
allow a rattlesnake of our selection
to bite him wherever we might
prefer the wound to be inflicted,
proposing then to antidote the poison by means of Echinacea only.
This offer (or rather, challenge) we
declined" (Lloyd, 1917, p. 5).

King introduced *Echinacea
angustifolia* to the medical profession, stating that Meyer "enter-
tains a very exalted idea of his
discovery, which certainly mer-
its a careful investigation by our
practitioners . . . and should it be
found to contain only one-half the
virtues he attributes to it, it will
form an important addition to our
materia medica" (Meyer, 1887,
p. 209). Dr. King had confidence
in the drug, partly because it was
the only substance that brought
his wife relief from her "virulent
cancer" (Lloyd, 1917, p. 4).

Lloyd, on the other hand, was
skeptical of Meyer's claims and
hesitant to introduce the drug. It
was not until several years after
King introduced the drug to the

medical profession that he convinced the Lloyd brothers to put
a purple coneflower tincture on
the market. There was already
considerable demand for the tincture from physicians, and once it
was on the market, the demand
increased greatly. Lloyd claimed
in 1917 that tincture of Echinacea
was a "therapeutic favorite with
many thousand American physicians, and which is consumed
in larger quantities to-day than
any other American drug introduced during the past thirty years"
(ibid., p. 19). It appeared to be most
effective when the tincture of the
ground root was made with four
parts alcohol to one part water
(Beringer, 1911, pp. 324–25). The
best roots were believed to come
from "the prairie lands of Kansas
and Nebraska" (Felter, 1898, p. 83).

Interest in the purple coneflower
as a native medicinal plant spurred
Boyce and Kirkland to isolate the
volatile oil of the root in the pharmacy laboratory at the University
of Kansas in 1898 (Woods, 1930,
p. 611). The oil had the odor and
taste of the purple coneflower drug
introduced by the Lloyd brothers
eleven years previously.

Many doctors and researchers
reported success in treating various disorders with the tincture
of purple coneflower. Professor
H. W. Felter, for example, called
it "A corrector of the depravation
[*sic*] of the body fluids" (Felter,
1898, p. 84). But not all doctors
were convinced of its effectiveness. The Council on Pharmacy

and Chemistry, composed of the college educated, "Regular" or traditional physicians, reported in a 1909 *Journal of the American Medical Association*:

It is worth noticing—although it is not surprising—that these far-reaching claims have been made on no better basis than that of clinical trials by unknown men who have not otherwise achieved any general reputation as acute, discriminating and reliable observers. . . . In view of the lack of scientific scrutiny of the claims made for it, echinacea is deemed unworthy of further consideration until more reliable evidence is presented in its favor (Council on Pharmacy and Chemistry, 1909, p. 1836).

They also reprinted Meyer's label and associated his claim with the college-educated "Eclectic" physicians, such as King, Lloyd, and Felter.

In 1915 researchers Heyl and Hart found no physiologically active substances in the purple coneflower (Heyl and Hart, 1915, pp. 1769–78). Five years later, Couch and Giltner were unable to find evidence that it affected botulism, anthrax, rattlesnake venom, tetanus, septicemia, tuberculosis, or trypanosomiasis (Couch and Giltner, 1920, p. 63–84). However, conclusions from this last experiment were refuted by Beal in 1921. Beal's findings suggested some benefit from the use of the purple coneflower on a clinical basis (Beal, 1921, p. 229–32). The purple coneflower, specifically *E. angustifolia*, was used by some pharmacists, and it received a quasi-endorsement when it was listed in the *National Formulary* from 1916 to 1950.

SCIENTIFIC RESEARCH

Recent scientific research has not justified Meyer's extravagant claims, but it has shown the plant to have active medicinal components. Much of the research on the purple coneflower has been done in Germany, where there is greater scientific interest in medicinal plants because more liberal laws govern their commercial availability and use (Tyler, 1981, p. 281; Foster, 1991). These experiments have been conducted on *Echinacea angustifolia* as well as the similar and closely related *E. pallida* and *E. purpurea*. Increased cultivation of *E. purpurea* and *E. angustifolia* may be needed to meet the increased commercial demand for its roots and to alleviate the effects of overharvesting wild stands. Previously there was confusion over which species was being harvested, especially between *Echinacea angustifolia* and *E. pallida*. Also, at times the identification of the prairie species, *E. angustifolia*, has been confused with the eastern species, *E. purpurea*. This confusion may have accounted for some of the early variation in experimental results.

The first pharmaceutical company's research to attribute physiological activity to the purple coneflower was conducted by the Sandoz Company and published in Germany in 1950 (Stoll et al., 1950, pp. 1877–93). They found the root to possess mild antibiotic activity against *Streptococcus* and *Staphyloccus aureus*.

In 1971, a pentane-extracted oil from the root of *Echinacea angustifolia* and *E. pallida* was found to be inhibitory to Walker carcinosarcoma 256 and P-388 lymphocytic leukemia (Voaden and Jacobson, 1972, p. 619). Italian investigators found the wound-healing effects to be attributable to echinacin B (Bonadea et al., 1971, pp. 281–95). Echinacin B is a polysaccharide that temporarily increases hyaluronic acid, a substance that acts as a binding and protective agent, increases connective tissue, forms cells called fibroblasts, and thus results in beneficial wound-healing effects.

A purple coneflower product available in Germany in 1978, containing the juice of the fresh aerial parts of *Echinacea purpurea*, was found to make mouse cells 50–80 percent resistant to influenza, herpes, and vesicular stomatitis viruses (Wacker and Hilbig, 1978, p. 89). Perhaps the most important finding so far is the discovery of large, highly active polysaccharide molecules in both *E. angustifolia* and *E. purpurea* that possess immunostimulatory properties (Wagner and Proksch, 1985, pp. 133–53; Wagner et al., 1985, pp. 1069–75).

Stimulation of the immune system appears to be strongly influenced by dose level. Recent pharmacological studies indicate that a 10-mg/kg daily dose of the polysaccharide over a ten-day period is effective as an immunostimulant. Increases in the daily dosage beyond this level, however, resulted in "markedly decreased pharmacological activity" (Wagner and Proksch, 1985, p. 137; Wagner et al., 1985, pp. 1069–75). Other research has shown that the purple coneflower produces an anti-inflammatory effect and has therapeutic value in urology, gynecology, internal medicine, and dermatology (Wagner and Proksch, 1985, p. 141; Harnischfeger and Stolze, 1980, as cited in Moring, 1984).

The purple coneflower, *E. angustifolia*, also contains chemical compounds that are insecticidal. One such compound is toxic to mosquitoes and house flies; another substance, echinolone, disrupts insect development (Hartzell, 1947, pp. 21–34; Jacobson, 1954, pp. 125–29; Voaden and Jacobson, 1972, p. 619). Researchers in the Horticulture Department of South Dakota State University are currently attempting to identify the *Echinacea angustifolia* germplasm containing the highest level of echinolone. It will be used in manufacturing an insecticide for the state's sunflower crop (Foster, 1991, p. 93).

For both Indians and Anglos, the purple coneflower has been the most widely and extensively harvested medicinal plant of the Prairie Bioregion. The pressure on wild stands of purple coneflower from harvesting has been intense during times of its greatest popularity. Dr. L. E. Sayre of the University of Kansas Pharmacy Department reported in 1897 that "students during the late summer and early fall months find in it a little profit at twenty-five cents a pound" (Sayre, 1897, p. 86). He reported that over 200,000 pounds of the dried root, worth over $100,000 (with the price rising to 50 cents per pound), were harvested in Kansas during 1902, mostly in the northwest part of the state (Sayre, 1903, p. 211). Since it takes eight-to-ten (or more) dried roots to equal one pound, about two million roots were harvested that year. The effect of this enormous harvest on the current population and distribution of the plant is unknown.

In 1902, Sayre wrote to Rodney True, who directed the investigations of drug and medical plants at the Department of Agriculture in Washington, D.C., asking that the government protect this plant against extermination (ibid., p. 212). True suggested that it be cultivated commercially. However, the demand for purple coneflower root apparently waned before the

purple coneflower was threatened with extinction and before any significant cultivation occurred in the region. The plant must be fairly resilient, since it is still common in many locations.

The demand for purple coneflower roots for medicinal use seems to have a cycle as unpredictable as the drought cycles in the region. Ronald McGregor of the University of Kansas Botany Department reported that in 1965, with a sudden research demand for *Echinacea* root, over 25,000 pounds of dried root were harvested (McGregor, 1968, pp. 115–16). At that time, *E. pallida* was the species preferred, although *E. angustifolia* was acceptable.

Interest in purple coneflower roots declined after 1965, but has increased recently. Steven Foster reports that because of excessive harvesting, purple coneflowers have been decreasing along Missouri roadsides (Foster, 1991, p. 118). In 1987 the Missouri legislature passed a law to reverse this trend by prohibiting the harvest of three *Echinacea* species—*E. pallida*, *E. purpurea*, and *E. paradoxa*—on state parkland, state forest lands, along state highways, or in wildlife areas (Berman, 1987, p. 2).

As a result of longstanding scientific interest in the purple coneflower in Germany and concern for proper identification and loss of wild stands, there is now renewed interest in cultivating the purple coneflower. When it is grown from seed, it takes three to four years for roots to reach harvestable size (Foster, 1991, p. 81). To increase the speed and frequency of germination, seeds must be stratified for two to four months. To stratify the seeds, wrap them in wet peat moss and place them in a plastic bag in the refrigerator. Seeds should be barely covered with soil when planted. Seedlings have little vigor and must be carefully weeded and watered.

Yields for cultivated, dried roots of three-year-old *Echinacea purpurea* grown at Trout Lake, Washington, were 131 kg/ha (1,200 lbs/ acre) (ibid.). Yields for the purple coneflower, *E. angustifolia*, are not available but probably would be smaller because the plant is smaller. Apparently there is no commercial production of the purple coneflower within its native range, as the commercial need is currently being met by production from the West Coast and from the harvest of wild stands.

Purple coneflowers can also be propagated by division of the crowns. This technique, which I investigated in greenhouse and field experiments, results in stronger plants initially and eliminates the tedious nurturing and tending of the slow-growing seedlings. When roots are harvested for use, the crown can be divided to make one to five "plantlets." These can be grown in flats in the greenhouse during the winter to re-establish their root systems, then replanted in the field the following spring for another round of production.

The purple coneflower is often grown simply for its ornamental value, especially for its showy flowers, but the ornamental possibilities of *Echinacea* have not been fully explored. The best possibility for obtaining a new cultivar is in the hybrids between *Echinacea purpurea* and *E. angustifolia* DC. var. *angustifolia*, whose progeny are compact, rounded, bushy plants about two feet in diameter (McGregor, 1968, p. 116). There are numerous cultivars of *Echinacea purpurea*; 'the King' and 'Sombrero' are available in the United States, and more are available in Germany.

Erigeron philadelphicus
Fleabane

Fleabane, daisy fleabane, Philadelphia fleabane, sweet scabious,
frostweed, fieldweed, and mourn-
ing widow.

INDIAN NAMES

The Mesquakie name for the
fleabane is "tcatca'mosikani"
(sneezing) (Smith, 1928, p. 213).
The Lakotas have three names
for the fleabane, *Erigeron annuus*
(L.) Pers.: "inijan pexuta" or "ini-
janpi" (sore mouth medicine),
and "onwahinjuntonpi" (tanning substance) (Munson, 1981,
p. 234). They also call the fleabane,
E. pumilus Nutt., "canxlogan hu
pteptecela" (short buffalo weed).
The Kiowas call the fleabane,
E. divergens T. & G., "a-kent-
ein" (white flower plant) (Vestal
and Shultes, 1939, p. 60). The
Cheyenne name for the fleabane,
E. peregrinus subsp. *callianthemus* (Greene) Cronq., is "ma hom'
a uts is se' e ao" (pink medicine)
(Grinnell, 1962, 2: 187).

SCIENTIFIC NAME

Erigeron philadelphicus L. is a
member of the Asteraceae (Sunflower Family). *Erigeron* comes
from the Greek "eri" (early) and
"geron" (old man). It refers to the
grayed and hairy pappus (the fluff
attached to the top of the seeds),
which becomes conspicuous soon
after the flowers fade. The species
name, *philadelphicus*, means "of
Philadelphia."

DESCRIPTION

Biennial or short-lived perennial herbs 2–7 dm (¾–2 ¼ ft) tall;
stems erect, smooth to hairy. Basal
leaves spatula-shaped, lobed, 2–
13 cm (¾–5 in) long, 0.6–5 cm
(¼–2 in) wide, margins toothed;
stem leaves gradually reduced upward, entire to toothed. Flower
heads numerous, in open clusters
at ends of stems, from May to Jul;
ray flowers up to 150, white to
pink or pale purple, 5–10 mm (³⁄₁₆–
⅜ in) long; disk flowers yellow.
Fruits sparsely hairy achenes, with
a tuft of slender bristles at the tip.

HABITAT

Fields, meadows, and disturbed
areas.

PARTS USED

Flowers and entire plant.

The Mesquakies powdered the disk flowers of fleabane, *E. philadelphicus,* to make a snuff. Sniffed into the nostrils, it caused sneezing and thus broke up a head cold or catarrh. Other tribes used the same procedure with the sneezeweed, *Helinium autumnale* L. The Mesquakies also mixed the disk flowers with the leaves of dotted beebalm, *Monarda punctata* L., and the stems of flowers of golden alexanders, *Zizia aurea* (L.) Koch, for this purpose (Smith, 1928, p. 213).

The Lakotas made a tea from the entire plant of the fleabane, *E. annuus,* to treat children with sore mouths and adults who had difficulty urinating. They also made a tea from an unidentified part of the fleabane, *E. pumilus* Nutt., for rheumatism, lameness, and stomach disorders. The blossoms were also mixed with the brains, gall, and spleen of a buffalo or other animal, then rubbed on the hide to bleach it in the tanning process (Munson, 1981, p. 234).

The Cheyennes steeped the dried roots, stems, and flowers of the fleabane, *E. peregrinus* subs. *callianthemus,* in hot water and had the patient, covered with a blanket, breathe the vapors of the steaming liquid. If the patient had an ache between the shoulders, the painful area was bathed with the liquid. It was sometimes drunk for backache, dizziness, or drowsiness (Grinnell, 1962, 2: 187).

The Kiowas believed that the fleabane, *E. divergens,* was an omen of good fortune and brought it into their homes (Vestal and Shultes, 1939, p. 60). The Navahos took some part of this plant internally to aid in the delivery of babies. They also used it for headache and as a snuff (Elmore, 1944, p. 96; Wyman and Harris, 1951, p. 47).

ANGLO FOLK USE

Samuel Stearns stated in his 1801 *American Herbal:* "The chief use of the flea banes is for destroying fleas and gnats, by burning the herbs so as to waste away in smoke" (Vogel, 1970, p. 305). Benjamin Smith Barton, in his 1810 *Collections for an Essay towards a Materia Medica of the United States,* called the fleabane, *E. philadelphicus,* a powerful diuretic and sudorific, useful in gouty and gravelly complaints (ibid.).

MEDICAL HISTORY

In his 1892 *Medicinal Plants,* Charles Millspaugh discussed the uses of fleabane and compared it to the horseweed, *Conyza canadensis* (L.) Cronq. (formerly called *Erigeron canadensis*): "The decoction has proven tonic, stimulant, astringent and diuretic, and been found useful in dropsies and many forms of urinary disorders, both renal and cystic,—such as gravel, diabetes, dysury, strangury, and urethritis; *E. heterophyllum*, and *Philadelphicum* have, however, greater power than *Canadense* in this direction" (Millspaugh, 1974, p. 319).

The fleabane, *E. philadelphicus*, was officially listed in the *U.S. Pharmacopoeia* from 1831 to 1882. The fleabane, *E. annuus*, contains a volatile oil (oil of fleabane), tannins, gallic acid, and a bitter extractive (Burlage, 1968, p. 43). Fleabanes may cause dermatitis in some people (Foster and Duke, 1990, p. 164).

CULTIVATION

Fleabanes have numerous small, attractive, daisy-like flowers, but they can be weedy and may not be desirable in the garden. Fleabanes are common in fields and meadows and are easily propagated by seed. Seeds can be planted in the fall or stratified and planted in flats in a greenhouse during the spring.

Eryngium yuccifolium
Rattlesnake Master

COMMON NAMES

Rattlesnake master, button snake-root, and water-eryngo.

INDIAN NAMES

The Mesquakie name for the rattle-snake master is "kisgu'paskwapi" (no translation given) (Smith, 1928, p. 248).

SCIENTIFIC NAME

Eryngium yuccifolium Michx. is a member of the Apiaceae (Parsley Family). *Eryngium* comes from the Greek "eryngion," a name used by Hippocrates, the Father of Medicine, for one of his medicinal plants. The species name, *yuccifolium*, means "yucca leaf."

DESCRIPTION

Stout perennial herbs 3–15 dm (1–5 ft) tall, with thickened, fibrous roots; stems solitary, branched above, smooth, waxy. Leaves alternate, firm, linear, parallel-veined, 1–8 dm (¼–2 ¾ ft) long, 1–3 cm (⅜–1 3⁄16 in) wide, gradually reduced up the stem, margins bristly. Flowers in dense, spherical clusters to 2.5 cm (1 in) in diameter, on short stalks at tips of stems, from Jun through Sep; petals tiny, white. Fruits egg-shaped, 4–8 mm (⅛–5⁄16 in) long, slightly scaly, with 2 small segments.

HABITAT

Prairies and rocky, open woodlands.

PARTS USED

Roots, leaves, and fruits.

INDIAN USE

The Mesquakies used the leaves and fruit of the rattlesnake master in their rattlesnake medicine song and dance. They also used the root as a medicine for bladder trouble and as an antidote to poisons other than rattlesnake venom (ibid.).

The botanist Thomas Nuttall traveled into the Arkansas Territory in 1819. He described the use of rattlesnake master, *Eryngium aquaticum*, by the Indians along the Arkansas River near its confluence with the White River: "February 3rd. . . . The prairie, in consequence of the late rains, appeared almost at once a continued sheet of water. I observed springing up, the *Eryngium aquaticum,* occasionally employed as a medicine by the inhabitants, acting as a diuretic, and in larger doses proving almost emetic" (Thwaites, 1905, 13:110).

MEDICAL HISTORY

The rattlesnake master was listed in Charles Millspaugh's *Medicinal Plants:*

This species was highly valued by the Aborigines as an alexiteric, and, combined with Iris versicolor, as a febrifuge and diuretic; since their time it has come into use by first the laity, then the physician, as a stimulant, diaphoretic, sialogogue, expectorant, diuretic, and alterative. A decoction of the root has been found useful in dropsy, nephritic and calculous disorders; chronic laryngitis and bronchitis; irritation of the urethra, vaginal, uterine, and cystic mucous membranes; gonorrhoea, gleet, and leucorrhoea; mucoid diarrhoea; local inflammations of the mucous membranes; exhaustion from sexual depletion with loss of erectile power, seminal emissions, and orchitis. By some physicians it has been preferred to Seneka snakeroot for its sphere, and by others it has been considered fully equal to Contrayerva. The powdered root is said to make a fine escharotic application to fungoid growths and indolent ulcerations, preventing gangrene, and stimulating them to

resolution (Millspaugh, 1974, pp. 245–56).

Millspaugh's reference to the use of Seneca snakeroot, *Polygala senega* L., suggests that rattlesnake master was also used as a snakebite remedy. The rhizome of the rattlesnake master was officially listed in the *U.S. Pharmacopoeia* from 1820 to 1873 as a diaphoretic, expectorant, and emetic.

SCIENTIFIC RESEARCH

Rattlesnake master is reported to have bitter aromatic constituents (Smith, 1928, p. 248). Apparently no research has been done on the effectiveness of rattlesnake master in the treatment on rattlesnake bites, but an extract of *Eryngium creticum* was found to be effective as an antivenin to the sting of the scorpion, *Leiurus quinuqestristus* (Afifi et al., 1990, pp. 43–48). This *Eryngium* grows in Jordan, where it is used by people in rural areas for scorpion stings.

CULTIVATION

The rhizome of the rattlesnake master (here called water-eryngo) was described in a 1907 U.S. Department of Agriculture publication titled *American Root Drugs:*

The stout rootstock is very knotty, with numerous short branches, and produces many thick, rather straight roots, both rootstock and roots of a dark-brown color, the latter wrinkled lengthwise. *The inside of the root-stock is yellowish white. Water-eryngo has a somewhat peculiar, slightly aromatic odor, and a sweetish, mucilaginous taste at first, followed by some bitterness and pungency.*

Collection, prices and uses.— *The root of this plant is collected in the autumn and brings from 5 to 10 cents a pound. Water-eryngo is an old remedy, and one of its early uses, as the several common names indicate, was for the treatment of snake bites (Henkel, 1907, p. 50).*

Rattlesnake master can be propagated by dividing the rootstock when dormant, or by planting stratified seed in the spring.

Eupatorium perfoliatum L.
Boneset

Boneset, throughwort, agueweed, wild sage, feverwort, vegetable antimony, and Indian sage. The name "boneset" is confusing, as it refers to its use in the treatment of flu, rather than for setting bones. As described by N. Chapman in his 1819 *Chapman's Discourses on the Elements of Therapeutics and Material Medica*:

> *Thirty years ago, we had throughout the United States, a singular catarrh, or species of influenza, which, in consequence of the sort of pain attending it, came to be denominated the "break bone fever." The eupatorium, acting as a diaphoretic, so promptly relieved this peculiar symptom, that it acquired the popular title of "bone-set," which it retains to the present moment (Chapman, 1819, cited in Lloyd, 1918, p. 4).*

INDIAN NAMES

The Mesquakie names for boneset are "skipwa'ishi mamitcakanakesiti" (sweet potato root and weeds with flowers round) and "manitowu'skw" (snake root) (Smith, 1928, p. 214).

SCIENTIFIC NAME

Eupatorium perfoliatum L. is a member of the Asteraceae (Sunflower Family). *Eupatorium* comes from the Greek "eupatorion," after Mithridates Eupator, King of Pon-

tus (134–63 B.C.). He was the first to use a plant of this genus for liver complaints, according to Pliny. The species name, *perfoliatum*, means "through leaf." It refers to the leaves, in opposite pairs, uniting at their bases so that the stem seems to grow through them.

DESCRIPTION

Perennial herbs 4–15 dm (1¼–5 ft) tall, with stout rhizomes; stems erect, long-hairy. Leaves opposite, simple, the bases usually encircling the stems, lance-shaped, 7–20 cm (2¾–8 in) long, up to 4 cm (1½ in) wide, margins coarsely toothed. Flower heads in flat-topped clusters on short branches at ends of stems, from Aug through Sep; small flowers tubular, white, 3–4 mm (²⁄₁₆–³⁄₁₆ in) long, with 5 lobes and protruding straplike styles. Fruits dry, 5-angled, hairy achenes.

HABITAT

Damp, low ground.

PARTS USED

Whole plant, flowers, leaves, and roots.

INDIAN USE

Boneset was used by many tribes in eastern North America for a wide variety of ailments, including colds, sore throat, fever, flu, chills, menstrual irregularity, epilepsy, gonorrhea, kidney trouble, rheumatism, and to induce vomiting (Shemluck, 1982, p. 331). The Mesquakies used boneset root "long ago" as a cure for snakebite (Smith, 1928, p. 214). A Mesquakie doctor named McIntosh used a tea of the foliage and flowers to expel worms. In the Great Lakes Bioregion, the Menominis used boneset to lower a fever (Smith, 1923, p. 30). The ethnobotanist Huron Smith believed that this use may have been learned from the white man—a rare example of Indians adopting an Anglo use of a medicinal plant.

ANGLO FOLK USE

Charles Millspaugh, in his 1892 *Medicinal Plants*, described the popularity of boneset:

There is probably no plant in American domestic practice that has more extensive or frequent use

than this. The attic, or woodshed, of almost every country farmhouse, has its bunches of the dried herb hanging tops downward from the rafters during the whole year, ready for immediate use should some member of the family, or that of a neighbor, be taken with a cold. How many children have winced when the maternal edict: "drink this boneset: it'll do you good," has been issued; and how many old men have craned their necks to allow the nauseous draught to the quicker pass the palate! The use of a hot infusion of the tops and leaves to produce diaphoresis, was handed down to the early settlers of this country by the Aborigines, who called it by a name that is equivalent to ague-weed (Millspaugh, 1974, p. 314).

Frederick Pursh, a noted English botanist who explored North America, stated in his 1814 *Pursh's Flora Americanae Septentrionalis*:

The whole plant is exceedingly bitter, and has been used for ages past by the natives and inhabitants in intermittent fevers. . . . I have stated a case of its efficacy in those diseases in a letter to William Royston, Esq., who inserted it in the Medical and Physical Journal. In which I stated the benefits derived from this plant, by myself and others during my stay in the neighborhood of Lake Ontario, when both the influenza and lake fever [similar to the yel-

low fever] were *raging among the inhabitants (Pursh, 1814, cited in Millspaugh, 1974, p. 3).*

Boneset was mentioned in nearly all early American books on medicinal plants. One of these, *Hand's House Surgeon and Physician*, published in 1820, recommended the following uses of boneset:

By different methods of preparation and management, it may be made to produce a variety of effects. A strong tea prepared by long steeping, or by boiling, and taken freely while warm, may, according to the quantity, be made either to produce perspiration and assist in raising phlegm from the lungs, or to purge, or to vomit. Taken cold, and in more moderate quantity, it gives strength. In one or other of these methods, it may be useful in common cold, influenza, malignant-pleurisy, low-fevers, agues, indigestion, and weakness in general, being managed as above directed, according to the effect desired (ibid.).

MEDICAL HISTORY

It is difficult to separate the Anglo folk use and early medical history of boneset. Although it was still widely used as a folk medicine in 1918 when John Uri Lloyd wrote "A treatise on Eupatorium Perfoliatum," its use has been discredited in more recent times. The use of dried boneset leaves and

flowering tops was listed in the *U.S. Pharmacopoeia* from 1820 to 1916 and the *National Formulary* from 1926 to 1950. The Food and Drug Administration classifies boneset as an Herb of Undefined Safety, stating that it "has a diaphoretic effect. Emetic and aperient in large doses. Household remedy never prescribed by the medical profession" (Duke, 1985, p. 188).

SCIENTIFIC RESEARCH

A clinical experiment in Germany compared the effectiveness of a homeopathic tincture of boneset to aspirin on fifty-three patients affected by the common cold. No significant differences were found between the two groups, indicating that the drugs were equally effective (Gassinger, Winstel, and Netter, 1981, pp. 732–33). Other German research indicates that boneset contains large polysaccharides that have significant immunostimulatory effects (Wagner et al., 1985, p. 1069). These compounds may explain its folk use as a cold remedy. Boneset also contains lactones and a bitter glycoside, eupatorin (Bolyard et al., 1981, p. 60). Boneset roots contain 7-hydroxy-6-dehydroxy-3-4-(Z)-farnescene and tridec-1-ene-3-5-7-9-11-pentyne. The aerial parts contain eufoliatorin, eufolitin, euperfolin, and euperfolitin. Boneset also contains xyloglucuran, which has been shown to stimulate pharmacological activity as an antitumor agent (ibid.; Herz et al., 1977, p. 2264; Vollmer et al., 1985, cited in Wagner and Proksch, 1985, p. 141). Toxic concentrations of nitrates have also been reported in the plant (Stephens, 1980, p. 152), along with toxic amounts of pyrrolizidine alkaloids (Smith and Culvenor, 1981, pp. 33, 144).

CULTIVATION

Boneset can be easily propagated by seed or division of the rootstock in the fall or spring. In the 1915 U.S. Department of Agriculture *Farmers' Bulletin* titled "Drug Plants Under Cultivation," W. W. Stockberger discussed its harvest:

The plants are cut late in the summer when in full bloom and the leaves and flowering tops stripped from the stem by hand and carefully dried without exposure to the sun. Yields of well-cultivated boneset are quite large and 2,000 pounds or more per acre of dry herb may be obtained under favorable conditions. The price for boneset is low, rarely exceeding 2 or 3 cents a pound. Since the demand is limited and the wild supply fairly available, the cultivation of boneset does not offer much prospect of profit (Stockberger, 1915, p. 16).

Boneset still offers little prospect for profit as a medicinal plant; however, it has a rich history and deserves a prominent location in the wildflower garden for its attractive cluster of white flowers in the late summer.

Euphorbia corollata
Flowering Spurge

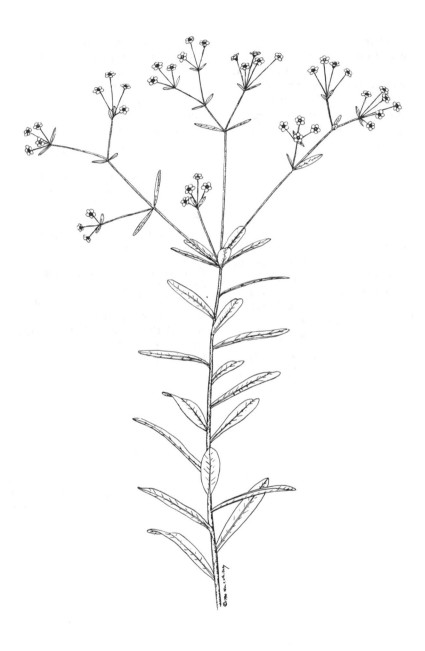

Flowering spurge, spurge, blooming spurge, milkweed (in reference
to the white, milky sap), white
pursley, and tramp's spurge.

INDIAN NAMES

The Mesquakie name for the
flowering spurge is "tcaposi'kuni"
(bowel movement) (Smith, 1928,
p. 220). The Omaha and Ponca
name for the thyme-leaved spurge,
Euphorbia serpyllifolia Pers.,
is "naze-ni pezhi" (milkweed)
(Gilmore, 1977, p. 47). The Pawnee
names for snow-on-the-mountain,
E. marginata Pursh, is "kari-
pika" (milkweed) or "kalipika
tsitsiks" (poison milkweed) (ibid.).
The Lakotas have two names for
snow-on-the-mountain. The first
is "asan'pi peju'ta" (milk medicine). The second, "ito'pta sa'pa
tapeju'ta" (black-footed ferret's
medicine), refers to the fact that
this plant grows in prairie dog
towns where the black-footed ferret, now an endangered species no
longer found in the wild, lived. The
black-footed ferret is sacred to the
Lakotas (Rogers, 1980, p. 45).

SCIENTIFIC NAME

Euphorbia corollata L. is a member of the Euphorbiaceae (Spurge
Family). *Euphorbia* comes from
the Greek "euphorbion," a plant
named after Euphorbos, a cele-
brated Greek physician of the
1st century B.C. The species

name, *corollata*, describes the
flowers. It comes from the Latin
"corolla," meaning "little crown"
or "garland."

DESCRIPTION

Perennial herbs 2–10 dm (¾–
3 ¼ ft) tall, with milky sap; stems
erect, 1 to several, smooth to
hairy, spreading-branched above.
Leaves alternate, simple, often
crowded, lance-shaped to elliptic, 2–6 cm (¾–2 ½ in) long, less
than 2 cm (¾ in) wide, margins
entire. Flowers in numerous
small, flowerlike cups at ends
of branches, each cup containing many tiny male flowers, a
single large female flower, and
5 white, petal-like appendages
around the lip of the cup; from
Jun to Oct. Fruits stalked, smooth,
3-lobed capsules containing 3
grayish seeds.

HABITAT

Dry rocky prairies, open woodlands, fields, roadsides, and disturbed areas.

PARTS USED

Root and leaves.

INDIAN USE

The Mesquakies pounded a half-inch piece of the root and boiled it in water to drink before breakfast as a laxative. It was also used for the treatment of rheumatism; after five or six doses, the ailment would disappear (Smith, 1928, pp. 220–21). The Mesquakies also used the flowering spurge root in mixtures with other plant roots. It was mixed with the purple cone-flower, *Echinacea pallida*, for use as a laxative. A tea made from the root mixed with the berries of the staghorn sumac, *Rhus typhina* L., and the bark of the bur oak, *Quercus macrocarpa* Michx., was drunk to expel pinworms.

The ethnobotanist Melvin Gilmore reported the Omaha and Ponca uses for the thyme-leaved spurge, *E. serpyllifolia*:

According to a Ponca informant this plant was boiled and the decoction drunk by young mothers whose flow of milk was scanty or lacking, in order to remedy that condition. This use of the plant is probably prescribed according to the doctrine of signatures. An Omaha informant said it was used

as a remedy in case of dysentery and abdominal bloating in children. For this purpose the leaves of the plant were dried and pulverized and applied after first cross-hatching the abdomen with a knife and then further abrading the skin with the head of a certain plant, the identity of which I do not know at present as I have not had a sample. Then the pulverized leaves were rubbed by hand on the abraded surface. It was said to cause a painful, smarting sensation and to act powerfully upon the bowels through the intervening tissues and to give relief (Gilmore, 1977, p. 47).

The Lakotas made a tea from snow-on-the-mountain, *E. marginata*, for mothers with insufficient breast milk (Rogers, 1980, p. 45). As noted by Gilmore above, this use may have been suggested in part by the plant's milky sap. The crushed leaves were also used by the Lakotas as a liniment for swellings.

In the Southwest, the Zunis used the thyme-leaved spurge, *E. serpyllifolia*, and the spurge, *E. albomarginata* T. & G., to increase the flow of milk in mothers (Stevenson, 1915, p. 51; Camazine and Bye, 1980, p. 372). They also used the thyme-leaved spurge as an emetic and as a purge.

ANGLO FOLK USE

At one time, vomiting was popularly regarded as a means of removing toxins and returning health to the body. The flowering spurge was one of the plants used to induce vomiting—but its properties were uncertain and its use was abandoned (Smith, 1928, p. 221).

MEDICAL HISTORY

In Dr. Finley Ellingwood's *A Systematic Treatise on Materia Medica and Therapeutics*, published in 1902, he described the flowering spurge as an agent to evacuate the stomach and listed its therapeutic uses:

Though Euphorbia acts as an emetic, it is but little used for that purpose, being too harsh in its action, including hydragogue catharsis at the same time. While in extreme doses it may cause acute gastro-enteritis, in small doses it stimulates normal functional activity of the stomach, influencing the glandular function of the entire gastro-intestinal tract. In the atonic dyspepsia of enfeebled conditions of the stomach, with bad breath, bad taste in the mouth, furred tongue, anorexia and constipation with a sense of weight in the stomach, and occasional colicky pains in the bowels, it is a good remedy. Ten drops of the tincture in two ounces of water, a teaspoonful every two hours, will relieve this common train of symptoms. It has been used in cholera infantum and other summer diarrhoeas of children with good results.

It is advised in the tenesmus of dysentery, and in the diarrhoea of exhausting diseases (Ellingwood, 1902, pp. 349–50).

The flowering spurge was officially listed in the *U.S. Pharmacopoeia* from 1820 to 1882. Its root was regarded as emetic in large doses, diaphoretic and expectorant in small doses. As a cathartic, it was limited by its tendency to produce nausea and was supplanted by other medicines.

SCIENTIFIC RESEARCH

The chemical constituents of various *Euphorbia* species include flavinoids, amino acids, alkanes, triterpenoids, and alkaloids. The diterpenes in the latex are irritant and vesicant to the skin and emetic and purgative when ingested. They are thought to be responsible for the plant's toxic effects. Diterpenes isolated from *Euphorbia* include: esters of phorbol, 12-deoxyphorbol, 12-deoxy-16-hydroxyphorbol, ingenol, 5-deoxy-ingenol, 20-deoxyingenol, resiniferotoxin, and tinyatoxin (Kinghorn and Evans, 1975, pp. 325–35). All parts of the plant contain some toxic substances and for some people, the milky sap may also cause dermatitis. In a study of sixty *Euphorbia* species native to Europe and Africa, only seven failed to produce an allergic skin reaction on mouse ears.

CULTIVATION

The flowering spurge can be propagated by both seeds and root division. Seeds are sometimes hard to find because they explode from their capsules when they are ripe.

When started from seed, the plants will bloom their second year. The roots may be divided in the late fall or early spring. They are brittle and must be handled carefully.

Glycyrrhiza lepidota
American Licorice

American licorice, wild licorice,
licorice, and dessert root.

INDIAN NAMES

The Pawnee name is "pithahatu-
sakitstsuhast" or "pilahatus" (no
translations given) (Gilmore, 1977,
p. 40; Gilmore, 1914, p. 4). The
Dakota name, "wi-nawizi" (jealous
woman), refers to the burrs, which
"take hold of a man" (Gilmore,
1977, p. 40). The Lakota name is
"wina'wizi ci'kala" (little cockle-
bur) (Rogers, 1980, p. 46). The
Cheyenne name, "haht' nowas-
spoph" (yellow-jacket stinger
plant), refers to both the color and
the burrs, which stick to a person like a yellow-jacket or wasp
(Grinnell, 1962, 2:178).

SCIENTIFIC NAME

Glycyrrhiza lepidota Pursh is a
member of the Fabaceae (Bean
Family). *Glycyrrhiza* is a Greek
word that means "sweet root." The
species name, *lepidota*, means
"scaly" and refers to the minute
scales on young leaves.

DESCRIPTION

Perennial herbs 3–10 dm (1–3 ¼ ft)
tall, with deep, woody rhizomes;
stems branched, gland-dotted.
Leaves alternate, pinnately compound; leaflets 7–21, oblong to
lance-shaped with sharp points
at tips, up to 5 cm (2 in) long,

surfaces scaly when young and
dotted with glands later. Flowers
in narrow, elongate groups among
leaves, from May to Aug; petals 5,
white or yellowish, top 1 larger
and erect, lower 2 boat-shaped, 2
wings at sides. Fruits dry, oblong,
1–2 cm (⅜–¾ in) long, covered
with hooked prickles; seeds olive
green to brown, smooth.

HABITAT

Prairies, pastures, disturbed areas,
and along railroad rights-of-way.

PARTS USED

Roots and leaves.

INDIAN USE

For diarrhea and upset stomach,
the Cheyennes drank a medicinal tea made from the peeled,
dried roots of the American licorice. The leaves were used for
the same purpose as well as their
drying effect (Hart, 1981, pp. 28–

29). The roots of the American licorice were also chewed by the Cheyennes in the sweat lodge and during the Sun Dance for their cooling effect.

The Lakotas used the roots as a medicine for flu. They also mixed the root with Canada milkvetch, *Astragalus canadensis* L., to treat the spitting of blood (Munson, 1981, p. 235; Rogers, 1980, pp. 45–46). The Dakotas steeped the leaves of American licorice in boiling water to make a topical medicine for earache. A tea of the root was used to reduce fever in children. The root was also chewed and held in the mouth to relieve toothache. Although the root is strong flavored at first, it tastes sweet after a while (Gilmore, 1977, p. 40).

The Blackfeet made a tea from the bitter-tasting root of the American licorice for coughs, chest pain, and sore throat. They also applied it to swellings (Hellson, 1974, pp. 72, 76). The Pawnees named one of their villages (along the Loup River in Nebraska near present-day Genoa) for the American licorice that grew there and probably used the plant as medicine (Gilmore, 1914, p. 4; Kindscher, 1987, p. 121). The Zunis chewed the root to keep the mouth sweet and moist (Camazine and Bye, 1980, p. 376), and the Bannocks chewed the root to strengthen the throat for singing (Murphey, 1959, p. 38). It was also eaten by the Cheyennes, Paiutes,

and other tribes as a sweet-tasting food (Kindscher, 1987, pp. 121–22).

ANGLO FOLK USE

Most of the folk use of licorice involves the Eurasian species, *Glycyrrhiza glabra* L. The two species are similar, and both contain the sweet-tasting substance glycyrrhizin. The earliest use of licorice, *G. glabra*, was recorded in the code of Hammurabi in 2100 B.C. (Gibson, 1978, p. 348). Since that time, it has been used as a remedy for a variety of ailments, including ulcers, scabies, indigestion, and inflamed stomach, and as a treatment for problems associated with the thorax, liver, lungs, and kidneys (Chandler, 1985, p. 422).

In the southwestern United States, Chicanos used the American licorice as a remedy for postparturition problems such as fever and as an emmenagogue (Curtin, 1976, p. 32).

MEDICAL HISTORY

American licorice was seldom, if ever, prescribed by doctors, but the closely related European species, *Glycyrrhiza glabra*, was used in early American medicine. The root was made into a tea and used to relieve inflammation of nasal and tracheal passages; its medicinal value was attributed to its ability to protectively coat the mucous membranes of these passages (Hart, 1976, p. 35).

More recently, the primary use of the wild licorice has been to mask unpleasant-tasting drugs. The licorice root was listed in the *U.S. Pharmacopoeia* from 1820 to 1975 and is still listed in the *British Pharmacopoeia* (Gibson, 1978, p. 348). The major use of wild licorice root in the United States, accounting for 90 percent of the imported roots, is flavoring and sweetening tobacco products, such as cigarettes, cigars, and pipe and chewing tobacco (Tyler, 1981, p. 138). Today the flavoring in most licorice candy is anise rather than licorice.

SCIENTIFIC RESEARCH

There has been considerable research devoted to the Eurasian licorice, *G. glabra*, but little study of the American licorice, *G. lepidota*. The primary constituent of both is the saponin glycoside, called glycyrrhizin or glycyrrhizic acid. Fifty times sweeter than sugar, it is available in a commercial form, ammoniated glycyrrhizin (ibid.; Trease and Evans, 1973, p. 443). The glycyrrhizin content of *G. glabra* varies from 6 to 13 percent, while the content of American licorice, *G. lepidota*, varies from 8 to 15 percent. The two are quite different when it comes to taste. The American licorice does not taste sweet like the licorice of commerce. I have chewed the root of the American licorice for several minutes, but it still tasted only faintly sweet.

Eurasian licorice root has been suggested as a vehicle for topical oral medications because it is sweet, and recent research shows that neither licorice, *G. glabra*, or glycyrrhizin promoted the growth of plaque-forming bacteria. In fact, glycyrrhizin markedly inhibited the growth of these bacteria when sugar (sucrose) was added (Segal et al., 1985, p. 79). Glycyrrhizin is reported to stimulate anti-inflammatory activity and anti-arthritic activity similar to that of hydrocortisone (Nikitini, 1966, cited in Gibson, 1978, p. 351; Cunitz, 1968, pp. 434–35; Gibson, 1978, p. 348). In addition, glycyrrhizin promoted the healing of wounds in laboratory rats. Other research has shown beneficial effects of glycyrrhizin on the liver and urinary tract (Gibson, 1978, pp. 348–51).

A Dutch physician reported in 1946 that the condition of many patients with peptic ulcer disease improved when treated with a dried licorice extract. A substance, carbenoxolone, which was synthesized from glycyrrhizin, was shown in medical tests in England to be effective in healing ulcers. In this experiment, eleven of thirty patients showed improvement, compared to only one in thirty in the control group (Lewis, 1974, pp. 460–61; Tyler, 1981, p. 139; Conn, Rovner, and Cohen, 1968, pp. 492–96). However, this treatment was accompanied by an adverse effect, swelling of the face and limbs, in 10 to 40 percent of the cases. These same symptoms have been reported in individuals who consume too much licorice in candy, in tobacco, or in the roots themselves. They have been labeled licorice-induced pseudoaldosteronism, because the effects are similar to those brought about by the excessive secretion of the adrenal cortex hormone aldosterone. Nevertheless, carbenoxolone was recognized in 1974 as "the only drug therapy that has been shown unequivocally to promote the healing of gastric ulcers." If it did not cause these side effects, the use of licorice and American licorice might be a common treatment for gastric ulcers today. Licorice can also cause high blood pressure and even heart failure (Chandler, 1985, p. 424).

CULTIVATION

Oliver Perry Medsger, in *Edible Wild Plants*, reported that he found American licorice growing near Indian villages in New Mexico as though it had once been cultivated (Medsger, 1966, p. 199). The American licorice is a spreading plant, weedy and aggressive. Michael Moore, in *Medicinal Plants of the Mountain West*, reported that in the early spring or late fall, pieces of the underground runners can be propagated. These pieces, which have scale-like buds, should be planted about 10 cm (4 in) deep in moist, well-drained soil. "With the right kind of growing conditions and a five-year headstart, this stout, fast-spreading plant will probably uproot the nearest house" (Moore, 1979, p. 97).

Grindelia squarrosa
Curly-top Gumweed

Curly-top gumweed, curly-cup
gumweed, rayless gumweed, and
broadleaf gumplant (the flower
heads have curly, leaf-like appendages on the sides, and the sap of
the plant has a sticky or gummy
consistency).

INDIAN NAMES

The Lakota name for the curly-
top gumweed is "pte ichi yuha"
(to make buffalo cows follow one
another) (Rogers, 1980, p. 36).
The Dakota name for the curly-
top gumweed is "pte-ichi-yuha"
(curly buffalo) (ibid.). The Pawnee
name is "bakskitits" (sticky
head), and the Omaha and Ponca
name is "pezhe-wasek" (strong
herb) (Gilmore, 1977, p. 81). The
Blackfeet name is "aks-peis"
(sticky weed) (McClintock, 1909,
p. 276). The Cheyenne name is
"ho?eeto'hkonah" (no translation
given) (Hart, 1981, p. 21).

SCIENTIFIC NAME

Grindelia squarrosa (Pursh) Dunal
is a member of the Asteraceae
(Sunflower Family). *Grindelia* is
named after David Hieronymus
Grindel (1776–1836), a professor of chemistry and pharmacy
in Dorpat, Estonia, who wrote
on pharmacological and botanical subjects. The species name,
squarrosa, means scabby, scaly,
or roughened, in reference to the

leaflike appendages that stick out
below the flower head.

DESCRIPTION

Sticky biennial herbs 1–10 dm (¼–
3 ¼ ft) tall; stems smooth, spreading to erect, usually single and
branched above. Leaves alternate,
simple, gland-dotted, spatula-
shaped to egg-shaped, ⅕–7 cm (⁹⁄₁₆–
2 ¾ in) long, 0.4–2 cm (⅛–¾ in)
wide, margins entire to coarsely
toothed. Flower heads few to
many, 2.5–4 cm (1–1 ½ in) wide,
at ends of branches, from Jul to
Oct; bracts of heads resinous and
strongly curled; ray florets yellow, up to 1.3 cm (½ in) long or
occasionally absent; disk flowers
yellow, sticky.

HABITAT

Disturbed areas, roadsides, railroads, and pastures.

Flower heads and leaves.

INDIAN USE

The Cheyennes boiled the flower heads of the curly-top gumweed as an external remedy for skin diseases, scabs, and sores. They also rubbed the gummy residue on their eyelids as an eye medicine, especially for snowblindness (ibid.). The Lakotas boiled curly-top gumweed with the fetid marigold, *Dyssodia papposa* (Vent.) Hitchc., to make a tea for the spitting of blood (Rogers, 1980, p. 37; Gilmore, 1977, p. 81). The Teton Dakotas made a tea of the plant that was given to children as a remedy for stomachache (ibid.). J. W. Blankenship, in his 1905 "Native Economic Plants of Montana," stated that the Sioux (both Lakotas and Dakotas) made a tea from the curly-top gumweed for kidney trouble (Blankenship, 1905, p. 12).

The Crows used the flowers of the curly-top gumweed to make a tea for coughs and postpartum pain, and sniffed the flowers up their nostrils for catarrh. They also made a hot poultice from the plant, which they applied to swellings (Toeineeta, 1970, cited in Shemluck, 1982, p. 333). Many tribes, including the Crows and Flatheads, drank curly-top gumweed tea for coughs (including whooping cough), pneumonia, bronchitis, asthma, and colds

(Hart, 1976, p. 32). Pete Beaverhead, a Flathead, reported that the old-timers drank it just to "pep them up." The Gros Ventres and the Shoshones made a curly-top gumweed tea to treat venereal disease (Shemluck, 1982, p. 333). The Poncas drank a tea made from the plant for tuberculosis (Gilmore, 1977, p. 81). The Blackfeet boiled the root and ate it for liver trouble (McClintock, 1909, p. 276).

The Crees in the Northwest Territories of Canada used some part of the curly-top gumweed to treat gonorrhea and to prevent pregnancy (Beardsley, 1941, p. 483). In the Southwest, the Zunis used the resin for relief from poison ivy rash (Shemluck, 1982, p. 334).

ANGLO FOLK USE

The curly-top gumweed tea was drunk by settlers for coughs (including whooping cough), pneumonia, bronchitis, asthma, and colds (Hart, 1976, p. 32; Duke, 1985, p. 220). It was also used by folk practitioners for cancers of the spleen and stomach.

MEDICAL HISTORY

In 1863, the use of the gumweed, *Grindelia robusta* Nutt., was promoted by a Dr. C. A. Canfield of Monterey, California, who learned of this west-coast species' use as a remedy for poison ivy, *Toxicodendron toxicarium* (Salisb.) Gillis, from the Indians. In 1875, James G. Steele of San Francisco contributed a paper to the American Pharmaceutical Association extolling the usefulness of the gumweed in treating poison ivy. As a result, its popularity increased substantially, and it was introduced as a medicine by Parke, Davis and Company of Detroit (Lloyd, 1921, p. 159). More recently, a lotion from a North American *Grindelia* species was available in Europe for dermatitis produced by poison ivy. The dried leaves and flower heads of several species of gumweed, including the curly-top gumweed, have been used historically as a sedative, an antispasmodic, and an expectorant (Duke, 1985, p. 220). These parts of the gumweed were officially listed in the *U.S. Pharmacopoeia* from 1882 to 1926 and the *National Formulary* from 1926 to 1960.

SCIENTIFIC RESEARCH

Curly-cup gumweed is about 20 percent resin, composed of grindelic-, oxygrindelic-, 6-oxygrindelic-, and 7-alpha-8 alpha oxodihydrogrindelic acids. In the resin-free portion of the plant, there is matricarianol and matricarianol acetate, with about 0.3 percent essential oil (largely borneol), tannin, saponins, the alkaloid grindelin, and p-oxybenzoic acid in the leaves (ibid.). In addition, several polyphenolic substances have been found, including vanillic and p-coumaric acid and querticin. Some of the substances may produce anti-inflammatory effects (Pinkas et al., 1978, pp. 97–104).

CULTIVATION

The curly-cup gumweed has attractive yellow flowers, but it is weedy and may not be desirable in a wildflower garden. It thrives on poor soil and can be propagated by seed or division of the root stock. In pastures cattle will not eat it.

Heuchera richardsonii
Alum Root

Alum root, American sanicle, and kalispell.

INDIAN NAMES

The Lakota names for the alum root are "canhlo' hsnasna'la" (weed bare) and "wahpe't'aga" (astringent, dries out mouth leaf) (Rogers, 1980, p. 58). The Blackfeet name for the alum root, *Heuchera parvifolia* Nutt. ex Torr. & Gray, is "apos-ipoco" (tastes dry) (McClintock, 1923, p. 320). The Cheyenne name for the alum root, *H. cylindrica* var. *ovalifolia* (Nutt. ex Torr. & Gray) Wheelock, is "e hyo' isse' e yo" (yellow medicine) (Grinnell, 1962, 2:176). The Mesquakie name for the alum root, *H. hirsuticaulis* (Wheelock) Rydb., is "kwakwate'wopamekie'shikekipeski'pak" (looks like grasshopper legs) (Smith, 1928, p. 246).

SCIENTIFIC NAME

Heuchera richardsonii R. Br. is a member of the Saxifragaceae (Saxifrage Family). *Heuchera* is named in honor of Professor Johann Heinrich Heucher (1677–1747), custodian of the Botanic Garden in Wittenberg, Germany. The species name, *richardsonii*, honors John Richardson, an English surgeon and botanist who accompanied the Franklin expedition to the Arctic.

DESCRIPTION

Perennial herbs 1.5–7 dm (½– 2 ¼ ft) tall; stems solitary and soft-hairy below to glandular above. Leaves basal, simple, long-stalked, the blades 2.5–10 cm (1–4 in) long, rounded to kidney-shaped, lower surfaces hairy, upper surfaces mostly smooth, margins prominently toothed and lobed. Flowers bell-shaped, green to greenish-yellow, 6–10 mm (¼–½ in) long, on long stalks that project above the leaves, from Jun to Jul. Fruits are capsules 7–15 mm (¼–⁹⁄₁₆ in) long, opening to release numerous tiny brown to black seeds.

HABITAT

Prairies, hillsides, rocky woods, and openings in woods.

PARTS USED

Roots and shoots.

INDIAN USE

Several species of the alum root were used similarly by Indians. The Lakotas used the tuberous roots of the alum root, *H. richardsonii*, to make a medicinal tea for treating chronic diarrhea. They also ground a powder from the roots to use on sores (Rogers, 1980, p. 58). The Blackfeet pounded the root of a related species, *H. parvifolia*, which they found growing in alkaline soil and gravel beds, to use fresh as a poultice for sores and swellings (McClintock, 1923, p. 320; Hellson, 1974, pp. 76–77). They also applied the chewed root to wounds and sores to control swelling. It was considered especially effective for mouth sores (cold sores and canker sores) in children.

The Cheyennes ground the roots of the alum root, *H. cylindrica*, to make a fine powder that was rubbed on the skin as a remedy for rheumatism or for sore muscles (Grinnell, 1962, 2: 176). This powder was described as "gummy," with a tendency to cling to the skin. They also powdered the top of the plant to make a tea which the patient drank as part of the same treatment.

The Arapahos also used the alum root, *H. cylindrica*, for unspecified medicinal purposes (Nickerson, 1966, p. 48). The Mesquakies used the foliage of the alum root, *H. hirsuticaulis*, as an astringent for healing sores (Smith, 1928, p. 246).

ANGLO FOLK USE

The alum root was used "in the treatment of serious diarrheas and other conditions where vegetable astringents are usually recommended" (ibid.).

MEDICAL HISTORY

The Indian and Anglo uses for this plant were identical. Benjamin S. Barton, a botanist and member of the faculty at the University of Pennsylvania, wrote in 1810 that the alum root, *H. americana*, "is one of the articles in the Materia Medica of our Indians. They apply the powdered root to wounds, ulcers, and cancers." He added that he did not believe that genuine cancer was cured by it, but he thought it certain "that it had proved very beneficial in some obstinate ulcers, which have been mistaken for cancer" (Vogel, 1970, p. 271). The dried root of this alum root was officially listed in the *U.S. Pharmacopoeia* from 1820 to 1882. It was used as an internal and external astringent, but has now been replaced by tannic acid. The alum root contains a large amount of tannin (Tehon, 1951, p. 64).

CULTIVATION

The small, spike-like flower clusters and green foliage make this an attractive border plant. The tiny seeds are best propagated soon after they mature. Otherwise, they should be stratified before planting. Mature plants can be divided with a sharp knife after they have matured in midsummer. Each division must include a root section with buds.

Coralbells, *H. sanguinea* Englem., consists of several named cultivars and is widely available as an ornamental plant. It is native to New Mexico, Arizona, and Mexico, and has bright red (but still small) flowers.

Ipomoea leptophylla
Bush Morning Glory

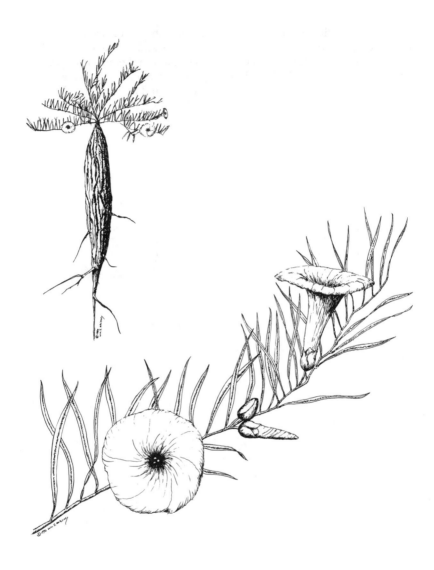

COMMON NAMES

Bush morning glory, big-root
morning glory, man root, man-of-
the-earth (these names refer to the
plant's human-sized roots), bush
moonflower, and wild potato vine.

INDIAN NAMES

The Pawnee name for the bush
morning glory is "kahts-tuwiriki"
(whirlwind medicine), referring to
the peculiar, twisted nature of the
root system (Gilmore, 1977, p. 58).
The Lakota name is "pezuta nige
tanka" (big stomach-medicine)
(Buechel, 1983, p. 440).

SCIENTIFIC NAME

Ipomoea leptophylla Torr. is a
member of the Convolvulaceae
(Morning Glory Family). *Ipomoea*
means "worm-like", and *leptophylla* means "fine, narrow leaf."

DESCRIPTION

Perennial herbs 0.3–1.2 m (1–
4 ft) tall, with enlarged, woody
roots; stems lying on ground or
erect. Leaves alternate, narrowly
lance-shaped to linear, 3–15 cm
(1¼–6 in) long, margins entire.
Flowers solitary or in groups of
2–3 on long stalks among leaves,
from May to Sep; petals fused and
funnel-shaped, 5–9 cm (2–3 ½ in)
long, purple-red to lavender-pink
with darker throats. Fruits dry,
oval, 1–1.5 cm (⅜–⅝ in) long; seeds

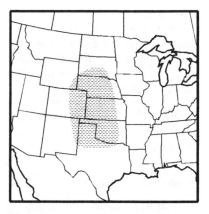

oblong, densely covered with short
brown hairs.

HABITAT

Sandy prairie, waste ground, roadsides, and stream banks.

PARTS USED

The root.

INDIAN USE

The Pawnees burned the enormous, human-sized roots of the
bush morning glory as a smoke
treatment for nervousness and
bad dreams (Gilmore, 1977, p. 58).
They also pulverized the dried root
and dusted it on the body with a
deer tail or feather brush to alleviate pain or to revive a person who
had fainted. The Lakotas scraped
off a portion of the root and ate it
raw for stomach trouble (Rogers,
1980, p. 43).

There were many uses for the

large root of the bush morning glory. In the days before matches, Indians in the Great Plains would start a fire in a portion of the dried root and let it smolder for later use as a punk for starting fires. The root was also used as an emergency food by the Pawnees, Cheyennes, Arapahos, and Kiowas (Kindscher, 1987, pp. 135–36).

MEDICAL HISTORY

The closely related species, big-root morning glory, *Ipomoea pandurata* (L.) G. F. W. Mey., was used as a medicine by early doctors, who apparently learned of it from the Indians. William Bartram, a Philadelphia botanist, reported that "the dissolvent and diuretant powers of the root . . . so much esteemed as a remedy for nephritic complaints, were discovered by the Indians to the inhabitants of Carolina" (Vogel, 1970, p. 324).

Henry Burlage reports on the use of the big-root morning glory in his *Index of Plants of Texas with Reputed Medicinal and Poisonous Properties*: "The root is cathartic, diuretic, hepatic, antivenomous, and lithontryptic; the tubers and roots of this trailing or climbing vine are diuretic, feebly cathartic, purgative, and were used by the American Indians as a food. The powdered root acts like rhubarb and requires that it be given in larger doses than jalap. It has been used in this country as a remedy for calculous affection and in cases of gravel" (Burlage, 1968, p. 60).

The tuberous root of the big-root morning glory was officially listed in the *U.S. Pharmacopoeia* from 1820 to 1863. It was primarily used as a powerful cathartic, but has since been replaced by other drugs.

Dr. L. E. Sayre of the Pharmacy Department at the University of Kansas studied the bush morning glory, *I. leptophylla*, in 1895, when its roots, along with those of the buffalo gourd, *Cucurbita foetidissima* H. B. K., were sent to him for analysis by "parties claiming for the roots remarkable tonic and aperient qualities" (Sayre, 1897, p. 85). He described the bush morning glory as follows:

It is a beautiful plant with a bushy head, bearing numerous large purple flowers, closely resembling those of the common cultivated morning glory of the gardens; the stems being numerous, branching, rarely attaining a height of a couple feet, but the root also enormous, often approaching the size of the wild pumpkin [buffalo gourd, C. foetidissima]. The roots of the wild pumpkin have been found of about seven feet in length and of proportional diameter. This root [the ipomea] is very difficult to powder, being very fibrous, and when in the powdered form has a very characteristic odor, yellowish color and intensely bitter taste; inhaled it produces sneezing (Sayre, 1895, p. 301).

Sayre reported in 1897 that "the analysis demonstrated the fact that the medicinal virtues, if any, resided in an oleo-resinous extractive, soluble in alcohol and in chloroform. Diluted alcoholic tinctures of the roots were very bitter, and fairly represented their virtues" (Sayre, 1897, p. 85).

SCIENTIFIC RESEARCH

The big-root morning glory, *I. pandurata*, contains a milky, resinous juice and the glucoside ipomoein (Tehon, 1951, p. 68).

CULTIVATION

The bush morning glory has beautiful pink-to-purple flowers and has been suggested as an ornamental plant for roadsides, parks, and recreation areas. It has been recommended for plantings in wildlife habitats as well, and for prairie restorations within the central and western portions of the Prairie Bioregion (Salac et al., 1978, p. 13). The bush morning glory could be developed as a cultivar for semiarid climates since its extremely large, starchy root makes it drought resistant. It can be propagated from seed or by division of the root crown.

Juniperus virginiana
Eastern Red Cedar

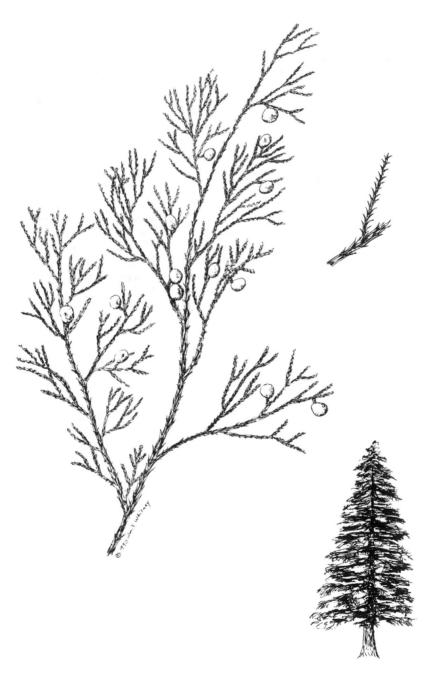

COMMON NAMES

Eastern red cedar, red cedar, cedar tree, juniper, juniper bush, savin, evergreen, cedar apple, and Virginia red cedar.

INDIAN NAMES

The Omaha and Ponca name for the red cedar is "maazi" and the Pawnee name is "tawatsaako" (no translations given) (Gilmore, 1977, p. 11). The Dakota name for cedar is "hante" or "hante sha"; "sha" means "red" (ibid.). The Comanche name is "ekawai:pv" (no translation given) (Carlson and Jones, 1939, p. 522).

SCIENTIFIC NAME

Juniperus virginiana L. is a member of the Cupressaceae (Cypress Family). *Juniperus* is the old Latin name for evergreen trees or shrubs. The species name, *virginiana*, means "of Virginia," where it was probably first seen by botanists.

DESCRIPTION

Pyramidal to columnar evergreen trees to 15 m (50 ft) tall; bark reddish-brown to gray, fibrous, and splitting into long, flat strips. Leaves opposite, simple, green to blue-green, scalelike and 0.2–0.3 cm (1⁄16–1⁄8 in) long or needlelike and 0.6–1.2 cm (1⁄4–1⁄2 in) long. Male and female cones on separate trees, from Apr to May; male cones yellowish-brown, papery,

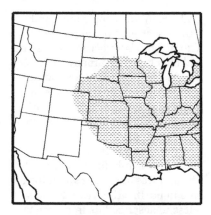

0.2–0.4 cm (1⁄16–3⁄16 in) long; female cones dark blue, waxy, berrylike, 0.4–0.7 cm (3⁄16–1⁄4 in) long, ripening Sep through Oct.

HABITAT

Prairie hillsides, fields, pastures, cemeteries, and occasionally woodlands.

PARTS USED

Leaves and berries.

INDIAN USE

The red cedar and other junipers were used by most tribes for incense in purification and ritual. The Dakotas boiled the fruits and leaves of the red cedar to make a tea that was drunk for coughs. For a cold, they would sit underneath a blanket and breathe the smoke and fumes from burning twigs (Gilmore, 1977, p. 11).

In 1849 and 1850, the Asiatic cholera was epidemic among the

Lakotas. Many people died, and others scattered in panic. Red Cloud, who later became a famous Lakota chief, tried many treatments for the cholera, including a decoction of cedar leaves which was drunk and also used for bathing. It was reported to have been a cure (ibid., p. 12).

For numerous tribes, the red cedar tree symbolized the tree of life and was burned in sweat lodges and in purification rites. Francis La Flesche described its importance to the Omahas:

An ancient cedar pole was also in the keeping of the We'zhinshte gens, and was lodged in the Tent of War. This venerable object was once the central figure in rites that have been lost. In Creation myths the cedar tree is associated with the advent of the human race; other myths connect this tree with the thunder. The thunder birds were said to live "in a forest of cedars. . . ."

There is a tradition that in olden times, in the spring after the first thunder had sounded, in the ceremony which then took place this Cedar Pole was painted, with rites similar to those observed when the Sacred pole was painted and anointed at the great tribal festival held while on the buffalo hunt (Fletcher and La Flesche, 1911, pp. 457–58).

The Kiowas chewed red cedar berries as a remedy for canker sores in the mouth. They also used the red, aromatic heartwood of the tree to make "love flutes" (Vestal and Shultes, 1939, p. 13). The Pawnees burned cedar twigs and inhaled the smoke as a remedy for nervousness and bad dreams (Gilmore, 1977, p. 12).

The Mesquakies made a medicine from the leaves of the red cedar which they called "mya'kapenatcigi" (they who are weak with illness) "anaposapi amenowatci" (they boil it, they drink it) (Smith, 1928, p. 234). They drank it to counteract weakness and as a convalescent medicine. They also used the wood of red cedar, mixed with unidentified material, as a seasoning for other medicines. The seasoning mixture was prepared in warm water and stirred with the fingers during preparation. The Mesquakie medicine man, John McIntosh, used the inner wood of red cedar as an inhalant for catarrh. He also used the berries as one of six ingredients in a remedy for lung troubles and fevers, and as one of three ingredients in a healing poultice for large external sores (ibid., pp. 194–95).

The Blackfeet made a tea from the berries of the Rocky Mountain juniper, *Juniperus scopulorum* Sarg., to stop vomiting. A Blackfeet remedy for arthritis and rheumatism was to boil Rocky Mountain juniper leaves in water, add one-half teaspoon of turpentine, and when cooled, rub the mixture on affected parts. The Blackfeet also drank a tea made from *Juniperus* root as a general tonic; mixed with *Populus* leaves, this root tea became a liniment for a stiff back or backache (McClintock, 1909, p. 276; Johnston, 1970, p. 305; Hellson, 1974, pp. 78, 83).

The Cheyennes steeped the leaves of the Rocky Mountain juniper and drank the resulting tea to relieve persistent coughing or a tickling in the throat. It was also believed to produce sedative effects that were especially useful for calming a hyperactive person. Cheyenne women drank the Rocky Mountain juniper tea to speed delivery during childbirth (Grinnell, 1962, 2: 170). The Cheyennes, along with the Flatheads, Nez Perces, Kutenais, and Sioux, made a tea from juniper boughs, branches, and fleshy cones which they drank for colds, fevers, tonsillitis, and pneumonia (Hart, 1976, pp. 5, 36).

Jeffrey Hart, in *Montana— Native Plants and Early People*, reported the mystic sacredness of juniper to the Cheyennes:

Charles Sitting Man, a Cheyenne, said that the Great Spirit has much respect for juniper because it seems to never grow old and remains green the year round. It therefore represented youthfulness, and they accordingly placed it centrally in many of their holy rites and purification ceremonies. Indians also admired it for the aromatic fragrance of its needles, which they burned as sacred incense; for the durability of its wood, which they found desirable for lance shafts, bows, and other items, and for the dark red seemingly dyed-in-blood color of its wood (Hart, 1976, p. 36).

Flutes made from juniper wood were highly regarded by the Cheyennes.

As a cure for asthma, the Gros Ventres ate whole juniper berries or pulverized them and boiled them to make a tea. They also made a preparation from the leaves mixed with the root which they applied topically to control bleeding (Kroeber, 1908, p. 226). The Crows drank this medicinal tea to check diarrhea and to stop lung or nasal hemorrhage. Crow women drank it after childbirth for cleansing and healing (Hart, 1976, p. 36).

ANGLO FOLK USE

Folk use of junipers can be traced to Europe, where the dwarf juniper or savin, *J. communis*, was used. This juniper, which occurs in both Europe and North America was listed in the 1636 Gerarde herbal, published in England:

The leaves of Savin boyled in Wine and drunke provoke urine, bring downe the menses with force, draw away the after-birth, expell the dead childe, and kill the quicke: it hath the like vertue received under the body in a perfume.

The leaves stamped with honey and applied, cure ulcers, stay spreading and creeping ulcers, scoure and take away all spots and freckles from the face or body of man or woman.

The leaves boyled in oile Olive, and kept therein, kill the worms in children, if you anoint their bellies therewith: and the leaves poudered and given in milke or Muscadell do the same (Gerarde, 1636, p. 1378).

Jacob Bigelow reported in his three-volume *American Medical Botany*, completed in 1820:

The leaves of Red cedar have a strong disagreeable taste, with some pungency and bitterness. The peculiar taste and odour reside, no doubt, in a volatile oil, which, however, is not readily separated by distillations in a small way. . . .

The botanical similarity of this tree to the Savin, which is an European shrub has already been mentioned. In their sensible and medicinal properties, they are equally allied. . . . As the American tree is frequently known throughout the country by the name of Savin, our apothecaries have been led to presume upon its identity with that medicine, and it has long been used in cases where the true Savin is recommended. Its most frequent use, however, is in the composition of the cerate [a salve] employed for keeping up the irritation and discharge of blisters (Bigelow, 1817, 1: 52).

The trappers of the upper Missouri River region apparently knew of the juniper from Europe, but also learned of its use from the Indians. They steeped the seeds of the creeping juniper, *Juniperus horizontalis* Moench, in hot water and drank the tea for kidney trouble (Blankenship, 1905, p. 13).

MEDICAL HISTORY

The young leafy twigs of the red cedar were officially listed in the *U.S. Pharmacopoeia* from 1820 to 1894 as a diuretic. The distilled oil of the red cedar has been officially listed as a reagent in the *U.S. Pharmacopoeia* since 1916. The dwarf juniper, *J. communis*, was officially listed in the *U.S. Pharmacopoeia* from 1820 to 1873 and the *National Formulary* from 1916 to 1960. In both publications it was listed as a diuretic. The oil of the dwarf juniper was described as a diuretic, emmenagogue, and genitourinary antiseptic.

SCIENTIFIC RESEARCH

The dwarf juniper, *J. communis*, has been the most widely used in medicine. Its volatile oil content varies from 0.2 to 3.42 percent (usually 1 to 2 percent in the berries), depending on geographic location, altitude, degree of ripeness, and other factors. The volatile oil is composed primarily of monoterpenes (about 58 percent), including alpha-pinene, myrcene, and sabinene as major components. The diuretic constituent is 4-terpinol or terpinen-4-ol (Leung,

1980, p. 208). Excessive doses may produce kidney irritation. Expectant mothers have been advised not to use junipers and their extracts as medicine because they increase intestinal movements and uterine contractions. Juniper oil is no longer recommended by the medical profession because of these problems and because safer and more effective drugs exist (Tyler, 1981, p. 133).

Berries of the dwarf juniper, *J. communis,* are the principal flavoring agent in gin and are also used in alcoholic bitters. Extracts and oils from juniper are used in many food products, including alcoholic and nonalcoholic beverages, frozen dairy desserts, candy, baked goods, gelatins, puddings, meat, and meat products (Duke, 1985, p. 256).

CULTIVATION

Red cedar and other junipers are often used as ornamentals for their evergreen foliage—most cemetery plantings include old red cedar trees and many younger dwarf junipers. The red cedar can be easily transplanted in the early spring before it starts its growth. It is especially well adapted to dry areas. There are numerous named varieties of junipers; *Hortus Third* lists thirty-two for the red cedar (Bailey and Bailey, 1976, p. 617).

Liatris punctata
Gayfeather

Gayfeather, blazing star, dotted
gay feather, Kansas gayfeather,
button snakeroot, rattlesnake master, and starwort. The common
names primarily refer to the showy
flower stalk.

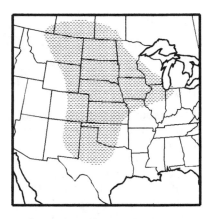

INDIAN NAMES

The Lakota name is "tat e' can-
nuga" (lumpy carcass or lumps
in carcass), somehow referring
to the similarity of the hardened
roots to deer excrement (Rogers,
1980, p. 38; Munson, 1981, p. 235).
The Blackfeet named it "mais-
to-nata" (crow-root) because it
was eaten by crows and ravens in
the autumn (McClintock, 1923,
p. 320). The Comanche name is
"atabitsenoi" (no translation given)
(Carlson and Jones, 1939, p. 522).
Both the Mesquakies and the
Prairie Potawatomis named the
blazing star "nipinuskwa" (summer weed) (Smith, 1928, p. 216).
The Omaha and Ponca names
for the gayfeather, Liatris aspera
Michx., are "aotashe" and "makan-
sagi"; both mean "medicine." The
Pawnee name for this species is
"kahtsu-dawidu" (round medicine)
(Gilmore, 1977, p. 81).

SCIENTIFIC NAME

Liatris punctata Hook. is a member of the Asteraceae (Sunflower
Family). The derivation of the
name Liatris is unknown. The
species name, punctata, is Latin

for "dotted" and refers to the tiny
dots on the leaves.

DESCRIPTION

Perennial herbs 1–8 dm (¼–2 ¾ ft)
tall; stems single or in clusters
from woody rootstocks. Leaves
alternate, linear, up to 15 cm
(6 in) long, closely spaced, arch-
ing upward, surfaces gland-dotted.
Flower heads as tufts arranged
in spikelike groups at ends of
branches, from Jul to Oct; flowers
are small, tubular, 9–12 mm (⅜–
½ in) long, pink-purple, with 5
pointed lobes and long straplike
styles protruding. Fruits dry, 10-
ribbed, 6–7 mm (approximately
¼ in) long, each with a tuft of
feathery bristles.

HABITAT

Prairies and native pastures.

PARTS USED

Primarily roots, but also leaves and entire plant.

INDIAN USE

The Lakotas pulverized the roots of the gayfeather and ate them to improve the appetite. For heart pains they powdered the entire plant and made a tea (Rogers, 1980, p. 38). The Blackfeet boiled gayfeather root and applied it to swellings (McClintock, 1923, p. 320). They often made a tea for stomachache, but sometimes they simply ate the raw root instead. The Comanches chewed gayfeather roots for the juice, a remedy for swollen testes (Carlson and Jones, 1939, p. 522). The Kiowa-Apaches pounded the cut-up roots, chewed them, made the chewed roots into a warm, damp pad, and placed it on a wound (Jordan, 1965, p. 118).

The Mesquakies and Potawatomis ascribed many virtues to gayfeather root (Smith, 1928, p. 216). As a tea, it was a valuable remedy when the urine was bloody and a cure for bladder trouble in women. Applied topically, it was a cure for scabies. The root was used alone in an unspecified manner to cure gonorrhea. This use also was mentioned by Edwin James on the Long expedition (see below).

The Mesquakies used the gayfeather, *L. aspera*, for bladder and kidney troubles. The Omahas, Poncas, and Pawnees also used this

gayfeather as medicine (Gilmore, 1977, p. 81; Gilmore, 1913a, p. 335). The Pawnees boiled the leaves and root together and fed the tea to children with diarrhea. The Omahas powdered gayfeather root and applied it as a poultice for external inflammation. They made a tea from the plant to treat abdominal troubles. The gayfeather was also used as food by the Kiowas, Tewas, and other tribes (Kindscher, 1987, pp. 143–45).

ANGLO FOLK USE

Gayfeather had only limited Anglo folk use, and that was probably learned from the Indians. Edwin James, botanist for the Stephen Long expedition, reported from near St. Louis on June 27, 1819, that the gayfeather, *L. pycno-stachya* Michx., "here called 'pine of the prairies,' which was now in full bloom, has a roundish tuberous root, of a warm somewhat balsamic taste, and is used by the Indians and others as a cure of gonorrhoea" (Thwaites, 1905, 14: 129).

Michael Moore, in *Medicinal Plants of the Mountain West*, noted recent folk uses for the gayfeather, *L. punctata*:

As a diuretic, to increase the volume of water in urine for mild bladder and urethra infections and water retention. Of some use in decreasing phosphates in the urine if used for an extended period of time. Contains inulin, a starch that is not metabolized but is considered of use as a mild kidney and liver tonic by herbalists and used clinically to test kidney function. The root is also a useful tea for throat inflammation and laryngitis, a tablespoon of the chopped root boiled for twenty minutes in a cup of water and drunk slowly. A useful cough syrup can be made from equal volumes of the chopped fresh root and honey, mixed in a blender or macerated by hand, boiled slowly for one-half hour and strained. In New Mexico the rootlets are burned like incense and the smoke inhaled for headache and nosebleeds or blown into the throat for tonsil inflammations (Moore, 1979, p. 47).

The roots were also used as a folk medicine for sore throats and as a cure for rattlesnake bite (Burlage, 1968, p. 49).

MEDICAL HISTORY

Finley Ellingwood, in his 1902 *A Systematic Treatise on Materia Medica and Therapeutics*, reported the medical use of the gayfeather, *L. spicata* (L.) Willd.:

Physiological Action—The agent has the properties, to a mild degree, of a bitter tonic. It is said to act as an antispasmodic to spasms of the muscular structure of the intestines, relieving spasmodic colic. It stimulates the kidneys and has been used in dropsies. It may be used in the later stages of fevers as an eliminant.
Therapy—Liatris stimulates the stomach mildly, and is a tonic and antispasmodic to the entire gastrointestinal apparatus, relieving colic and soothing irritation. After fevers and other acute prostrating diseases it is a useful remedy to assist in removing the products of disease and restoring healthy glandular action. Its eliminative action is quite marked, it having been often used in syphilis and scrofula.
It is a prompt diuretic, relieving kidney irritation and assisting in the removal of dropsical effusions, but we have more direct and efficient remedies (Ellingwood, 1902, p. 332).

SCIENTIFIC RESEARCH

The gayfeather, *L. spicata*, contains a volatile oil and a resin. Potentially allergenic sesquiterpene lactones have been isolated from *Liatris* species (Mitchell and Rook, 1979, p. 179).

CULTIVATION

The blazing purple flower spikes of gayfeather add a beautiful accent to the prairie's subtle colors. These plants are now recognized as attractive ornamentals—the flowers can now be ordered from florists. It is ironic that the gayfeather, native only to prairies and other open areas in North

America, is grown commercially in greenhouses in Europe and exported to florists in the United States.

The blazing star, *L. pycnostachya*, has the largest flower spikes, sometimes 60 cm (2 ft) long, and blooms in midsummer. The blazing star, *L. punctata*, is a compact plant, amazingly drought tolerant, that blooms in late summer and early fall. It can be grown in a sunny location, either from seeds or from root-cuttings planted in late fall or early spring. Seedlings will bloom either the second or third year.

Seeds are light weight—about 139,000 to a pound. Since the seeds have a high germination rate, only about three seeds are planted per square foot when a large area is being restored to prairie. In one experiment, a 96 percent germination rate was obtained after seeds were stratified, then germinated at 79°F. (Salac et al., 1978, p. 4).

Lithospermum incisum Lehm.
Puccoon

Puccoon, narrow-leafed puccoon, gromwell, narrow-leafed gromwell, and fringed puccoon (puccoon is an Indian word given to dye-yielding plants).

INDIAN NAMES

The Cheyenne name for the puccoon is "hoh'ahea no is' tut" (paralysis medicine) (Grinnell, 1962, 2: 185). The Blackfeet name is "pono-kau-sinni," which may translate as "turnip elk food" (McClintock, 1923, pp. 324–25; Johnston, 1970, p. 318). The Lakota name for the puccoon is "peju'ta sabsa'pa" (black medicine); their name for another species of puccoon, *Lithospermum carolinense* (Walt.) MacM., is "peju'ta ha sa'pa" (black skin medicine or bark medicine) (Rogers, 1980, pp. 40–41).

SCIENTIFIC NAME

Lithospermum incisum Lehm. is a member of the Boraginaceae (Borage Family). *Lithospermum* comes from the Greek word "lithospermon," which refers to the stony seed (technically a fruit) of a European species. The species name, *incisum*, refers to the margins of the petals, which are fringed.

DESCRIPTION

Perennial herbs 0.8–4.5 dm (3– 1½ ft) tall, with woody rootstocks;

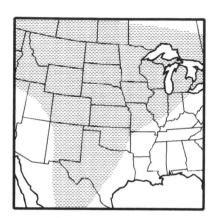

stems erect, simple or branched. Leaves alternate, simple, entire, linear to lance-shaped, 1.5–5 cm (½–2 in) long, 0.5–1 cm (3/16–3/8 in) wide. Flowers in slightly coiled clusters at ends of stems, from Apr to Jun; petals 5, fused and trumpet-like, with 5 fringed lobes, yellow. Fruits composed of 4 small, smooth, hard white nutlets.

HABITAT

Dry prairies, open woods, and disturbed sites.

PARTS USED

Leaves, roots, and stems.

INDIAN USE

The Blackfeet made an incense from the dried tops of the puccoon, *L. incisum*, which they burned during ceremonial events. A violet-colored dye was extracted from the roots (McClintock, 1909, p. 277; Blankenship, 1905, p. 14).

A red dye was obtained from the hoary puccoon by the Omahas and the Chippewas (Gilmore, 1977, p. 59; Densmore, 1974, pp. 370–71).

The Lakotas used the puccoon, *L. incisum*, in an unspecified treatment for hemorrhaging of the lungs (Munson, 1981, p. 236). They also made a powder from the black-skinned roots of the puccoon, *L. carolinense*, for chest wounds, such as gunshot wounds.

The Kiowa-Apaches made a tea from the roots for stomach trouble and diarrhea. For this treatment, they dug fully matured roots (which they noted had the greatest amount of dark-reddish pigment) and used the pieces, either chopped fresh or dried, then pounded. This medicine reportedly had a sweet flavor (Jordan, 1965, p. 119).

The Cheyennes ground the dried leaves, roots, and stems of the puccoon, *L. incisum*, to treat paralysis (Grinnell, 1962, 2: 185). Rubbed on the paralyzed limb, the powder acted as a counterirritant and caused a prickling sensation. This sensation was probably caused by the mechanical action of the extremely fine hairs that cover the plant. Sometimes the green plant was used for this purpose; in that case, the leaves were wrapped in a cotton cloth, crushed with the teeth, then rubbed on the affected areas.

To treat a person who was delirious, the Cheyennes made a tea from the leaves, roots, and stems and rubbed it on the patient's head and face. If a person was very sleepy but needed to stay awake, the plant was used as a stimulant. It was finely chewed by a medicine man or woman "who spits and blows the medicine in the patient's face and rubs some of it over the heart" (ibid.).

The Cheyennes also made a salve from the powdered and moistened leaves and stems of the puccoon, *L. ruderale* Dougl. ex Lehm., to relieve rheumatic and other pains where the skin is not broken. They believed it best to keep this mixture on the injured part at all times. Since this was usually not possible, frequent applications were made.

The Assiniboins knew that the puccoon, *L. ruderale*, suppressed menstrual flow. They concluded that the plant would therefore cause bleeding elsewhere in women, such as the lungs (Johnston, 1970, p. 318).

The puccoon, *L. ruderale*, was a favorite diarrhea remedy for the Shoshones in Nevada. It was also used as a contraceptive for women. For this purpose, a cold water tea was made from the roots; if drunk daily for a period of six months, it insured sterility thereafter (Train, Henrichs, and Archer, 1941, p. 102). It has also been suggested that Comanche women used an unknown species of *Lithospermum* as a form of birth control (Vogel, 1970, p. 242).

The seeds of the puccoon, *L. ruderale*, were among the most abundant plant remains excavated at the Lodaiska site near Denver, Colorado. It is believed that they were used by the people at this site as a contraceptive (Galinat, 1959, pp. 106–7).

In the Southwest, the Navahos took the puccoon, *L. incisum*, internally (method not specified) as a remedy for coughs and colds (Elmore, 1944, p. 96). The Zunis made a medicine from this species, as reported in 1915 by Matilda Stevenson, one of the first women field anthropologists:

The medicine is administered by Kwe'lele, one of the three patron gods of the Great Fire fraternity, to relieve sore throat and swelling of any part of the body.

The root is ground to a powder in the morning, on a ceremonial grinding-stone, in the room of the patient, and gathered into a deerskin sack. The remainder of the plant is made into a tea by boiling in water, which is given warm to the patient as soon as made. After the tea has been drunk the stone upon which the root was ground is heated, a small quantity of water is poured on the stone, and when the water is boiling Kwe'lele loosens the medicine which adheres to the stone, and, lifting the latter with both hands, rubs it over the affected part of the body of the patient. The tea is again given at noon, and Kwe'lele returns at sunset with his two godly impersonators and with much

ceremony applies the powdered root medicine to the parts affected (Stevenson, 1915, p. 56).

MEDICAL HISTORY

The European puccoon, *L. arvense* L., has been used in central Europe as an oral contraceptive because it suppresses the menstrual cycle (Trease and Evans, 1973, p. 364).

SCIENTIFIC RESEARCH

The puccoon is one of the plants that has been studied in the search for a simple and inexpensive method of birth control. Extracts of puccoon, *L. ruderale*, apparently contain a natural estrogen and suppress the secretion of gonadotropins from the pituitary gland (Stone, 1954, pp. 31–33). Some species of *Lithospermum* contain tannins which provide some protection from irritants and may account for the use of the puccoon as a topical skin remedy (Camazine and Bye, 1980, pp. 384–85). Several *Lithospermum* species have been found to contain naphthaquinone derivatives, and *L. officinale* was found to contain toxic pyrrolizidine alkaloids (Rizk, 1986, pp. 18–19).

CULTIVATION

The puccoon has attractive flowers, and if it were easier to propagate, it would be used more often as an ornamental. To improve seed germination, soak fresh seed in hot water before planting. Seedlings are often weak and die easily, and transplanting is often unsuccessful. Root cuttings 5 cm (2 in) long, taken in the fall and treated with a root hormone, will produce some success. The cuttings should be planted right side up, 5 cm (2 in) deep.

Lobelia inflata
Lobelia

Lobelia, Indian tobacco, wild tobacco, asthma weed, gagroot, vomit-wort, puke weed, emetic herb, bladder pod, low belia, and eyebright.

INDIAN NAMES

The Mesquakie and Prairie Potawatomi name for the cardinal flower, *Lobelia cardinalis* L., is "inote'wi" (Indian tobacco) (Smith, 1928, p. 231). The Mesquakie name for the great lobelia, *L. siphilitica* L., is "wapiskitce'piki" (white roots).

SCIENTIFIC NAME

Lobelia inflata L. is a member of the Campanulaceae (Bellflower Family). *Lobelia* was named after Mathieu de Lobel (1538–1616), a Flemish physician and herbalist who wrote on botanical subjects. The species name, *inflata*, means "puffed up" or "swollen," in reference to the enlarged seed capsule.

DESCRIPTION

Annual herbs 2–8 dm (¾–2 ¾ ft) tall; stems hairy below but often smooth above. Leaves simple, alternate, elliptic to lance-shaped, 4–9 cm (1½–3 ½ in) long, gradually reduced up the stem, margins toothed. Flowers inconspicuous, in short, spikelike groups extending above leaves, from Jul to Oct; petals 5, fused into a short, whitish

tube, opening into two bluish lips. Fruit egg-shaped, enclosed by the fused and inflated sepals, splitting into 2 segments to release numerous minute seeds.

HABITAT

Rich soil in woodlands and open woods.

PARTS USED

Leaves, tops, seeds, and roots.

INDIAN USE

Dr. Ferdinand V. Hayden, in his "Botany Report to the U.S. Secretary of War," reported that the Crow Indians in the Yellowstone Valley of Montana were cultivating *Lobelia inflata* for their religious ceremonies. This location is several hundred kilometers (miles) west of its current distribution (Hayden, 1859, p. 739).

The Mesquakies made ceremonial use of both the cardinal

flower, *L. cardinalis*, and the great lobelia, *L. siphilitica*, as love medicines (ibid., pp. 231–32). The roots were finely chopped and mixed into the food of a quarrelsome couple without their knowledge. This, they believed, would avert divorce and make the pair love each other again.

The Pawnees also used the cardinal flower as a love charm. Its root and flowers were combined with ginseng, *Panax quinquefolium* L., wild columbine, *Aquilegia canadensis* L., wild parsley, *Lomatium foeniculaceum* (Nutt.) Coult. & Rose, and red-earth paint. The ethnobotanist Melvin Gilmore reported how this love charm worked:

The possession of these medicines was supposed to invest the possessor with a property of attractiveness to all persons, in spite of any natural antipathy which might otherwise exist. When to these were added hairs obtained by stealth through the friendly offices of an amiably disposed third person from the head of the woman who was desired, she was unable to resist the attraction and soon yielded to the one who possessed the charm (Gilmore, 1977, pp. 54, 77).

Gilmore reported in 1919 that the cardinal flower and lobelia (*L. inflata*) were found in Nebraska only within the old Pawnee domain. Noting that the isolated areas where it was found were near old Pawnee village sites, he

concluded that the plant was introduced into Nebraska by humans (ibid.). James Mooney reported that Cherokee medicine men were cultivating the cardinal flower in 1932 as a medicinal plant (Mooney, 1891, p. 91).

After referring to the works of Long, Catlin, Nuttall, and others, John Uri Lloyd and Curtis Gates Lloyd stated in their 1886 *Drugs and Medicines of North America* that, "with exception of the Penobscot Indians, the evidence is altogether against the reiterated assertion that Lobelia inflata is a drug handed down to us from the American Indians." Still, James Duke finds references to medicinal use of this lobelia by the Cherokees, Micmacs, and Senecas (Lloyd and Gates, 1886, p. 87; Duke, 1985, p. 87).

While on the Lewis and Clark expedition to the Pacific Ocean, Meriwether Lewis wrote in his journal that the Chippewas (whom they did not visit on their journey) used the "simples," lobelia and sumac, in treating gonorrhea and syphilis, and that they were both "effecatious and sovereign" (Will, 1959, p. 293). The botanist Constantine Rafinesque described *L. inflata* in 1828 as one of the Indians' "puke weeds, used by them to clear the stomach and head in their great councils" (Rafinesque, 1830, p. 23).

ANGLO FOLK USE

Lobelia was much more widely used and acclaimed by colonists, settlers, and some doctors than it had been by the Indians. It was an early domestic remedy commonly used as an emetic and cathartic, and to treat asthma, nerves, coughs, and many other ailments (Duke, 1985, p. 281). The Reverend Manasseh Cutler produced the first written record of the use of lobelia when he referred to it as "emetic weed" in the 1785 *American Academy of Science* (Lloyd, 1921, p. 184).

Lobelia's popularity as well as its notoriety can be credited to the doctor Samuel Thomson (1760–1843). Lobelia was one of his specific remedies, used as an emetic. He was arrested in 1809 and charged with murder for allegedly administering a fatal dose of lobelia. He was acquitted due to lack of evidence of his intent to harm the patient and lack of proof that lobelia was a poison (Foster, 1984, p. 119).

MEDICAL HISTORY

Because of the attention that Thomson received, doctors took sides in the controversy and became either followers or disbelievers. The majority were the latter. Nevertheless, both groups used lobelia as an expectorant and an emetic. The dried tops and leaves were officially listed in the *U.S. Pharmacopoeia* from 1820 to 1936

and the *National Formulary* from 1936 to 1960.

SCIENTIFIC RESEARCH

The alkaloid lobeline is the primary active ingredient. It is poisonous in large doses. Lobeline hydrochloride is used in the resuscitation of newborn infants (Trease and Evans, 1973, p. 602).

Several of the commercial products that help people quit smoking contain lobeline. The action of lobeline is similar to that of nicotine in that it excites and paralyzes the nerve cells (Bolyard et al., 1981, pp. 52–53). While a person is quitting smoking, lobelia can offer some of the same benefits as nicotine. Lobeline is also an ingredient in several commercial products used to revive persons from drug overdoses. Lobelia leaves have been smoked as a psychoactive drug for their mildly euphoric, yet stimulating effect (Duke, 1985, p. 280).

Fatal overdoses of lobelia have been reported resulting from improper use of this drug as a home remedy (Bolyard et al., 1981, p. 53). Due to the poisonous alkaloid lobeline, lobelia is on the Food and Drug Administration's list of poisonous plants (Ballentine et al., 1985, p. 41). Besides lobeline, the plant contains lobelianin (a pungent volatile oil), at least fourteen pyridine alkaloids, lobelanine, lobeanidine, isolobelanine, volatile oil, inflatin, and lobelic acid.

Lobelias are often grown in flower gardens. Several, including the red-flowered cardinal flower and the giant lobelia, have named cultivars. The lobelias can be propagated by seed, division, or layering. The tiny seeds should be planted in fine soil, but not covered, because they need some sunlight to germinate. Whether planted in flats or outdoors, fall sowing will give the best results. Transplanting or division of the crown can be done either in the late fall or early spring.

For the drug market, lobelia is harvested when in full flower or as soon as some of the older seed pods are mature. According to results from an experiment in eastern Kentucky, yields of the dried lobelia, *L. inflata*, were 1,700 pounds per acre. The 1,700 pounds of lobelia would, in turn, yield about 17 pounds of lobeline. In 1970, the selling price for dried lobelia ranged from 25 to 80 cents per pound, which indicates gross profits of $425 to $1,360 per acre (Krochmal, Wilken, and Chien, 1972, pp. 216–20).

Mentha arvensis L.
Mint

Mint, field mint, wild mint, brook mint, Indian mint, and horse mint.

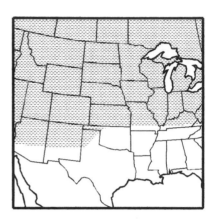

INDIAN NAMES

The Cheyennes have two names for mint, "mahpe'-moxe'shene" (water mint or perfume) and "he heyuts'tsihiss' ots" (vomiting medicine) (Hart, 1981, p. 27; Grinnell, 1962, 2: 186). The Omaha and Ponca name is "pezhe nubthon" (fragrant herb), and the Pawnee name is "kahts-kiwahaaru" (swamp medicine) (Gilmore, 1977, p. 60). The Lakotas also had two names for mint, "cejaka" or "sejake" (mint) and "can pezuta cikala" (little wood medicine) (Munson, 1981, p. 236). The Blackfeet name is "sax ika-kitsim" (quick smell) (McClintock, 1923, p. 324). The Gros Ventre name is "waasowahaan" (Kroeber, 1908, p. 226), and the Arapaho name is "paquanah" (no translations given) (Nickerson, 1966, p. 50).

SCIENTIFIC NAME

Mentha arvensis L. is a member of the Lamiaceae (Mint Family). *Mentha* is a name used by Theophrastus in the first century B.C. for a mint, probably peppermint. The word comes from the name of a Greek nymph, Minthe, who was changed into a mint plant by the jealous Persephone because Minthe was in love with Pluto.

The species name, *arvensis*, means "occurring in a cultivated field."

DESCRIPTION

Perennial herbs 3–5 dm (1–1¾ ft) tall, with creeping rhizomes; stems square, slightly hairy to smooth, sometimes branched, often clustered. Leaves opposite, simple, gland-dotted and strongly aromatic, narrowly lance-shaped to oval, 2.5–12 cm (¼–¾ in) long, gradually reduced upward, margins toothed and slightly hairy. Flowers in dense clusters along the stem, from Jul to Sep; petals fused at base into a short tube, separating into 4 lobes, 4.5–6.5 mm (⅛–¼ in) long, white to lavender. Fruits dry, hard, 0.7–1.3 mm (approximately ¹⁄₁₆ in) long, yellowish-brown.

HABITAT

Moist or wet soil of stream banks, lake margins, prairie ravines, and low woods in the northern latitudes of the northern hemisphere.

Leaves, stems, and roots.

INDIAN USE

All the Indian tribes of the Upper Missouri River region used the wild mint to relieve gas. For this purpose it was steeped in water and drunk (Gilmore, 1977, p. 60). They also used mint to make a beverage and a deodorant.

The Cheyennes used the mint to prevent vomiting by making a tea from the boiled leaves and smaller stems and drinking it slowly. It was also drunk to strengthen heart muscles and to stimulate vital organs (Grinnell, 1962, 2: 186; Hart, 1981, p. 27). Mint foliage was used in ceremonies, but had a variety of practical uses as well: Mint was a home deodorizer, a perfume, an ingredient in hair oil, and a flavoring in beverages. The chewed leaves placed on the body were reputed to improve one's love life.

The Lakotas made a beverage tea from the leaves and a stronger tea from the roots to treat headache (Buechel, 1983, pp. 461, 799). For stomach trouble the Kiowas frequently chewed the fresh leaves or drank a mint tea (Vestal and Shultes, 1939, p. 49).

The Blackfeet chewed and swallowed about a teaspoon of the dried mint leaves to treat heart ailments and chest pains (Johnston, 1970, p. 318). The Flatheads, Kutenais, and other tribes drank mint tea for colds, coughs, fevers, and similar complaints (Hart, 1976, p. 64). Mint was also used medicinally by the Gros Ventres and Pawnees (Kroeber, 1908, p. 226; Dunbar, 1880, p. 340).

The diluted oil of peppermint was sold as a trade item by trappers and traders to the Indian tribes. Since the Indian tribes were already familiar with the native mint, they valued the more potent oil. It was extracted by distillation in England and sold or traded in distinctive, clear green or blue glass vials with raised letters, ESSENCE OF PEPPERMINT and BY THE KINGS PATENT. These glass vials have been found in numerous archaeological sites, including those of the Ottawas, Potawatomis, Arikaras, Chippewas, Kickapoos, Omahas, and Pascagoulas (Bard, 1982, p. 37). These sites date from about 1760 to 1850. At an Arikara cemetery near Leavenworth, Kansas, a vial was found buried with a five-year-old girl, perhaps as a final medicinal offering.

ANGLO FOLK USE

Most of the mints that have been used are from Europe, where there has been a long history of folk use. Two-to-three thousand varieties have been created from numerous hybrids. Of these, peppermint, *Mentha x piperita* L., is probably the most popular herbal tea consumed today in North America.

MEDICAL HISTORY

The various mints are no longer prescribed by the medical profession, but their volatile oil is used in some products. In earlier days, doctors used peppermint as a stomachic, stimulant, tonic, and carminative. Peppermint tea was drunk to relieve insomnia, upset stomachs, nervous tension, migraines, colds, cramps, and many other minor ailments (Foster, 1985, pp. 125–27). Today, peppermint oil is used in many antipuretic preparations for burns and sunburn. It is also used to treat poison ivy rash, diaper rash, athlete's foot, and as a pharmaceutical aid, for flavoring. The volatile oil of the mint, *M. arvense*, and other species, was listed in the *U.S. Pharmacopoeia* from 1882 to 1950.

SCIENTIFIC RESEARCH

Because of the commercial importance of the mint oils, mints have been studied more than any other oil-producing plants (Tyler, 1981, p. 120). The native North American mint, *Mentha arvensis*, contains a volatile oil from which pulegone and thymol or carvacrol have been isolated (Vogel, 1970, p. 340). The volatile oil is toxic, if taken internally, and can cause dermatitis (Foster and Duke, 1990, p. 188). Menthol is extracted from a Japanese variety of this species now cultivated in various parts of the world. A recent study showed that when the fragrance of peppermint, *M. piperita*, was provided at the work place, it was generally associated with superior overall work performance accuracy (Warm, Dember, and Parasuraman, 1990, pp. 17–18).

CULTIVATION

All the mints are easily propagated from cuttings of stems or division of the runners. Cuttings can be rooted in water before planting. Mints prefer a moist location, but will grow almost anywhere if periodically watered. They are very hardy once started and can become a weed in a flower bed.

Monarda fistulosa L.
Beebalm

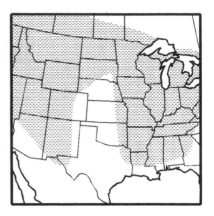

COMMON NAMES

Beebalm, bergamot, horsemint, American horsemint, long-flowered horsemint, Oswego tea, purple bergamot, oregano, plains bee balm, and fern mint.

INDIAN NAMES

The Dakota names are "hehaka ta pezhuta" (elk medicine) and "hehaka to wote" (food of the elk) (Gilmore, 1977, p. 59). The Dakotas also have a name for a second variety, "wahpe washtemna" (fragrant leaves). The Omaha and Ponca name is "pexhe pa" (bitter herb), and they refer to the second variety, which they used as a fragrant pomade for the hair, as "izna-kithe-ige" (no translation given). The Pawnees have names for four varieties of beebalm. The lowest form they call "tsusahtu" (ill-smelling); the second is "tsostu" (no translation given); the third is "tsakus tawirat" (shot many times still fighting); and the fourth, the most desirable, is "parakaha" (fragrant) (ibid.). The Cheyenne names are "wi' us kimohk' shin" (bitter perfume) and "mo in' a mohk' shin" (horse perfume) (Grinnell, 1962, 2: 186). The Blackfeet call it "ma-ne-ka-pe" (young man) (McClintock, 1923, p. 321). The Mesquakie name for beebalm is "menaskwa'kuki meskwanaki" (smelling and red berries) (Smith, 1928, p. 225), and the Kiowas call it "po-et-on-sai-on" (perfume plant) (Vestal and Shultes, 1939, p. 49).

The Osage name is "nidsida" (no translation given) (Munson, 1981, p. 236).

SCIENTIFIC NAME

Monarda fistulosa L. is a member of the Lamiaceae (Mint Family). *Monarda* is named after Nicholas Monardes, a sixteenth-century physician of Seville, who wrote about medicinal and other plants of the New World. The species name, *fistulosa*, means "tubular," in reference to the shape of the flowers.

DESCRIPTION

Perennial herbs 3–12 dm (1–4 ft) tall, with creeping rhizomes; stems square, usually hairy above, sometimes branched, often clustered. Leaves opposite, simple, gland-dotted and fragrant, lance-shaped to narrowly triangular, 3–10 cm (1 1/4–4 in) long, lower surfaces hairy, margins toothed to nearly entire. Flowers in round

156

clusters at ends of branches, from Jun to Sep; petals fused at base into a tube, separating into 2 lips, upper one slender and slightly arched, lower one bent backward, 2–3.5 cm (¾–1⅜ in) long, pale lavender to dark lavender, rarely white. Fruits dry, hard, 1.5–2 mm (approximately ¹⁄₁₆ in) long, brownish or blackish.

HABITAT

Prairie hillsides, pastures, roadsides, stream banks, and occasionally in open woods, usually in rocky soil.

PARTS USED

Leaves, flower clusters, and roots.

INDIAN USE

The Lakotas drank a tea made from the flower clusters as a remedy for fevers and colds. A tea from the leaves was used for whooping cough and other coughing; it was also considered good for people who had fainted (Munson, 1981, p. 236; Rogers, 1980, p. 50). The Lakotas wrapped boiled leaves in a soft cloth and placed it on sore eyes overnight to relieve pain. Chewed leaves were placed on wounds under a bandage to stop the flow of blood.

The Dakotas used the beebalm for the same purposes and made a tea from either the leaves or the flowers for abdominal pain (Gilmore, 1977, p. 59). Dr. F.

Andros, who lived and worked among the Winnebagos and Dakotas for many years, wrote in 1883 that both tribes used a horse mint as a stimulant. (He identified the plant as *Monarda punctata*, but it was probably beebalm, *M. fistulosa*, or spotted beebalm, *M. pectinata* Nutt.) "This I saw them use in cases of Asiatic cholera, which prevailed among them, using it both internally and externally— very hot. I think they were as successful as I was in the treatment" (Andros, 1883, p. 118).

The women of both the Sioux and the Flatheads reportedly drank a tea made from the leaves of beebalm after childbirth (Blankenship, 1905, p. 17). The Winnebagos also boiled the leaves and applied them to pimples and other skin eruptions on the face (Gilmore, 1977, p. 59).

The Blackfeet made an eyewash from beebalm blossoms and warm water. They also bound the flower heads over a burst boil and removed them when the wound had healed (McClintock, 1923, p. 321; Hellson, 1974, pp. 67, 72, 77, 84). They drank a tea made from the plant to control coughs and soothe the kidneys. They chewed the roots for swollen neck glands, and applied pieces of the plant to cuts. A tea made from a mixture of wild onions, *Allium* species, and beebalm was drunk to induce vomiting. The Blackfeet expression for vomiting is "break it," implying that the sickness was forced from the body by vomiting.

157

The Mesquakies used beebalm mixed with other plants as a cure for the common cold (Smith, 1928, p. 225). They also made numerous preparations from the dotted beebalm, *M. punctata* L., and combinations of other plants for headaches, colds, and catarrh, and to revive an unconscious patient.

In their medicinal use of the plants, the Kiowas did not distinguish between beebalm, *M. fistulosa*, and the spotted beebalm, *M. pectinata*. They crumpled the leaves of both, mixed them with spittle, and applied the resulting lotion to soothe and cool insect bites and stings (Vestal and Shultes, 1939, p. 49).

The Crows found beebalm tea helpful in treating respiratory problems (Hart, 1976, p. 70). It was also used as medicine by the Flatheads, Kutenais, and Pawnees (ibid.; Dunbar, 1880, p. 340). Several tribes in the region used the beebalm as a perfume for their hair, bodies, homes, or horses. It was also occasionally used as a beverage tea or as a seasoning (Kindscher, 1987, pp. 150–51).

ANGLO FOLK USE

Whether they discovered its medicinal value through experimentation or learned of it from the Indians, pioneers viewed beebalm as an important folk remedy. It was used to treat headache and fever (Burlage, 1968, p. 93). The ethnobotanist Huron Smith stated that *Monarda* "is an aromatic stimu-

lant, diaphoretic and carminative, occasionally used by the white man for flatulent colic, nausea and vomiting, and the diarrhoea resulting from a cold" (Smith, 1928, p. 225).

MEDICAL HISTORY

Constantine Rafinesque, a medical botanist and explorer, wrote in 1830 concerning *Monarda punctata*:

The whole plant has a grateful smell somewhat similar to Dittany and Balm; much stronger when bruised. The taste is pungent, warm, bitterish &c. . . . Schoepf long ago recommended this plant in intermittent fevers . . . The oil become an official article, kept in shops . . . as a rubefacient liniment in chronic rheumatism, paralytic affections, cholera infantum, difficulty of hearing, periodical headache, and typhus. It must be dissolved in alcohol and rubbed. A liniment made with camphor and opium, cured the periodical headache. . . . It relieves the gastric irritability in cholera infantum, by bathing the abdomen and limbs. . . . Internally, two drops of oil in sugar and water, act as a powerful carminative, and stop emesis or profuse vomiting. The plant is used in New Jersey in cholic, and gravel as a diuretic, being often united to onion juice in gravel and dropsy (Rafinesque, 1830, pp. 37–38).

The leaves and tops of *M. punctata* were officially listed in the *U.S. Pharmacopoeia* from 1820 to 1882. Monarda oil, the principal active constituent of the plant, was officially listed during the same period. It was used internally as a carminative and diaphoretic, and externally in liniments as a stimulant, counterirritant, and vesicant. Thymol, which can be derived from *M. punctata*, *M. fistulosa*, and *M. didyma*, was officially listed in the *U. S. Pharmacopoeia* from 1882 to 1950 and has been listed in the *National Formulary* since 1950. It has been used as an antifungal, antibacterial, and anthelmintic, especially for hookworm.

SCIENTIFIC RESEARCH

Most thymol today is produced in the laboratory. In addition to thymol, both beebalm and dotted beebalm contain limonene, carvacrol, and cymene (Foster, 1985, p. 67). A sweet variety of beebalm, *M. fistulosa* var. *menthaefolia* (Graham) Fern., has been found in Manitoba (Marshall and Scora, 1972, pp. 1845–48). Geraniol, an important perfume component previously unreported in *Monarda*, was found to compose 72–93 percent of the steam-distilled oil of

this variety. Production potential per acre might be great enough to make geraniol from this variety competitive with the synthetic form (Simon and Beliveau, 1986, p. 120).

CULTIVATION

A handsome ornamental, beebalm is an easy plant to grow in the garden. Melvin Gilmore believed that beebalm was inadvertently propagated by Indians of the Missouri River region, who used it widely and spread its seeds when they transported the plants after harvesting them (Gilmore, 1977, p. 7).

Many varieties of the red-flowered beebalm, *M. didyma* L., have been selected for their colorful flowers. These and the native beebalm are easy to propagate by dividing the roots or planting the tiny seeds in spring. They should be sown about 0.5 cm (¼ in) deep. Seedlings will bloom the second year, and plants established by division may bloom the same year.

Established plants send out side shoots in all directions and will crowd out adjacent plants over time. Division of the clumps is one method of preventing this. Beebalm is attractive to bees, and they feed on the flowers quite heavily.

Oenothera biennis
Evening Primrose

COMMON NAMES

Evening primrose, common evening primrose, wild evening primrose, field evening primrose, tree primrose, fever plant, night willow-herb, king's cure-all, large rampion, scurvish, scabish. (The name "evening primrose" was given to this plant because the flowers open in the evening and have the light-yellow color of the English primrose or cowslip, *Primula veris*.)

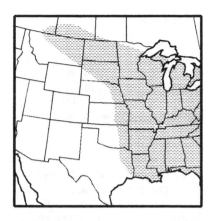

INDIAN NAMES

The Lakota name is "canhlo'gan hu'nla" (rattle weed) (Rogers, 1980, p. 52). The Potawatomi name is "owesa'wanakuk" (yellow top) (Smith, 1933, p. 66). The Blackfeet names for the alkali lily, *Oenothera caespitosa* Nutt., are "oskpi-poku" (sticky root) and "ap-aksibokn" (wide leaves) (McClintock, 1923, p. 320).

SCIENTIFIC NAME

Oenothera biennis L. is a member of the Onagraceae (Evening Primrose Family). *Oenothera* is a name that Pliny used for a plant (now unknown) reputed to produce sleep when its juice was drunk in wine. The species name, *biennis*, means "lasting for two years," indicating that the plant is a biennial.

DESCRIPTION

Biennial herbs 4.5–21 dm (1½–7 ft) tall, arising from taproots; stems single, short-hairy, and spreading-branched. Leaves alternate, simple, often red-spotted, 5–30 cm (2–12 in) long, 1.3–7.6 cm (½–3 in) wide, margins entire to toothed. Flowers numerous, in dense, spike-like groups at ends of stems, from Jul through Oct; petals 4, yellow, joined at the base into a 2.5–5 cm (1–2 in) long tube, separate and flaring at end. Fruits hairy, cylindrical capsules to 4 cm (1½ in) long, splitting at the tip to release many small, angular seeds.

HABITAT

Disturbed habitats, such as fields, roadsides, pastures, and weedy flood plains.

PARTS USED

Seeds, root, and the whole plant.

The tiny seeds of the evening primrose were used as an unspecified medicine by the Forest Potawatomis (Smith, 1933, p. 66). The Flambeau Ojibwas used the whole plant, soaked in warm water, to make a poultice to heal bruises (Smith, 1928, p. 376).

The Omahas also made a poultice from some part of the four-point evening primrose, *O. rhombipetala* Nutt. ex T. & G. (Gilmore, 1977, p. 352). The Blackfeet pounded the root of the alkali lily, *O. caespitosa*, and applied it wet to swellings and sores to reduce inflammation (McClintock, 1923, p. 320). The Kayenta Navahos applied the ground alkali lily to correct a prolapsed uterus (Wyman and Harris, 1951, p. 33). They also made a dusting powder from the flowers to relieve soreness caused by chafing.

In *Medicinal Plants of the Mountain West*, Michael Moore discussed the folk use of the evening primrose, *O. biennis:*

The root, fresh or dried, is chopped and boiled slowly in twice its volume of honey to make a cough syrup both soothing and antispasmodic. A tablespoon every three or four hours as needed. The tops can be used similarly. The herb possesses diuretic function and both root and herb have a sedative effect on some individuals. *It has some laxative effect and can suppress both skeletal and smooth muscle pain, particularly in the reproductive organs. Evening Primrose is variable in its effects, both because of locality and species and because of personal sensitivities, but it can be a prime remedy for some individuals. As common as the plant is, it should be tried. Some of its effects can be attributed to the physiologically active amounts of potassium nitrate present in all parts of the plant. It also functions to some degree as a stimulant to the vagus nerve (Moore, 1979, p. 75).*

Constantine Rafinesque, in his 1830 *Medical Flora of the United States*, stated that the evening primrose leaves are effective for healing when "bruised and applied to wounds. Flowers fragrant and phosphorescent at night" (Rafinesque, 1830, p. 247). B. B. Smythe, a professor of medical botany in Kansas, reported in 1901 that the evening primrose root was an alterative, astringent, and a demulcent (Smythe, 1901, p. 202).

Extracted oil from evening primrose seeds has been shown to be effective in treating atopic eczema, premenstrual syndrome, alcoholism, elevated cholesterol levels, Sjogren's syndrome, mild hypertension, and scleroderma (Horrobin, 1984, pp. 13–17). The oil in the seeds of the evening primrose contains gamma-linolenic acid and linoleic acid, which may be useful for the treatment of burns, wounds, or skin lesions (Erichsen-Brown, 1979, p. 430). The oil has recently become popular in the health food market, primarily for reducing cholesterol. However, the Food and Drug Administration has given the oil "disapproving attention," claiming it is "unaware of any evidence to establish the safety and effectiveness for such claims" (Ballentine and Maifarth, 1987, p. 34).

CULTIVATION

The evening primrose is easily propagated by seed planted either in the fall or in the spring. Seeds planted in the fall will make a rosette that will overwinter and send up a flower stalk in the summer. The evening primrose has spikes of attractive yellow flowers, followed by capsules containing large numbers of seeds. If these seeds are allowed to disperse, the plants can become weedy.

Polygala senega
Seneca Snakeroot

Seneca snakeroot, Senega, Seneca root, rattlesnake root, and mountain-flax.

INDIAN NAMES

The Mesquakie name for the Seneca snakeroot is "wesat-cakika'kuk" (head dress of an Indian) (Smith, 1928, p. 236).

SCIENTIFIC NAME

Polygala senega L. is a member of the Polygalaceae (Milkwort Family). *Polygala* is a classical Latin name for the milkwort, from the Greek "polys gala" (much milk). Pliny reported, "taken in drink, it increases the milk in nursing women." The species name, *senega*, refers to the Seneca Indian tribe.

DESCRIPTION

Perennial herbs 1–5 dm (¼–1¾ ft) tall, with thick rootstocks; stems erect, several to many, minutely hairy, unbranched. Leaves alternate, simple, entire, sessile, lowest ones scalelike, upper ones lance-shaped to linear, 3–8 cm (1³⁄₁₆– 3 ⅛ in) long, 0.5–3.5 cm (³⁄₁₆–1⅜ in) wide. Flowers in cylindrical groups at ends of stems, white, less than 4 mm (³⁄₁₆ in) long, from May to Jul. Fruits slightly hairy capsules, about 4 mm (³⁄₁₆ in) long, each one containing 2 black seeds.

HABITAT

Open woods, prairies, with preference for limestone or chalky soils.

PARTS USED

The root.

INDIAN USE

The Seneca Indians made a tea from this plant as a remedy for coughs, sore throat, and colds as well as snakebite (Youngken, 1924, p. 497), but it was for this last use that the colonists named it Seneca snakeroot. It was one of the first plants whose medicinal use was learned from the Indians. The Winnebagos and Dakotas also used Seneca snakeroot as an antidote for snakebite, insect stings, and other poisons (Andros, 1883, p. 118). Both the Mesquakies and Potawatomis used the boiled root to treat heart trouble (Smith, 1928, p. 236). The white milkwort, *Polygala alba*, was an article of barter among the Plains Indian tribes. The Sioux used it for earache (Blankenship, 1905, p. 18).

John Dunn Hunter wrote *Memoirs of a Captivity among the Indians of North America* in 1824, after his capture by the Kickapoos, and subsequently by the Osages and Kansas. He described their use of the Seneca snakeroot:

in cold infusions, during the remission of fevers, which are attended with great prostration of strength, and in diseases of the pulmonary organs.

They also give it warm, in combination with various other drugs, with a view to promote the sweating process, or to discharge the collection of mucus from the trachea and lungs.

They esteem it very highly in their female complaints, and also in disease of their children when there is great difficulty of breathing (Hunter, 1957, p. 201).

In the Great Lakes Bioregion, the Chippewas made a medicine from a mixture of the Seneca snakeroot, sage (*Artemisia frigida* Willd.), groundplum milkvetch (*Astragalus crassicarpus* Nutt.), and the wild rose (*Rosa arkansana* Porter). It was used as a tonic and stimulant and was prepared in the following manner:

A quart of water is heated and about ⅓ of a teaspoon of the mixed ingredients is placed on the surface of the water at the 4 sides of the pail. A very little of the first

(principal ingredient) is placed on top of each. The ingredients soon dissolve. A stronger decoction was secured by boiling. The medicine was taken 4 times a day, the dose being small at first, and gradually increased to about a tablespoonful (Densmore, 1974, pp. 364–65).

ANGLO FOLK USE

The Seneca snakeroot was a popular folk medicine in the eastern United States. Its use was based primarily on its medical use by early doctors.

MEDICAL HISTORY

The history of the introduction of the Seneca snakeroot into the medical profession is told by Charles Millspaugh:

About the year 1735, John Tennent, a Scotch physician, noted that the Seneca Indians obtained excellent effects from a certain plant, as a remedy for the bite of the rattlesnake; after considerable painstaking and much bribing, he was shown the roots and given to understand that which is now known to be Seneca Snakeroot was the agent used. Noting, then, that the symptoms of the bite were similar in some respects to those of pleurisy and the latter stages of peripneumonia, he conceived the idea of using this root also in those diseases. His success was such that he wrote to Dr. Mead, of London, the results of his experiments. His epistle was printed at Edinburg in 1738, and the new drug favorably received throughout Europe, and cultivated in England in 1739. The action of Seneka was claimed to be that of a stimulating expectorant, thus claiming usage in the latter stages of croup, pneumonia, humid asthma in the aged, etc.; also, when pushed to diuresis and diaphoresis, it was found valuable in rheumatism, anasarca from renal troubles, amenorrhoea, dysmenorrhoea, and kindred complaints. Among the German physicians Seneka received praise in the treatment of ophthalmia after the inflammatory period had passed; and was claimed by Dr. Ammon to prevent the formation of cataract, and promote the formation of pus in hypopyon. The use of Seneka against the poisonous effects of rattlesnake bites, and those of rabid animals [Barton], is not warranted by the results so far gained, at least in civilized practice (Millspaugh, 1974, p. 176).

The dried root of Seneca snakeroot was officially listed in the U.S. Pharmacopoeia from 1820 to 1936 and the National Formulary from 1936 to 1960.

SCIENTIFIC RESEARCH

Fresh Seneca snakeroot has a pleasant odor, similar to wintergreen, because it contains approximately 0.1 percent methyl salicylate. However, the active ingredient in Seneca snakeroot is a complex mixture of triterpenoid saponins that range in concentration from 6 to 10 percent in the root. "Saponins act by local irritation of the lining of the stomach, thus causing nausea which in turn stimulates both bronchial secretions and the sweat glands. Large doses cause vomiting and purging" (Tyler, 1981, p. 211). The triterpenoid saponins and the hydrolysis of senegrin, a crude saponin, yield senegenic acid, polygalic acid, senegenin, presenegenin, hydroxysenegrin, and glucose (Bolyard et al., 1981, p. 115). Polygalic acid gives the plant sternutatory properties. Seneca snakeroot shows uterine stimulant activity on experimental animals and was 98.5 percent effective as an inhibitor of stress-induced gastric ulcers in rats. It continues to be used in Europe in syrups, lozenges, and tea mixtures for controlling coughs and related throat irritations.

CULTIVATION

The USDA's "Drug Plants Under Cultivation," written in 1915, offered instructions for growing Seneca snakeroot:

Seneca can be grown in good garden soil or in rather firm, stony soil provided it contains a fair proportion of leaf mold or very well-rotted manure. Shade is not essential, although the plant thrives in partial shade or under modified forest conditions. Roots for propagation may be obtained from dealers or may be collected from the wild in autumn or early spring. If set 15 inches apart in rows, the plants may be readily cultivated until they reach a marketable size. The seeds ripen in June and may then be planted, or they may be stratified by mixing with sand and buried in boxes or flower pots in moist soil until the following spring, when they may be sown in seed beds or shallow boxes of loam and leaf mold. The seedlings when old enough to be handled safely may be transplanted to the permanent beds and set in rows to facilitate cultivation. In cold situations they will probably need to be protected during the first winter after transplanting. A light covering of straw or pine needles will be sufficient to protect them from severe frost.

The plant is slow in growth, but experiments thus far indicate that about four years are required to obtain marketable roots. The roots should be dug in the fall, thoroughly cleaned, and dried. There are no reliable data on the probable yield. Seneca root is in constant demand, and collectors usually receive [in 1915] from 35 to 50 cents a pound (Stockberger, 1915, pp. 34–35).

Research interest in Seneca snakeroot in Europe, Japan, and the United States has created a demand for this plant, particularly in Canada. In 1987 commercial wholesalers in Winnipeg estimated that they handled about 10,000 kg (22,000 lbs) (Briggs, 1988, p. 199).

Prunus virginiana
Chokecherry

COMMON NAMES

Chokecherry, common chokecherry, wild cherry, and choke-
berry. (The fruit is very astringent
or puckery; hence the "choke" part
of its name.)

INDIAN NAMES

The Omaha and Ponca name
for the chokecherry is "nonpa-
zhinga" (little cherry) (Gilmore,
1977, p. 36). The Pawnee name
is "nahaapi nakaaruts" (cherry
tree) (ibid.). The Lakota called it
is "canpa'-hu" (bitter-wood stem)
(Rogers, 1980, p. 57). The Blackfeet names are "pukkeep" (choke
cherry) and "puckkeep" (the berry)
(Johnston, 1970, pp. 313–14). The
Cheyenne name is "monotse"
(berries) (Hart, 1981, p. 35).

No translations were given for
the following names, but most
of them would probably translate as "chokecherry." The Mesquakie name is "makwi'minuni"
(Smith, 1928, p. 242); the Kiowa
is "o-hpan-ai-gaw" (Vestal and
Shultes, 1939, p. 30); the Crow
is "malupwa"; the Flathead is
"schla scha" (Blankenship, 1905,
p. 19); the Assiniboin is "cham-
pah" (Denig, 1855, p. 583); and the
Osage is "goonpa" (Munson, 1981,
p. 237).

SCIENTIFIC NAME

Prunus virginiana L. is a member of the Rosaceae (Rose Family).
Prunus is from the Greek "prou-
nos," an ancient name for the plum

tree. The species name, *virginiana*,
means "of Virginia."

DESCRIPTION

Shrubs or small trees 20–60 dm
(6–20 ft) tall, often forming thickets; small branches red-brown to
dark brown. Leaves alternate, egg-
shaped to broadly elliptic, 4–12 cm
(1 5/8–4 3/4 in) long, upper surfaces
dark green and lustrous, lower surfaces grayish-green, usually hairy
along veins, margins toothed.
Flowers in dense, elongated groups
at ends of branches, from Apr
through May; petals 5, separate,
rounded, 3–4 mm (1/8–3/16 in) long,
white. Fruits fleshy, round, 8–
11 mm (5/16–7/16 in) in diameter,
red or bluish-purple to black, each
containing 1 seed.

HABITAT

Rich soils, thickets, fence rows,
roadsides, borders of woods, sandy
and rocky soil on hillsides, and
ravine banks.

Primarily the bark, but also the twigs, roots, unripe fruit, and fruit juice.

Chokecherries were the most important wild fruit to the Indians of the Prairie Bioregion, who used the dried, crushed berries in their meat-fat-chokecherry mixture known as pemmican (Kindscher, 1987, pp. 177–82). The Indians of this bioregion used chokecherries to treat an array of ailments. The Blackfeet drank chokecherry juice for diarrhea and sore throat (Hell-son, 1974, p. 68). They also made a tea from the inner bark of the chokecherry and the service berry, *Amelanchier alnifolia* Nutt., which they drank as a purge. Blackfeet mothers drank the tea in order to pass its medicinal qualities to their nursing babies through their milk. They also administered it to their children periodically as an enema. A willow (*Salix* species) tea was used to counteract the laxative effect of the chokecherry. A tea was made from the boiled bark of the chokecherry, mixed with roots of the Western Sweet Cicely, Northern Valerian, and Sixocasim [Indian Horehound], and taken internally (McClintock, 1909, p. 277).

The Sioux (Blankenship, 1905, p. 19), Crows, Gros Ventres, and other tribes (Hart, 1976, p. 43) drank a tea made from boiled bark to treat various stomach com-

plaints, diarrhea, and dysentery. The Poncas used the same treatment and also pulverized the dried fruit to make a tea specifically for diarrhea (Gilmore, 1977, p. 37). The Crows used the bark to cleanse sores and burns, but only certain tribal members had the authority to perform the medicinal applications (Hart, 1976, p. 43).

The Sioux chewed the dried roots and placed them in wounds to stop bleeding (Blankenship, 1905, p. 19). The Mesquakies used a root bark tea as a sedative for stomach problems and as a rectal douche for hemorrhoids (Smith, 1928, p. 242). In 1724 an anonymous author reported that the Illinois and Miamis chewed the bark of the cherry tree root and held it against the gums as a cure for scurvy (Erichsen-Brown, 1979, p. 158). Arikara women drank chokecherry juice in cases of postpartum hemorrhage (Gilmore, 1930, p. 74); as an alternative treatment, they made a tea from the pulverized gum that exudes from chokecherry tree wounds mixed with the root of the red false mallow, *Sphaeralcea coccinea* (Pursh) Rydb.

Indian tribes that lived outside the Prairie Bioregion also made extensive use of the chokecherry and wild black cherry, *P. serotina*, as medicines. These plants

were often used interchangeably as cough medicines, antidiarrheals, cold remedies, and so on. The Mohegan and Ojibwa, for example, used a boiled black cherry bark tea to make a cold remedy while the Paiute used the choke-cherry bark for this purpose. The Delaware made a stimulating tonic from the black cherry bark, while the Thompson Indians and Potawatomi used the choke-cherry bark this way (Moerman, 1982, p. 49).

ANGLO FOLK USE

The medicinal use of chokecherry and wild black cherry was common knowledge to many early American emigrants. In 1785 Reverend Manasseh Cutler wrote one of the first accounts of the medicinal use of the wild black cherry: "Black cherry, an infusion or tincture of the inner bark, is given with success in Jaundice" (Erichsen-Brown, 1979, p. 158).

The mother of Meriwether Lewis was known as a "yarb" (herb) doctor in Albemarle County, Virginia, so Lewis had been exposed to the preparation and use of many plant-derived medicines (Will, 1959, pp. 273–97). Before he and William Clark led their government-sponsored expedition to the Pacific Ocean, he also received further medical instructions from Benjamin Rush, a doctor and statesman. The following incident occurred on June 11, 1805, after Lewis and his men killed four elk along the Marais River in Montana:

I determined to take dinner here, but before the meal was

prepared I was taken with such violent pain in the intestens, that I was unable to partake of the feast of marrowbones. my pain still increased and towards evening was attended with a high fever; finding myself unable to march. I determined to prepare a camp of some willow boughs and remain all night. having brought no medecine with me I resolved to try an experiment with some simples; and the Choke cherry which grew abundantly in the bottom first struck my attention; I directed a parsel of the small twigs to be geathered striped of their leaves, cut into pieces of about 2 Inches in length and boiled in water un-till a strong black decoction of an astringent bitter tast was produced; at sunset I took a point [pint] of the decoction and ab[o]ut an hour after repeated the d[o]ze by 10 in the evening I was entirely relieved from pain and in fact every symptom of the disorder forsook me; my fever abated, a gentle perspiration was produced and I had a comfortable and refreshing nights rest (Thwaites, 1905, 2: 142).

MEDICAL HISTORY

In volume two of *Medical Flora or Manual of Medical Botany of the United States*, published in 1830, Constantine Rafinesque stated that both the chokecherry and the wild black cherry are medicinally active.

The bark is bitter astringent, contains Prussic acid, tannin, gum and mucus. Tonic, febrifuge, sedative. Very useful in fevers, agues, hectic fever, dyspepsia, lumbar abscess, chronic asthma and hysteria, cardialgy, &c . . . heat drives off the Prussic acid. Bark of the root stronger. Reduces pulse from 75 to 50. In large doses narcotic and vermifuge (Rafinesque, 1830, p. 253).

In 1855 Catherine Trail wrote in *The Canadian Settler's Guide* that the bark of the chokecherry "is tonic and bitter: when steeped in whiskey it is given for ague. No doubt it is from this that the common term of 'taking his bitters,' as applied to dram drinking, has been derived. Bitter indeed are the effects of such habits upon the emigrant" (Erichsen-Brown, 1979, p. 159).

The bark of the chokecherry and the wild black cherry was listed in the *U.S. Pharmacopoeia* from 1820 to 1970. Although they are distinct species, they were listed as synonymous in some editions of the *Pharmacopoeia*. For about a century, wild black cherry was recommended as a tonic and stimulant as well as a cough remedy. In 1921, John Uri Lloyd wrote that "No more popular bark of a native tree, excepting sassafras, is known to home medication" (Lloyd, 1921, p. 257).

Today wild cherry is mainly used in cough medicine for its mild sedative properties and pleasant taste. It is no longer used medicinally, as more effective medicines have replaced it. It is currently listed in the *U.S. Pharmacopoeia* as a pharmaceutical aid, a flavoring agent. It is a good vehicle for more potent, nasty-tasting drugs, but it has been replaced in many medicines by saccharin and NutraSweet, which are sweeter, easier to use, and more consistent.

SCIENTIFIC RESEARCH

One of the constituents of chokecherry and wild black cherry bark is the cyanogenic glucoside, amygdalin. With the addition of water, it chemically breaks down to form prunasin and then hydrocyanic acid (Trease and Evans, 1973, p. 112). This cyanide is highly toxic; it can be lethal to livestock that eat the leaves of chokecherries or wild black cherries (Kingsbury, 1964, p. 366). Fortunately, livestock generally avoid these plants unless there is little else for them to eat. People have also been poisoned and even killed by consuming large numbers of the seeds of other *Prunus* species plants—apricots, bitter almonds, and even apples—that also contain large amounts of hydrocyanic acid. The hydrocyanic acid content of chokecherry and wild black cherry bark is low compared to these other sources.

Many medicines are therapeutic in small doses and poisonous

in large; their measure of safety and effectiveness lies between those two doses. Since individual reactions vary greatly, it is best not to take any chances with this substance.

CULTIVATION

The bark of the chokecherry and wild black cherry is collected in the fall when it is the most medicinally active. It is stripped from the wood with a sharp knife. The inner portion has a reddish color and an odor of bitter almonds or benzaldehyde. The bark is dried and stored in an airtight container.

It is quite probable that Indians propagated chokecherries and moved them to convenient locations for harvesting. Later, the prairie pioneers transplanted them from the wild to their farmsteads.

Chokecherries are also valuable as habitat and food for wildlife.

They have been planted in shelter belts on the Great Plains for that reason and for their drought tolerance. They attract birds, raccoons, and even large game. On July 29, 1842, the explorer John Charles Frémont reported from the Oregon Trail near what is now Casper, Wyoming, that on the banks of the river "the cherries are not yet ripe, but in the thickets were numerous fresh tracks of the grizzely bear, which are very fond of this fruit" (Jackson and Spence, 1970, p. 243).

The chokecherry and the wild black cherry have attractive clusters of pendulant white flowers in the spring. They grow best in a sunny location with a rich soil. They can be transplanted from the wild in the early spring, or can be grown from seed. Cultivars are available at some nurseries, including a yellow-fruited chokecherry named "Xanthocarpa."

Psoralea tenuiflora
Wild Alfalfa

Wild alfalfa, slender-flowered scurf pea, many-flowered scurf pea, and scurfy pea.

INDIAN NAMES

The Dakota name for the wild alfalfa is "tichanicha-hu" (no translation given) (Gilmore, 1977, p. 41). The Lakota have two names for the wild alfalfa, "wahpo'kijate" (branched leaf) and "ti'canicahu tanka" (large silver-leafed psoralea [*Psoralea argophylla*]) (Rogers, 1980, pp. 47, 48). Their name for the silver-leafed psoralea is "ti'canicahu" (long-billed curlew stem), which somehow refers to "one that doesn't have a home," perhaps in reference to the habits of the long-billed curlew. The Cheyenne name for the silver-leafed scurfpea is "to'wan i yuhk ts" (to make cold medicine) (Grinnell, 1962, 2: 178).

SCIENTIFIC NAME

Psoralea tenuiflora is a member of the Fabaceae (Bean Family). *Psoralea* means "scabby," and refers to the glandular dots that cover the plant. The species name, *tenuiflora*, means "thin, slight, few, flowers," and refers to the flowers, which are both small and sparse.

DESCRIPTION

Perennial herbs 1.5–12 dm (½– 4 ft) tall, with deep, woody roots;

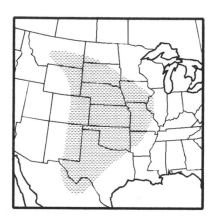

stems erect, appressed-hairy, 1 to several, ridged, branched. Leaves alternate, gland-dotted, palmately compound; leaflets 3–5, lance-shaped to elliptic, entire, 1.3–5 cm (½–2 in) long, less than 1.3 cm (½ in) wide. Flowers in open to dense, cylindrical groups at ends of branches, from May to Sep; petals 5, light blue to bluish-purple, upper 1 larger and erect, lower 2 boat-shaped, 2 wings at sides. Fruits smooth, gland-dotted, 5–9 mm (³⁄₁₆–³⁄₈ in) long, each containing a single brown, kidney-shaped seed.

HABITAT

Prairies, pastures, and open woods.

PARTS USED

The root and leaves.

INDIAN USE

The Lakotas made a tea from the root of the wild alfalfa for headache, and they burned the root as incense to repel mosquitoes. The Dakotas boiled the root of wild alfalfa, along with two unidentified roots, to make a medicine for tuberculosis (Gilmore, 1977, p. 41). From the tops of the plant, they made garlands that were worn on very hot days to protect the head from the heat of the sun.

The silver-leafed scurfpea, *P. argophylla*, was also used as medicine by many tribes. The Mesquakies made a tea from the root to cure chronic constipation (Smith, 1928, p. 230). George Bird Grinnell described the use of the silver-leafed scurfpea by the Cheyennes:

The leaves and stems are ground fine and boiled in water, and the tea is drunk. To cure a high fever, the leaves and stem ground to powder are also mixed with grease and rubbed all over the body. Dr. Rusby has said that the medicinal properties of this plant are not known to science, but it is a near relative of species having active and important properties, though not much used in medicine. Its use as a febrifuge is of great interest and very suggestive (Grinnell, 1962, 2: 178).

The silver-leafed scurfpea was also used by the Dakotas as a horse medicine (Rogers, 1980, p. 47). Meriwether Lewis of the Lewis and Clark Expedition reported that "a decoction of the plant is used by the Indians to wash their wounds" (Blankenship, 1905, p. 20).

The prairie turnip, *Psoralea esculenta*, was the most important wild food used by the Plains Indians (Kindscher, 1987, pp. 184–89). It was used as a medicine by the Blackfeet, who brewed a tea from the dried roots to treat sore throat, chest problems, and gastroenteritis (Hellson, 1974, pp. 68, 72, 80, 82). They applied the chewed root to sprains and fractures, and blew it into a baby's rectum to treat gas pains. For removing matter in the eye, the root was chewed and the spittle was applied to the eye; then a heated cloth or soft hide was kept on the eye until the patient felt confident to remove it. For earache, the root was used in the same way, with earplugs fashioned from cloth or buffalo wool. They also chewed the root to relieve sore throat.

The Arapahos gathered the lemon scurfpea, *P. lanceolata* Pursh, in April or May and chewed its roots to reduce hoarseness. They also rubbed the oily, aromatic leaves on the skin as a moisturizer, and bathed the head with a tea made from the leaves for headaches. They mixed the leaves with the blossoms of sneezeweed, *Dugaldia hoopesii* (Gray) Rydb., to produce an inhalant for headaches (Nickerson, 1966, p. 48; Murphey, 1959, p. 38). The Arapahos also chewed the fresh leaves of the sneezeweed for a clearer throat and voice.

B. B. Smythe, professor of medical botany at the Kansas Medical College from 1891 to 1896, reported that *P. tenuiflora* and *P. argophylla* were "cathartic and nervine" (Smythe, 1901, p. 204).

SCIENTIFIC RESEARCH

As a group, the scurfpeas, *Psoralea*, contain a substance known as psoralen, a linear furocoumarin that has been reported to cause photodermititis (Frohne and Pfander, 1984, p. 122). Research is being conducted on psoralen because of its potential for use in psoriasis and leukemia and possibly certain immune diseases, such as AIDS (Duke, 1987, pp. 524–26).

CULTIVATION

The wild alfalfa and other scurfpeas can be most easily propagated from seed. Germination may be aided by filing a notch in them to break through the hard seed coat. Cuttings and division of the root stock may also be successful.

Ratibida columnifera (Nutt.) Woot. & Standl.
Prairie Coneflower

Prairie coneflower, Mexican hat, columnar prairie coneflower, and longhead coneflower.

INDIAN NAMES

The Dakota name for the prairie coneflower is "wahcha-zi chikala" ("flower, yellow, little" or "little sunflower") (Gilmore, 1977, pp. 78–79). The Lakotas have two names for the prairie coneflower: "napo'stan" (thimble), in reference to the thimble-shaped seed head; and "asan'pi iya'tke" (used to drink milk with), as the top was reportedly used as a nipple (Buechel, 1983, pp. 92, 355). The Cheyenne name for the prairie coneflower is "shi' shin o wuts' tse i yo" (rattlesnake medicine) (Grinnell, 1962, 2: 188–89).

SCIENTIFIC NAME

Ratibida columnifera (Nutt.) Woot. & Standl. is a member of the Asteraceae (Sunflower Family). The origin of the name *Ratibida* is unknown. The species name, *columnifera*, refers to the columnar cluster of disk flowers in the center of the flower.

DESCRIPTION

Perennial herbs 3–10 dm (1–3 ¼ ft) tall, with stout taproots; stems erect, appressed hairy, 1 to several, ribbed, sometimes branched. Leaves alternate, stalked, 2.5–

13 cm (1–5 in) long, up to 7.5 cm (3 in) wide, pinnately divided and occasionally twice so, with unequal linear segments. Flower heads columnar, up to 5 cm (2 in) long, at the ends of long stalks, from Jun to Sep; ray flowers 4–11, golden yellow to purplish-brown, about 2.5 cm (1 in) long, drooping; disk flowers purplish-brown, abundant. Fruits short, gray, flattened achenes tipped with 1–2 bristles.

HABITAT

Prairies, open disturbed areas, and roadsides.

PARTS USED

Leaves and stems.

INDIAN USE

The Lakotas made a tea from the stalks and leaves to cure a stomachache or a pain in the side. A tea made from the flower tops was used to relieve headache (Rogers, 1980, p. 89). The Lakotas used an unspecified part of the plant to stop hemorrhaging from external wounds or internal causes. A song accompanied their use of this plant (Densmore, 1936, pp. 264–65; Buechel, 1983, p. 355). The Dakotas used the prairie coneflower flowers along with other unidentified plants in the preparation of a remedy for chest pains and other ailments. Mixed with other unidentified plants it became a remedy for wounds. The Dakotas considered the plant very fragrant and also made a beverage tea from the leaves (Gilmore, 1913b, p. 368).

The Cheyennes boiled the leaves and stems to make a yellow solution that was applied externally to rattlesnake bites to relieve the pain and to draw out the poison. The same fluid was reported to provide quick relief in cases of poison ivy (Grinnell, 1962, 2: 189).

CULTIVATION

The prairie coneflower, also called Mexican hat, is an attractive ornamental and one of the easiest wildflowers to propagate from seed. The percentage of seeds that will sprout can be increased by a cold treatment—chilling the seeds at 4°C (40°F) for nine weeks, then germinating them at 27°C (80°F). Grown from seed, the plants will bloom in their second year (Art, 1986, p. 216). They also can be easily propagated by division. The prairie coneflower prefers full sun, well-drained soils, and is very drought tolerant.

Rhus glabra
Smooth Sumac

Smooth sumac, smooth upland
sumac, and dwarf sumac. The
aromatic sumac is also called
skunk-bush sumac, pole-cat
bush, stinking hazel, ill-scented
sumac, squaw berry, squaw bush,
lemonade sumac, and three-lobed
sumac. (The name sumac and its
various spellings and pronuncia-
tions—sumach, shumac, shumack,
summaque, and shoemake—are
said to be of Arabic origin.)

INDIAN NAMES

The Kiowa name for the smooth
sumac is "maw-kho-la" (tobacco
mixture) (Vestal and Shultes,
1939, p. 39). The Dakota, Lakota,
Omaha, and Ponca name is "chan-
zi" (yellow wood), the Winnebago
name is "haz-ni-hu" (water-fruit
bush), and the Pawnee name is
"nuppikt" (sour top) (Gilmore,
1977, pp. 47–48). The Cheyenne
name is "no' anio ni mai' ki mins"
(mixing ingredients), in reference
to its use in smoking (Grinnell,
1962, 2: 180). The Mesquakie
name is "pekwana'nomishi" (no
translation given) (Smith, 1928,
p. 255). The Comanche name is
"dimeyov" (no translation given)
(Carlson and Jones, 1939, p. 524).

The Lakota name for aromatic
sumac is "canun'kcemna," which
refers to a bush with a bad smell
(like human excrement) (Rogers,
1980, p. 255). The Kiowa name
is "dtie-ai-pa-yee-'go" (bitter red
berry) (Vestal and Shultes, 1939,

p. 39). The Cheyenne name is "ho
a to' o nuts" ("smoke issues," in
reference to prayers in ceremonials) (Grinnell, 1962, 2: 180). The
Comanche name is "datsipv" (no
translation given) (Carlson and
Jones, 1939, p. 524).

SCIENTIFIC NAME

Rhus glabra L. is a member of the
Anacardiaceae (Cashew Family).
Rhus comes from the Greek
"rhous," the name for a bushy
sumac. The species name, *glabra*,
means "smooth," in reference to
the stems and leaves.

DESCRIPTION

Shrubs 3–5 m (9–15 ft) tall; forming loose colonies or dense thickets. Leaves alternate, stalked,
pinnately compound; leaflets
11–31, lance-shaped to elliptic, 7–9 cm (2 ¾–3 ½ in) long,
upper surfaces dark green and
shiny, lower surfaces dull, margins toothed. Flowers small, in

large branched groups at ends of branches, sometimes male and female flowers separate, in May and Jun; petals 5, greenish. Fruits red, hairy, rounded, 3.5–4.5 mm (⅛–³⁄₁₆ in) in diameter, ripening Aug through Sep.

Rhus aromatica Ait., aromatic sumac, differs in having leaves with only 3 leaflets and yellow flowers. The fruits are very similar to those of *R. glabra*, although clusters are usually smaller.

HABITAT

Upland prairies, pastures, borders and openings of woods, country roads, and along railroads.

PARTS USED

Leaves, bark, roots, and fruits.

INDIAN USE

Both the smooth and aromatic sumac were used by many tribes as medicine. The Pawnees boiled the fruits of the smooth sumac as remedy for painful menstruation and for bloody diarrhea (Gilmore, 1977, p. 48). In addition to their use of the roots to make a yellow dye, the Omahas had several medicinal uses for the smooth sumac. Ethnobotanist Melvin Gilmore reported:

An Omaha medicine-man, White Horse, said the fruits were boiled to make a styptic wash to stop hemorrhage in women after parturition, and that a de-

coction of the root was used to drink in case of retention of urine and when urination was painful. An Omaha said that a poultice made by bruising the leaves was applied wet in case of poisoning of the skin, as by some irritant vegetal oil. In case the leaves could not be had, the fruits were soaked and bruised, the application being kept moist with the water in which the fruits had been soaked (ibid.).

The Omahas also steeped the fruits and root together to make a wash for sores (Gilmore, 1913a, p. 334). Dr. Edwin James, botanist for the Long expedition, reported in 1819 that the Omahas used the smooth sumac in their smoking mixture:

The Kinnecanick, or as the Omawhaws call it, Ninnegahe, mixed or made tobacco, which they use for smoking in their pipes, is composed partly of tobacco, and partly of the leaves of the sumack [R. glabra]; but many prefer to the latter ingredient, the inner bark of the red willow [Cornus stolonifera Michx.]; and when neither of the two latter can be obtained, the inner bark of the arrow wood [Viburnum] is substituted for them. These two ingredients are well dried over the fire, and comminuted together by friction between the hands (Thwaites, 1905, 15: 122).

Many other tribes used smooth sumac leaves in a smoking mixture, the roots for a yellow dye, and the berries in an acidic-tasting, flavorful beverage (Kindscher, 1987, pp. 191–94).

The Kiowas also used the smooth sumac leaves in a smoking mixture that was esteemed by some members of the tribe as a tuberculosis medicine. However, a medicine-man and peyote-leader explained that "it was not a medicine but was used to 'purify' the body and mind so the peyote, the real medicine, could effect a cure more easily" (Vestal and Shultes, 1939, p. 38). The Mesquakies used the root bark of the smooth sumac as a rubefacient. They boiled and drank a sumac root tea which they also fed to invalids as an appetizer (Smith, 1928, p. 200).

John Dunn Hunter, who lived with the Kickapoos, Osages, and Kansas, wrote that one of these tribes called the astringent root (most probably *R. glabra*) "hon-kos-kao-ga-sha" (it stops the blood flowing out) and described its use:

This is a shrubby plant, growing in abundance in the edges of the prairies and hillsides through the Western country. Its principal virtue consists in its astringent properties which it possesses in a very high degree. It is one of their favourite remedies in stopping bleeding from wounds; the dried root is powdered and put on the mouths of the bleeding vessel and a bandage bound over it. The indians have great confidence in it. They use it very much both internally in form of tea, and externally as a wash in female

complaints. But by far the most efficacious purpose to which this root is applied, is to stop the spitting of blood; an affection which frequently exists amongst them, in consequence of their long and hurried marches. They seldom travel without it; a half tea spoonful in cold water is the dose. I know it to be a highly valuable article in their materia medica (Hunter, 1957, p. 371).

An even older use of the smooth sumac has been found in the Ozark Bluff-dweller culture. A preserved human coprolite, 20-to-30 centuries old, of an Ozark Bluff-dweller was found to be full of sumac fruits, indicating that his or her last food or medicine was sumac fruits (Wakefield and Dellinger, 1936, pp. 1412–13).

The Cheyennes dried the leaves of the aromatic sumac, *R. aromatica*, and mixed them with tobacco, red willow dogwood, *Cornus stolonifera* Michx., and bearberry, *Arctostphylos uva-ursi* (L.) Spreng., to make a smoking mixture (Hart, 1981, pp. 14, 40). They boiled the leaves to treat a head cold and make a diuretic tea. Another medicine made from the plant was used to stop bleeding. Not only were the fruits chewed for relief from toothache, they were also used to protect the hands when removing dog meat from a boiling pot. The plant was also used as a horse medicine. Some Cheyennes claimed that this plant "was received from the Great Spirit and was given to a medicine man." The Kiowa also ate the whole berries of the aromatic sumac as a cure for stomach trouble and influenza (ibid.).

The Blackfeet dried aromatic sumac berries, ground them, and dusted the powder on the pustules of smallpox "in a vain attempt to treat the disease" (Johnston, 1970, p. 315). The Comanches chewed the bark of the aromatic sumac and swallowed the juice as a treatment for colds (Carlson and Jones, 1939, p. 534).

ANGLO FOLK USE

Folk use of the various sumac species can be traced to Europe, where related species were used similarly. The 1636 Gerarde herbal stated the uses of the European coriar sumac, *R. coriari*:

The leaves of Sumach boiled in wine and drunken, do stop the lask, the inordinat course of womens sicknesses, and all other inordinat issues of bloud.

The seed of Sumach eaten in Sauces with meat stop all maner of fluxes of the belly, the bloudie flix, and all other issues, especially the Whites of women.

The decoction of the leaves maketh haires blacke, and is put into stooles to fume upward into the bodies of such as that have the Dysenterie, and is to be given to them also to drinke.

The leaves made into an ointment or plaister with hony and vinegar stayes the spreding nature of gangrenes. . . .

The drie leaves sodden in water until the decoction be as thicke as honey, yeeld forth a certaine oilinesse which performeth all the effects of Licium.

The seed is no less effectuall to be strewed in pouder upon their meats which are Coeliaci [diarrhea] or Dysenterici.

The seeds pouned, mixed with hony and the powder of oke coles, healeth the hemorrhoides.

There issueth out of a shrub a gum, which being put into the hollowness of the teeth, taketh away the paine, as Dioscorides saith (Gerarde, 1636, p. 1,475).

With this and similar information available to pioneers and settlers, it is not surprising that many of them used the native sumac in treating a variety of ailments. The smooth sumac was also used as a chew-stick to clean the teeth, a use also reported from the Ozarks (Elvin-Lewis, 1979, p. 445).

MEDICAL HISTORY

In 1830, Constantine Rafinesque reported some of the early medical uses of the *Rhus* species (excluding the poisonous species) in the eastern United States:

Roots antisyphilitic used by Indians, dye wood reddish. Leaves have much tannin, make the Morocco leather, dye wool and silk black, good astringent for all fluxes. Bark and berries make ink. Fresh roots used for rheumatism, spirituous infusion rubbed with flannel. Gum similar to copal *[resin from tropical trees] cures toothache put in hollow teeth. Indian flutes made of the stems. Berries used in dysentery, rheumatism, dysurea, sorethroat, putrid fevers, hemorrhage, gangrene, &c. they have an agreeable acid taste, make a cooling drink infused in water. Efflorescence on them used as salt and vinegar: it is malic acid. Seeds in powder used for piles and wounds. The juice removes warts and tetters, is the fine red mordant of Indian dyes. . . . Kinikah of western tribes is root and leaves haf mixt with their tobacco, used also for dropsy* (Rafinesque, 1830, pp. 256–57).

The bark of the smooth sumac root was also used by nineteenth-century physicians to make poultices for burns by pounding and then boiling it in a mixture of equal parts milk and water (Bolyard et al., 1981, p. 31). They also made a tea of the root bark to treat various ailments, including gonorrhea, leucorrhea, diarrhea, hectic fever, dysentery, cankers of the throat or mouth, and scrofula; they drank a root tea to cure coughs and consumption.

The berries of the smooth sumac were listed as an official medicine in the *U.S. Pharmacopoeia* from 1820 to 1916 and 1926 to 1936 and in the *National Formulary* from 1916 to 1926 for use as a sore throat gargle, an astringent, and a tonic.

SCIENTIFIC RESEARCH

The sumacs all contain large amounts of tannin, which acts as an astringent and may be the basis for their apparent effectiveness in treatment of burns and other injured tissues. However, tannins can also cause damage to the liver; consequently, their use today is limited. The tannic acid content in the leaves of the smooth sumac ranges from 15 to 27 percent (Vestal and Shultes, 1939, p. 38). The smooth sumac also contains calcium bimalate, gallotannic acid, malic acid, oil resin, oleoresin, sugar, starch, and gum.

Smooth sumac collected from the Missouri Ozarks was found to contain a highly active antibiotic substance that is effective in preventing tooth decay and treating other ailments (Lewis and Elvin-Lewis, 1977, pp. 218, 238). Chew-sticks can be easily made by cutting off a small stem several inches long, removing the outer bark, and chewing on the tip to soften the fibers, which can then be used to massage the gums. Other woody plants, such as the dogwoods, *Cornus florida* L. and *C. drummondii* C. A. Meyer, can be used similarly and may be preferred because they are not so bitter.

CULTIVATION

Smooth sumac is an attractive ornamental plant that can be cultivated both for its beauty and for its wide array of uses. Besides the showy red berries in the fall, the leaves also turn from dark green to a brilliant red. One cultivar of smooth sumac, called 'Flavescens,' has yellow foliage in the fall. Aromatic sumac is a smaller shrub whose fragrance some find attractive and others find skunky smelling. It also has attractive fall foliage. Both varieties can be grown from seed or transplanted root cuttings. They are considered aggressive in pastures and wildlife plantings because they spread by clonal suckers that form colonies. The staghorn sumac, *R. typhina*, found in eastern North America, is also frequently used as an ornamental for its colorful fall foliage.

Rosa arkansana
Wild Rose

COMMON NAMES

Wild rose, prairie wild rose, sunshine rose, Arkansas rose, meadow rose, and pasture rose.

INDIAN NAMES

The Dakota name is "onzhin-zhintka" (rosebush); the Omaha and Ponca name is "wazhide" (no translation given); and the Pawnee name is "pahatu" (red) (Gilmore, 1977, p. 33). The Arapaho name for *Rosa woodsii* is "ya-no" (no translation given) (Nickerson, 1966, p. 48). The Cheyenne name for the rose hip of *Rosa woodsii* is "hih' nin" (to pour out), referring to pouring out water, flour, or grain. This is also their name for the tomato (Grinnell, 1962, 2: 177). The Blackfeet names for *Rosa acicularis* are "kine" (rose berries) and "apis-is-kitsa-wa" (tomato flower) (McClintock, 1923, p. 321). The reason for these comparisons to the introduced tomato is not clear. The Mesquakie names for *Rosa blanda* Ait. are "sipitia'mini" (berry) and "kishipi'iminaki" (to itch like the hemorrhoids) (Smith, 1928, p. 242).

SCIENTIFIC NAME

Rosa arkansana Porter is a member of the Rosaceae (Rose Family). *Rosa* is the Latin name for rose. The species name, *arkansana*, means "of Arkansas."

The very similar rose species are known to hybridize, and there

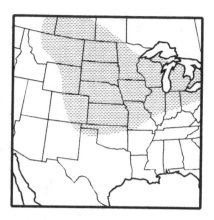

is no evidence that these species were distinguished by the Indians. For these reasons, *Rosa arkansana* is discussed as the main species. Other species names are given when they were noted in the literature.

DESCRIPTION

Shrubs 1–5 dm (¼–1½ ft) tall; branches with slender prickles. Leaves alternate, pinnately compound; leaflets 9–11, egg-shaped to elliptic, 1–4 cm (⅜–1⅝ in) long, lower surfaces usually hairy, upper ⅔ of margins toothed. Flowers in groups of 3 or more at ends of branches, from May to Aug; petals 5, separate, rounded, 1.5–2.5 cm (⅝–1 in) long, pink to white or rarely deep rose. Fruits dry, plump, with hairs along one side; seeds 15–30, enclosed in fleshy covering (hip) that turns red when ripe in late Aug to Sep.

Prairies, ravine and stream banks, bluffs, thickets, along roads and railroads.

PARTS USED

Roots, stems, bark, fruit (hips), and insect-caused galls.

INDIAN USE

The wild rose was widely used by the Indians as a medicine and, in some cases, as an emergency food as well (Kindscher, 1987, pp. 200–204). As discussed here, the wild rose is a group of similar species that are known to hybridize.

The Omahas steeped the fruits (rose hips) or roots of *Rosa arkansana* to make a wash to treat inflammation of the eyes (Gilmore, 1977, p. 33; Fletcher and La Flesche, 1911, p. 584). From the lower parts of the stems, the Pawnees collected insect galls, spherical swellings of plant tissue that develop in response to insect damage. The galls were charred and crushed to make a dressing for burns (Gilmore, 1977, p. 33). Galls were found in the archaeological remains of the Hill Site (near present-day Guide Rock, Nebraska), which was occupied by the Pawnees in the early 1800s (Wedel, 1936, p. 59).

In the Great Lakes Bioregion, the Chippewas made a tea from the wild rose, *Rosa arkansana*, and used the berries for food and dis-

eases of the eye (Densmore, 1974, p. 292). They also used the inner bark of the roots of the wild root (*Rosa sp.*) and the red raspberry, *Rubus idaeus* L., to treat cataracts:

These two remedies are used successively, the first for removing inflammation, and the second for healing the eye. They are prepared in the same way, the second layer of the root being scraped and put in a bit of cloth. This is soaked in warm water and squeezed over the eye, letting some of the liquid run into the eye. This is done 3 times a day (ibid.).

The wild rose was a well-known medicine of the Cheyennes. They boiled the inner bark or the root of *Rosa woodsii* to make a tea that was valued in treating diarrhea and stomach trouble (Hart, 1981, p. 36). To make an eyewash for treating snow blindness, the Cheyennes and Flatheads boiled the petals, stem bark, or root bark of *Rosa* sp. (Hart, 1976, p. 62). The Crows boiled the crushed roots of *Rosa* sp. to make a hot compress that was used to reduce swellings. They also sniffed the vapor from this brew for nosebleed, drank it to stop bleeding in the mouth, and gargled and swallowed some of it to treat tonsillitis and sore throat (ibid.).

The Arapahos made a beverage tea from the wild rose bark of *Rosa woodsii* and used the seeds "to produce a drawing effect for muscular pains" (Nickerson, 1966, p. 48). The Blackfeet made a drink from the root of the wild rose (*Rosa acicularis*) for children with diarrhea (McClintock, 1923, p. 321). The Mesquakies ate the skin of the rose hip of *R. blanda* for stomach trouble. They also boiled the whole fruits down to make a syrup that was used to relieve itching anywhere on the body, but especially for hemorrhoids (Smith, 1928, pp. 242–43).

ANGLO FOLK USE

In Appalachia, the wild rose (*Rosa* sp.) is used to treat jaundice by boiling the root in water. This tea is drunk straight or mixed with equal parts of whiskey. One table-spoon is taken three times a day until the condition is improved. A root tea is used to treat hives on babies (Bolyard et al., 1981, p. 127).

Michael Moore, a folk medicine practitioner from New Mexico, re-ported these uses for the wild rose (*Rosa* sp.) in his 1979 *Medicinal Plants of the Mountain West*:

A good treatment for diarrhea; five to ten flowers or buds steeped in hot water for twenty minutes and drunk as often as needed, gen-erally every two or three hours, be-ginning at least twelve hours after the onset. . . . Rose buds are also one of the safest and most widely used eyewashes, acting as a mild astringent, giving tone to the tis-sues, and shrinking capillary inflammation and redness. Two or three flowers, steeped in a half cup of water until it reaches body temperature and then strained well, is sufficient (Moore, 1979, pp. 141–42).

MEDICAL HISTORY

Constantine Rafinesque reported the following medicinal uses of the wild rose in 1830: "Roots, gall, buds, and fruits all astrin-gent, sweetish, corroborant, used in dysentery and diarrhea. . . . Blos-soms of red roses similar, styptic, have gallic acid, fine conserves" (Rafinesque, 1830, p. 258).

SCIENTIFIC RESEARCH

Fresh rose hips may contain up to 1750 milligrams of vitamin C per 100 grams; by comparison, an equal quantity of oranges contains only 71 milligrams of vitamin C (Arnason, Herbda, and Johns, 1981, p. 2239; Watt and Merrill, 1963, p. 41). Three fresh rose hips may contain as much vitamin C as a whole orange (Phillips, 1979, p. 123). However, the amount of vitamin C in dried rose hips varies greatly, depending on where they were grown, when they were col-lected, and how they were dried and stored. Consequently, some commercial sources of dried rose hips contain almost no vitamin C (Tyler, 1981, p. 186).

In addition to vitamin C, rose hips are about 11 percent pectin, and 3 percent malic and citric acid combined. These substances may be responsible for the mild laxative and diuretic effects of the drug. Rose hips also contain vitamin A, riboflavin, nicotinic acid, carotene, flavonol glycosides, and tannin (Bolyard et al., 1981, p. 128).

CULTIVATION

Wild roses are a lovely addition to a wildflower garden, although sometimes difficult to propagate. Seeds should be sown or stratified soon after harvest, but many will not germinate until the second year. Mature wild roses have roots that may extend 6 m (20 ft) deep, so they are difficult to move without disturbing the root system. Dividing the root stock and taking cuttings from green growth are easier methods of propagation and often successful.

Salix humilis
Prairie Willow

Prairie willow, willow, dwarf willow, dwarf prairie willow, low willow, cone willow, and bush willow.

INDIAN NAMES

The Mesquakie name for a lowland variety of prairie willow is "sopika"; their name for an upland variety is "soso'pika" (no translations given) (Smith, 1928, p. 245). The Blackfeet name for willow, *Salix* species, is "o-che-pes" or "otsipis" (Johnston, 1970, p. 310). The Dakota name for willow is "wahpe-popa"; the Winnebago name is "uhi"; and the Pawnee name is "kitapato" (Gilmore, 1977, p. 121). The Kiowa names are "sen-a," "ai-pee-a-'gaw," and "sen-ya-daw" (Vestal and Shultes, 1939, p. 19). The Cheyenne name is "meno?keo?o" (Hart, 1981, p. 37).

SCIENTIFIC NAME

Salix humilis Marsh is a member of the Salicaceae (Willow Family). *Salix* is the classical Latin name for the willow. The species name, *humilis*, means "low-growing" or "dwarf."

DESCRIPTION

Colonial shrubs 5–30 dm (1½– 10 ft) tall; young branches brown and hairy. Leaves alternate, simple, lance-shaped, 6–10 cm (2⅜–4 in) long, upper surfaces green and smooth, lower surfaces silvery-

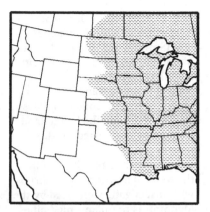

white and hairy, margins entire. Male and female flowers in separate groups on different plants, from Apr to May. Fruits are small, hairy capsules that open to release tiny seeds, each with a tuft of long, silky hairs at the base.

HABITAT

Upland sites in prairies and sparse woods, especially in sandy soil.

PARTS USED

Leaves and stems.

INDIAN USE

The Indians used many species of willow as medicine and for a variety of other purposes as well: making dye, furniture, mats, baskets, drums, stirrups, tipi pegs and pins, fox and fish traps, hunting lodge poles, and meat-drying racks.

The Mesquakies made a tea from the root of the prairie willow or dwarf willow for treatment of diarrhea and for giving enemas (Smith, 1928, p. 245). John McIntosh, a Mesquakie medicine man, also used the leaves of the plant found in upland locations to stop hemorrhaging. (The Mesquakies distinguished an upland from a lowland variety of this species.)

In the Great Lakes Bioregion, the roots of prairie willow shrubs with insect galls were used by the Menominis to make a medicine for spasmodic colic, dysentery, and diarrhea (Smith, 1923, p. 52).

The Blackfeet made a tea from the crushed fresh root of *Salix* species to treat internal hemorrhage, throat constrictions, swollen neck glands, bloodshot or irritated eyes, and for symptoms described as "waist trouble" (Hellson, 1974, pp. 68, 74, 78, 82). The twigs were also gathered and preserved. Steeped in boiling water, they were made into a tea to cure fever or alleviate pain (Johnston, 1970, p. 310; Blankenship, 1905, p. 23).

The Cheyennes drank a tea from the peach leaf willow, *Salix amygdaloides* Anderss., for diarrhea and other ailments (Hart, 1981, p. 38). They also fastened a strip of willow bark around a cut to stop the bleeding. Unbranched willow stems were wrapped around waists, heads, wrists, and ankles of dancers in the Sun Dance because they grow near water and were believed to have the capacity to help thirsty dancers.

Jeffrey Hart has described additional medicinal uses of the willow:

Nez Perce and Crow Indians, historical allies, once used the willow as an emetic in conjunction with the sweatbath. Mickey Old Coyote, a Crow, said that they chewed willow stem tips to induce vomiting. Nez Perces used willow twigs "to clean out their insides." They tied three smooth sticks together and thrust them down the throat, the resulting vomiting producing a green bile. They believed that this bile caused a tired feeling and by forcing it out, a man would feel more energetic, light, and strong; he could easily face hardships and warfare. [Nez Perce women, incidentally, never practiced this remedy.] Crow Indians also chewed willow bark to clean teeth, to prevent cavities, and to relieve headaches (Hart, 1976, p. 67).

Willows, *Salix* species, were also used by many other Indian tribes, including the Choctaws, Delawares, and Cheyennes, as chew sticks to clean the teeth. The shining willow, *Salix lucida* Muhl., was favored by the Osages, Delawares, and Cherokees for this purpose (Elvin-Lewis, 1979, p. 446).

The Kiowas made a tea of willow leaves which they rubbed on the body to cure pneumonia and relieve rheumatic aches. They also chewed the bark to relieve toothache (Vestal and Shultes, 1939, p. 19). The Comanches burned the stems of the willow and used the ashes to treat sore eyes (Carlson and Jones, 1939, p. 533). To restore themselves both physically and mentally, the Dakotas drank a willow-bark tea (Andros, 1883, pp. 116–18).

John Dunn Hunter, who spent most of his life with the Indians in the Prairie Bioregion, reported that the willow or "green twig" that commonly grows on the banks of rivers and water courses "is considered valuable in colds, and asthma; they give a warm infusion at night, with a design to excite perspiration. The roots are used for anthelmintic purposes, and the inner bark as a febrifuge" (Hunter, 1957, p. 378).

ANGLO FOLK USE

The folk use of willows has a long history in Europe. In Appalachia, a tea made from the small branches was reported to cure headache, fever, colds, kidney trouble, and bed wetting in children. A leaf tea was drunk for dysentery and used as a wash for irritated skin (Bolyard et al., 1981, p. 131).

Michael Moore wrote in *Medicinal Plants of the Mountain West*:

The value of Willow lies in the glycosides salicin and populin, as well as the ever present tannin. Its uses are many, but most specifically in the reduction of inflammations of joints and membranes.

Useful for headache, fevers, neuralgia, and hay fever. The glycosides are excreted in the urine as salicylic acid, salicyl alcohol, and related compounds; this renders the tea useful for urethra and bladder irritability, acting as an analgesic to those tissues. Most of our plants are not particularly potent and a fair amount of the bark or stem is needed. Up to an ounce a day can be consumed in tea if needed, although, as in any substance with the ability to alter body functions, take not more than is needed for the problem. Willow bark is a strong but benign antiseptic, and a good poultice or strong wash is made of the fresh or dried herb. (Moore, 1979, p. 161).

Chicanos in New Mexico chewed willow leaves or small branches with the bark removed to harden the gums in cases of pyorrhoea (Curtin, 1976, p. 105).

MEDICAL HISTORY

Constantine Rafinesque wrote in 1830: "Valuable prolific genus. . . . Bark of all bitter astringent, febrifuge and antiseptic . . . in many cases, contains tannin, gluten and salicin similar to Quinine, 3 doses of 6 grains of Salicin have cured agues" (Rafinesque, 1830, p. 260).

The bark of the yellowstem white willow, *Salix alba* L., indigenous to Europe but naturalized in North America, and the native black willow, *Salix nigra* Marsh., have been used in medicine as

197

an astringent. Salicin, the well-known pain killer present in all willows, was officially listed in the *U.S. Pharmacopoeia* from 1882 to 1926 and the *National Formulary* from 1936 to 1955. Aspirin, acetyl salicylic acid (a closely related compound), and other synthetic substitutes have been popular since the late 1800s.

SCIENTIFIC RESEARCH

Salicin occurs in the bark, leaves, and buds of the willow and is used as an antirheumatic drug. Through hydrolysis salicin becomes saligenin, an analgesic (Bolyard et al., 1981, p. 131). When salicin is taken internally, it probably decomposes into salicylic acid, which is used in ointments for skin diseases. Its action is mostly keratolytic; antibacterial and fungicidal activities are secondary. *Salix* species also contain salinigrin, quercitin, sucrose, tannin, salicoside, and aesioside.

CULTIVATION

Willow trees are easily propagated by making cuttings or transplanting small trees. Generally they do well in any moist location, but are short lived. The prairie willow is a drought-tolerant shrub that has attractive "pussy-willow" buds in the early spring.

Silphium laciniatum
Compass Plant

Compass plant, rosin weed, gum weed, and pilot weed.

INDIAN NAMES

The Omaha and Ponca names are "zha-pa" (bitter weed) and "makan-tanga" ("big medicine" or "root"); the Pawnee names are "kahts-tawas" (rough medicine) and "nakisokiit" or "nakisu-kiitsu" (pine water), perhaps in reference to the piney-tasting sap) (Gilmore, 1977, p. 80). The Lakota name is "cansin'sinla" (little tree sap) (Rogers, 1980, p. 39); the Mesquakie name is "peke'wakwa" (gum) (Smith, 1928, p. 216).

SCIENTIFIC NAME

Silphium laciniatum L. is a member of the Asteraceae (Sunflower Family). *Silphium* comes from the Greek "silphion," a plant of the Carrot Family that was used as medicine by the Greeks. In 1753, Linnaeus transferred the name to this genus. The species name, *laciniatum*, describes the leaves which are "cut" into narrow strips or lobes.

DESCRIPTION

Coarse perennial herb 10–30 dm (3 ¼–10 ft) tall, with massive woody rootstocks; stems erect, stiff-hairy, resinous, usually single and unbranched. Leaves alternate, stiff, stalked below, gradually re-

duced up the stem; basal leaves prominent, up to 4.5 dm (1 ½ ft) long and 3 dm (1 ft) wide, deeply pinnately divided, with the segments mostly linear and coarsely toothed. Flower heads 5–10 cm (2–4 in) wide, bell-shaped, in spike-like groups above the basal leaves, from Jun to Sep; ray flowers yellow, numerous, up to 4 cm (1 ½ in) long; disk flowers yellow. Fruits broad, flattened achenes about 1.3 cm (½ in) long, notched at the tip.

HABITAT

Open prairies and roadsides, especially in areas of mild disturbance.

PARTS USED

Stems and root.

INDIAN USE

From the pounded root the Pawnees made a tea for "general debility." This tea was also used by the Santee Dakotas to rid horses of worms and by the Omahas and Poncas as a horse tonic (Gilmore, 1977, p. 80).

The Omahas used the dried root of the compass plant to alleviate head colds or pain in any part of the body in a treatment called "ashude-kithe." In this treatment, fat and some of the dried root were placed on hot coals. The affected body part was then covered with a skin or blanket and placed over the coals so the smoke would "permeate the affected part" (Gilmore, 1913a, p. 334; Gilmore, 1977, p. 80).

The Omahas and Poncas also believed lightning is common wherever the compass plant abounds, so they did not make their camps in such places. They also burned the dried root during electrical storms to avoid being struck by lightning (Gilmore, 1977, p. 80).

The Mesquakies boiled the smaller roots of the compass plant and drank the cooled liquid as an emetic. The children of several of these tribes (including the Mesquakies) used the resinous sap as a chewing gum (Smith, 1928, p. 217). William Bartram, a Quaker botanist from Philadelphia, toured the South in 1788 and observed that the Creeks used

a tall species of Silphium [the stem of which was often cracked or split from the weight of its flowers] from whence exudes a gummy or resinous substance, which the sun and air harden into semi-pellucid drops or tears of a

pale amber color; this resin possesses a very agreeable fragrance and bitterish taste . . . is chewed by the Indians and traders, to cleanse their teeth and mouth, and sweeten their breath (Vogel, 1970, p. 104).

The cup plant, *Silphium perfoliatum* L., was also used medicinally. It can be distinguished from compass plant by its cup-shaped leaves and square stems. A Winnebago name for this plant is "rakeni-ozhu" (weed that holds water), in reference to the cup-shaped junction between the leaves and the stem; another name is "rake-paraparatsh" (square weed). One Omaha and Ponca name for the plant, "zha-baho-hi" (with angled stem), also refers to its square stem, unusual for a plant of the Sunflower Family. The Omahas and Poncas also called it "zha tanga" (big weed). These tribes used the root as a smoke treatment, inhaling the fumes for head colds, nerve pains, and rheumatism (Gilmore, 1977, p. 80). One Winnebago medicine man reported that a root tea was used as an emetic for cleansing and purification after accidental ceremonial defilement and before beginning a buffalo hunt or other important undertaking (ibid.).

The Mesquakies used the cup plant root to alleviate vomiting during pregnancy and to reduce profuse menstruation (Smith, 1928, p. 217). The Menominis, Potawatomis, and Ojibwas lived outside cup plant's native range in Wisconsin, but obtained the plant from Iowa, where it grew naturally in the 1920s. They propagated it and cultivated it in medicinal plant gardens on their reservations (ibid.; Smith, 1928, p. 365).

ANGLO FOLK USE

One use of the compass plant relates to its name. Early pioneers apparently used the leaves of the plant, which are often oriented in a north-south direction, to help them find their way on cloudy days. A recent study showed that over half of the 460 compass plant leaves measured were within 10 degrees of a north-south line (Martin, 1988, pp. 1–2). The leaves are also unusual in that they are often in a vertical position. These factors help the compass plant maximize photosynthesis without risking lethal leaf temperatures.

MEDICAL HISTORY

The compass plant and other *Silphium* species were used by doctors during the nineteenth century and the first few decades of this one. They were used as an antipyretic, diuretic, emetic, expectorant, tonic, styptic, antispasmodic, and stimulant, and for their diaphoretic properties

(Smythe, 1901, p. 204). Dr. L. D. Havenhill of the Pharmacy Department of the University of Kansas reported in 1922 that "Silphium—rosin weed—is another drug which is supplied to some extent from Kansas. It is quoted at 4 cents per pound for the root" (Havenhill, 1919, p. 38).

SCIENTIFIC RESEARCH

An extract and an ointment made from cup plant, *S. perfoliatum*, were found to increase the healing rate of burns (Kuyantseva and Davidyants, 1988, pp. 36–38).

CULTIVATION

Compass plant has unique foliage and attractive sunflowerlike flowers in the mid to late summer. It can be propagated most easily by planting stratified seed in the spring. Year-old plants may have only one leaf, since much of the plant's carbon and energy is invested in the development of an extensive root system. Plants grown from seed will bloom the second or third year. Mature cultivated compass plants often become large and top heavy and have a tendency to fall over. A site with some competition or poor soil will yield smaller plants and may actually be advantageous.

Solanum triflorum
Cut-leaved Nightshade

Cut-leaved nightshade and nightshade.

INDIAN NAMES

The Lakota name for the cut-
leaved nightshade is "canhlogan
skiski'ta" (rough weed) (Rogers,
1980, p. 60). The Blackfeet name
is "omaka-ka-tane-wan" (gopher-
berries), perhaps because this
nightshade is frequently found in
prairie dog towns (McClintock,
1923, p. 321). The Comanche name
is "de:petetsi" (no translation
given) (Carlson and Jones, 1939,
p. 524).

SCIENTIFIC NAME

Solanum triflorum Nutt. is a
member of the Solanaceae (Nightshade Family). *Solanum* is the
name Pliny used for a member of
the nightshade family, supposedly
Solanum nigrum L. The species
name, *triflorum* (three-flowered),
describes the blossoms, often
borne in clusters of three.

DESCRIPTION

Strong-smelling annual herbs 3–
4 dm (1–1 ¼ ft) tall; stems typically
much branched from the base,
somewhat hairy. Leaves alternate,
deeply pinnately divided, 2–5 cm
(¾–2 in) long, about 2 cm (¾ in)
wide. Flowers in groups of 2–3,
arising from bases of leaves, 8–
12 mm (⁵⁄₁₆–½ in) wide, from May

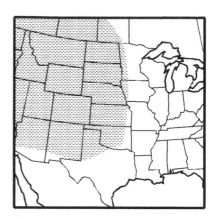

through Sep; petals 5, white, fused
at the bases. Fruits small, spherical, black berries containing tiny
yellowish seeds.

HABITAT

Rocky prairie hillsides, prairie dog
towns, pastures, fields, roadsides,
and waste places.

PARTS USED

The berries and root.

INDIAN USE

The Lakotas used the berries of
the cut-leaved nightshade in the
treatment of stomachache (Rogers,
1980, p. 60). The Blackfeet boiled
the berries of this nightshade and
fed them to children with diarrhea (McClintock, 1923, p. 321).
The Comanches used an unspecified part of a nightshade (*Solanum*
species) as a general tonic and
tuberculosis remedy (Carlson and
Jones, 1939, p. 524).

In the Southwest, the Zunis
made a tea from the buffalo bur,
S. rostratum Dun., by placing a
pinch of the powdered root in a
small quantity of water. It was
drunk for nausea but did not act
as an emetic (ibid.; Stevenson,
1915, p. 60). They also chewed the
root of the silver-leaf nightshade,
Solanum elaeagnifolium Cav.,
and placed it in the cavity of an
aching tooth.

ANGLO FOLK USE

The related European black nightshade, *S. nigrum* L., has a long
history of use as a medicine. Millspaugh reported in 1892:

*This species has been used in
general practice, especially as a
resolvent, from A.D. 54 [Diosco-
rides] to within a few years. The
principal use of the plant has been
in dropsy; gastritis; glandular en-
largement; nervous affections;
general inflammations of mucous
membranes; herpetic, scorbutic,
and syphilitic eruptions; and
as a narcotic. The Arabs use the
bruised leaves, with adeps, as an
application to burns, bullae, and
felons. In Dalmatia the root is
used to cure hydrophobia, and if
fried in butter and eaten to produce sleep; while in Bohemia the
blossoming plant is hung over the
cradle of infants to act as an hyp-
notic. Orfila claims the extract
equal in power and energy to lac-
tucarium. In Spain patients are
often said to be cured of phythisis*

*by burying them up to the neck in
garden loam, then, after removal,
rubbing the body thoroughly with
an ointment of the leaves of this
species (Millspaugh, 1974, p. 489).*

MEDICAL HISTORY

The only native nightshade in the
Prairie Bioregion used by medical doctors was the horse nettle,
S. carolinense L. Its fruits or berries were used as a sedative and an
antispasmodic by doctors. It was
listed in the *National Formulary*
from 1916 to 1936.

SCIENTIFIC RESEARCH

Although some species of *Solanum*
are partially edible (the tubers
of potatoes, for example), most
species contain alkaloids that are
poisonous to humans and livestock. *Solanum* poisoning has
reportedly caused sickness and
death in humans. Even potatoes
that have turned green as a result
of exposure to sunlight are poisonous due to their solanine content.
The horse nettle, *S. carolinense*,
contains the alkaloids solanine,
solaneine, and solanidine (Tehon,
1951, p. 107), but the amount of
poisoning differs between species
and also between plants. In general, the alkaloid content in the
plant decreases in this order: unripe fruit > leaves > stems > ripe
fruit (Frohne and Pfander, 1984,
p. 217). These alkaloids are probably the most important chemical
constituent in terms of medicinal

properties. In a screening process for antibacterial activity, the dried fruit of the horse nettle was found to produce antibacterial activity against a common bacteria, *Pseudomonas* species (Pitts, Thompson, and Hoch, 1969, p. 379).

CULTIVATION

Most of the nightshades are annuals. Besides being poisonous, many are also weedy. Their cultivation is also unadvisable because their fruits may appear edible to inquisitive children.

Sphaeralcea coccinea
Scarlet Globe Mallow

Scarlet globe mallow, red false mallow, and globe mallow.

INDIAN NAMES

The Dakota and Lakota name for the red false mallow is "heyoka ta pezhuta" (medicine of the "heyoka" [contrary medicine men]) (Gilmore, 1977, p. 51). The Cheyenne name for the red false mallow is "wi ke isse' e yo" (sweet medicine) (Grinnell, 1962, 2: 180).

SCIENTIFIC NAME

Sphaeralcea coccinea (Pursh) Rydb. is a member of the Malvaceae (Mallow Family). *Sphaeralcea* comes from the Greek "sphaira" and "alkea" meaning "spherical" "mallow." The species name, *coccinea*, means "scarlet."

DESCRIPTION

Perennial herbs 0.7–3 dm (¼– 1 ft) tall, with creeping, woody rootstocks; stems 1 to several, gray-green, covered with tiny star-shaped hairs. Leaves alternate, simple, stalked, 1.3–6.4 cm (½–2 ½ in) long, divided into 3– 5 wedge-shaped lobes. Flowers solitary or in short terminal clusters, from Apr to Aug; petals 5, 0.6–1.9 cm (¼–¾ in) long, reddish-orange to brick red. Fruits dry, splitting into 10 wrinkled, kidney-shaped segments, each one containing a few brown seeds.

HABITAT

Dry prairies, plains and hills.

PARTS USED

Entire plant, tops, or leaves.

INDIAN USE

This plant, like others of the Mallow Family (okra, purple poppy mallow, and the mallow formerly used in marshmallows) contains a mucilaginous substance. Because of this, "the Dakota *heyoka* utilized it by chewing it to a paste, which was rubbed over hands and arms, thus making them immune to the effect of scalding water, so that to the mystification and wonderment of beholders these men were able to take up pieces of hot meat out of the kettle over the fire" (Gilmore, 1977, p. 51). The purpose of these shocking and amusing feats was probably to encourage trust in the *heyoka*'s abilities, a great asset in healing. The plant was also chewed, then applied to inflamed sores and wounds as a cooling, healing salve.

Members of the Cheyenne Contrary Society also used the red false mallow in their ceremonies (Hart, 1981, p. 31); for this purpose, they chose plants that had four flower stems to represent the four directions. They also finely ground the entire plant—leaves, stem, and roots—and steeped it in water to make a sweet-tasting tea that was mixed with bad-tasting medicines to make them more palatable (Grinnell, 1962, 2: 180). In modern medicine, substances like sugar, peppermint, and wild cherry are used for this purpose and called pharmaceutical aids.

In cases of postpartum hemorrhage, Arikara women were given a mixture of pulverized red false mallow and the gum exuded from the chokecherry tree, *Prunus virginia* L. (Gilmore, 1930, p. 74). The Comanches made a tea from the red false mallow that was used to reduce swellings (Carlson and Jones, 1939, p. 534).

In the Southwest, the Navahos used the red false mallow as one of their principal Coyoteway ceremonial medicines (Wyman and Harris, 1951, p. 32). They used it as a lotion to treat skin diseases, a tonic to improve the appetite, a medicine for rabies, and an ingredient in a ceremonial fumigant. The red false mallow was also pulverized and dusted on sores, and Navajo singers used it to strengthen their voices.

ANGLO FOLK USE

The red false mallow has been used as a folk medicine in New Mexico by both Anglos and Chicanos. Michael Moore, in *Medicinal Plants of the Mountain West*, reports that the plant, also called *Yerba de la Negrita*, may be used as:

A demulcent and emollient. The crushed leaves can be made into a plaster or poultice for any skin inflammation and make a soothing shoe liner for sore or blistered feet. The fresh leaves and flowers can be chewed or the dried plant brewed for tea to soothe a sore throat and hoarseness as well as minor irritability of the stomach and small intestine. A traditional New Mexican first aid for internal hemorrhoids is a little bolus of Yerba de la Negrita leaves, a pinch of punche ('Tobacco'), and saliva used as a suppository. The whole plant can be used in the same manner as marshmallow root, particularly for lower urinary tract inflammations. A cup of tea drunk three times a day until the complaint subsides; even better when combined with a few leaves of Uva Ursi, Manzanita, or Pipsissewa (Moore, 1979, p. 168).

CULTIVATION

The scarlet globe mallow can be propagated by seed, by division, or by cuttings.

Verbena hastata
Blue Vervain

Blue vervain, wild verbena, false vervain, American vervain, wild hyssop, iron-weed, blue vervain, and simpler's joy.

INDIAN NAMES

The Dakota name is "chanhalogo pezhuta"; "pezhuta" translates as "medicine." The Omaha and Ponca name is "pezhe makan" (herb medicine) (Gilmore, 1977, p. 59). The Mesquakie name is "pasan-kwe'tuk" (fine hair woman root), in reference to the fine, hairlike roots (Smith, 1928, p. 193).

SCIENTIFIC NAME

Verbena hastata L. is a member of the Verbenaceae (Vervain Family). *Verbena* is the classical name for branches of laurel, olive, myrtle, cypress, and other trees used in religious rites. The species name, *hastata*, comes from the Latin "hastatus" and means "armed with a spear." It refers to the divergent basal lobes of some of the lower leaves, which give them the appearance of a halberd spear.

DESCRIPTION

Perennial herbs 5–23 dm (1½–7½ ft) tall; stems erect, rough-hairy, unbranched or branched above. Leaves opposite, simple, lance-shaped to broadly egg-shaped, 4–18 cm (1½–7 in) long, 1–11 cm (⅜–4⁵⁄₁₆ in) wide, margins coarsely toothed and often lobed at the base. Flowers in dense, cylindrical spikes at ends of branches, from May to Sep; petals 5, joined at the base into a shallow funnel but with flaring lobes, blue to bluish-purple, less than 5 mm (³⁄₁₆ in) wide. Fruits composed of 4 slender, reddish-brown nutlets, each containing a single seed.

HABITAT

Moist prairies and meadows, low open woodlands, stream banks, around springs and seepage areas, and roadsides.

PARTS USED

Leaves, roots, and flowering tops.

INDIAN USE

The Teton Dakotas boiled the leaves of the blue vervain to make a drink to treat stomachache; the Omahas used the leaves for a beverage tea (Gilmore, 1977, p. 59).

The Mesquakies used the root of the blue vervain as a remedy for fits (Smith, 1928, p. 58).

In the Great Lakes Bioregion, the Menominis made a tea from the roots to clear up cloudy urine (Smith, 1923, p. 58). The Chippewas took the dried, powdered flowers as a snuff to stop nosebleed (Densmore, 1974, pp. 356–57).

ANGLO FOLK USE

Folk use of the European vervain species, *V. officinalis*, has a long history in Europe, where some of the North American folk uses originated. The Reverend Manasseh Cutler reported in 1785: "It is said that the surgeons of the American army, at a certain period when a supply of medicine could not be obtained, substituted a species of verbena for an emetic and expectorant and found its operation kind and beneficial" (Erichsen-Brown, 1979, p. 293).

Constantine Rafinesque in his 1830 *Medical Flora of the United States* reported:

Our best medical sp. is V. hastata *(simpler's joy)* . . . emetic expectorant, tonic, a good substitute for Eupatorium *[boneset]*, but much weaker, used in agues and fevers. Said by Thompson to be next to Lobelia *for an emetic in tea or powder, to check fevers and incipient phthisis. . . . Was the holy herb of the Greeks and Druids, used as panacea, in incantations and to drive evil spirits* (Rafinesque, 1830, p. 274).

Michael Moore reported in *Medicinal Plants of the Mountain West*:

Vervain is broadly active medicinally, serving as a sedative, diaphoretic, diuretic, bitter tonic, and antispasmodic. It is one of the best palliatives for the onset of a virus cold, particularly with upper respiratory inflammation. It will promote sweating, relax and soothe, allay feverishness, settle the stomach, overall producing a feeling of relaxed well-being. It is especially useful for children who become fidgety and cranky when first feeling ill, running around in a droopy, hyperactive fashion, or for the child who has spent three hours in bed and is bored to tears but by no means well enough to play in the snow. The dose for children is one-half to one teaspoon as needed, for adults up to a tablespoon. Larger quantities of Vervain can produce nausea and vomiting and in fact it was formerly employed as an emetic. The tea is an effective sedative for insomnia and, like Hops, will settle a nervous stomach. In treating sprains and deep bruises, the tea will aid in reabsorption of blood from the ruptured tissues, two or three cups a day for at least three or four days. The tea is bitter and can be made more palatable if combined with lemon grass, lemon balm [especially good], peppermint, or wintergreen tea. The latter may counteract the diaphoretic properties of Vervain. Sweeten with honey if needed (Moore, 1979, p. 160).

MEDICAL HISTORY

The dried aboveground part of *V. hastata* was officially listed in the *National Formulary* from 1916 to 1926 as a diaphoretic and expectorant.

SCIENTIFIC RESEARCH

The blue vervain contains the glucosides verbenalin and hastatocide, a bitter constituent, and tannin. In the laboratory, verbenalin shows uterine stimulant activity (Tehon, 1951, p. 117; Rimpler, 1970, p. 491; Farnsworth et al., 1975, p. 577).

CULTIVATION

All of the vervains are easily grown from seed or by division in the late fall or early spring. Many species are considered undesirable perennial weeds in pastures. Cattle don't eat them (probably due to their bitterness), and they tend to increase when an area is heavily grazed. Some of the larger-flowered varieties, such as the sprawling Dakota vervain, *V. bipinnatifida*, and the upright hoary vervain, *V. stricta* Vent., are quite showy, have long blooming periods, and should be considered for planting in ornamental gardens.

Veronicastrum virginicum
Culver's Root

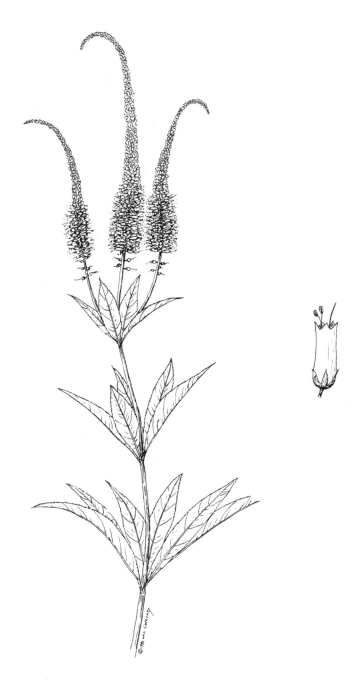

Culver's root, Culver's physic,
Bowman's root, Brinton root
(these names all refer to the practitioners who popularized it), physic
root (the root was used as a purgative), black root, leptandra, tall
speedwell, high veronica, and
whorly wort.

INDIAN NAMES

The Mesquakie names for Culver's root are "witcikatcapi sikuni"
(black snake root) and "maka-
te'wakwi" (black root) (Smith,
1928, p. 247). The Missouris and
Osages called it "hini," and the
Delawares called it "quitel" (no
translations given) (Lloyd, 1921,
p. 181).

SCIENTIFIC NAME

Veronicastrum virginicum (L.)
Farw. is a member of the Scrophulariaceae (Figwort Family). The
genus name *Veronicastrum* indicates its similarity to the genus
Veronica, specifically the Asiatic *Veronica spicata*. The species
name, *virginicum*, means "of
Virginia." The common name
leptandra comes from *Leptandra virginica*, an earlier scientific
name for the same plant. Before
that name was used, it was called
Veronica virginica, the name
under which it was listed in the
first *U.S. Pharmacopoeia* in 1820.

DESCRIPTION

Perennial herbs 8–15 dm (2 ½–
5 ft) tall, often in colonies; stems
erect, smooth to hairy, sometimes branched above. Leaves
whorled, 3–7 per node, simple,
lance-shaped, 7–14 cm (2 ¾–5 ½ in)
long, 1–3 cm (⅜–1 ³⁄₁₆ in) wide,
margins toothed. Flowers in dense
spikes at ends of branches, from
Jun to Aug; petals white to pale
pink, fused at the base into a short
tube, the lobes separate. Fruits
woody, egg-shaped capsules, opening to release numerous tiny, light
brown seeds.

HABITAT

Rich woods and moist prairies.

PARTS USED

The roots.

The Osages, Missouris, Delawares, and other Indians used Culver's root as a tea for its violent purgative effect (ibid., pp. 180–81). The Dakotas and Winnebagos used it to treat snakebite (Andros, 1883, p. 118). Culver's root was a valuable remedy for the Mesquakies, who used it to cure fits and constipation, and to dissolve gravel in the kidneys (Smith, 1928, p. 247). They brewed a root tea to treat ague; it was also drunk by women who were weak or in labor.

In the Great Lakes Bioregion, the Menominis used Culver's root as a strong purgative and "reviver." The ethnobotanist Huron Smith reported: "This is only one of many such revivers and is always found with evil medicines, so that a sorcerer can undo his work." Culver's root was also found in medicine bags and war bundles. It was used to purify people, animals, medicine, and weapons that had been defiled by a person who had just experienced a death in the family (Smith, 1923, pp. 53–54). The Chippewas steeped five roots in a quart of water to make a tea that was both a purgative and a blood cleanser (Densmore, 1974, pp. 346–47).

ANGLO FOLK USE

Culver's root was used by early doctors and in home medicine as a purgative, emetic, alterative, cholalogue, and as a substitute for the use of mercury (primarily as a purgative) (Vogel, 1970, p. 298). It was used in treating a variety of ailments, including liver disorders, bilious fever, pleurisy, and venereal diseases. The use of Culver's root was popularized by Peter Smith, who stated in his 1813 *Indian Doctor Dispensatory* that his father had used Culver's root to cure pleurisy "with amazing speed" (Lloyd, 1921, p. 181).

MEDICAL HISTORY

Constantine Rafinesque reported in his 1830 *Medical Flora*:

The root alone is medical; it is bitter and nauseous, and is commonly used in warm decoction as purgative and emetic, acting somewhat like the Eupatorium *and* Verbena hastata; *some boil it in milk for a milder cathartic, or as a sudorific in pleurisy. A strong decoction of the fresh root is a violent and disagreeable, but effectual and popular remedy in the Western States, for the summer bilious fevers. Some physicians depend upon it altogether (Rafinesque, 1830, pp. 21–22).*

Dr. Finley Ellingwood described several uses for Culver's root or leptandra in his 1902 *Materia Medica and Therapeutics*:

In malarial conditions no cathartic is more efficient than Leptandra. It may be given in full doses, and there is no irritation from its action. It certainly in-

creases the discharge of bile and stimulates and greatly improves the function of the liver.

In ague when quinine is given as an antiperiodic, if from one-fourth to one grain of Leptandra be given with each dose in the intermission, the effects are much more marked and the influence is more permanent. It is demanded in malarial fevers of all kinds, and especially in remittent fever. It is given alone at the onset of the attack as a laxative and in the remission, in small doses in conjunction with the antiperiodic, proving a most valuable auxiliary to the treatment. As an addition to vegetable tonics when malarial conditions prevail, it improves the tone of the entire gastro-intestinal canal and increases the functional activity of the glandular organs. In some cases small doses in wine will produce excellent results.

In the treatment of jaundice it is a valuable auxiliary, and combined with the tonics here indicated its influence is most desirable. It clears the skin, produces black alvine evacuation, and assists in overcoming the entire train of symptoms.

Leptandra has no superior in a case of this character and must be used freely to be appreciated. It is certainly underestimated (Ellingwood, 1902, p. 392).

Culver's root was listed in the U.S. Pharmacopoeia from 1820 to 1840 and from 1860 to 1916, and in the National Formulary from 1916 to 1955. The dried roots and rhizomes were recommended for cathartic and emetic purposes.

Culver's root is potentially toxic. Charles Millspaugh reported in his 1982 Medicinal Plants:

Full doses of the recent root of Leptandra cause dimness of vision, vertigo, vomiting, and purging of bloody or black, tarry, papescent feces. Dr. Burt's experiments with from 1 to 40 grains "Leptandrin" and 20 to 160 drops of the fluid extract gave the following symptoms: Headache, smarting of the eyes and lachrymation; yellow-coated tongue; nausea, burning and distress in the stomach; severe abdominal pains with great desire for stool; profuse black, fetid discharges from the bowels; general lassitude; hot, dry skin; and sleepiness.

Leptandra proves itself to be a severe irritant to the gastric and intestinal mucous surfaces, and a stimulant to the absorbent system (Millspaugh, 1974, p. 446).

SCIENTIFIC RESEARCH

Culver's root contains an intensely bitter, nauseous substance called leptandrin that was originally isolated by Wayne in 1859. It also contains a volatile oil, tannin, gum, and a resin (ibid.; Tehon, 1951, p. 445).

The 1907 U.S. Department of Agriculture publication, "American Root Drugs," offered the following advice for collecting the root as medicine: "The rootstock and roots should be collected in the fall of the second year. When fresh these have a faint odor, resembling somewhat that of almonds, which is lost in drying. The bitter, acrid taste of Culver's-root also becomes less the longer it is kept, and it is said that it should be kept at least a year before being used. The price paid to collectors ranges from 6 to 10 cents a pound" (Henkel, 1907, p. 60).

The short life span of the roots, only three years, affects not only the harvest of the root for medicine, but also its propagation. William Chase Stevens reported in his 1961 *Kansas Wildflowers*:

Digging up a plant in midsummer we discover that the underground system consists of a series of similar, horizontal rhizome segments provided with stout, fibrous roots, the youngest segment bearing at its front end the upright foliar and flowering shoot of the season and being connected at its rear end with the segment of last year that now shows the scar where the shoot it bore last year came away; and this segment of last year is in turn connected at its rear end with the segment of year-before-last, which still shows the scar of its upright shoot. These segments are all alive, and since none older than 3 years is present we realize that each segment dies soon after the completion of its third year of life. While it is the terminal bud of a segment that produces the foliar-flowering shoot, it is a lateral bud that sometime in the fall gives rise to a new segment. The best time to transplant Culver's physic, therefore, is when the leaves begin to ripen in late summer, for then new segments that are to produce the foliar-flowering shoots of the following summer can grow forth and send out their roots without subsequent molestation (Stevens, 1961, p. 292).

This graceful plant is an attractive ornamental that can be planted in either full sun or shade. It is most easily propagated by division of the rootstock in the late summer or fall. Often transplants will bloom the following year. The plant can also be propagated by seed and by cuttings.

Yucca glauca
Small Soapweed

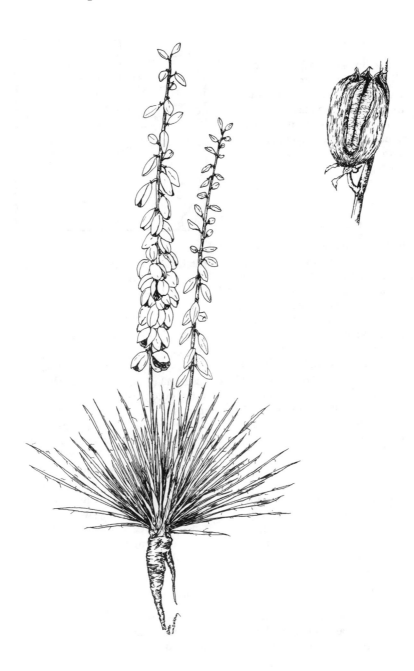

COMMON NAMES

Small soapweed, soapweed, soap-well (these three names refer to the use of the root as a soap substitute), yucca, beargrass, New Mexican Spanish pamilla, amole, Spanish bayonet, dagger plant, and Adam's needles (these last three names refer to the sharp, pointed leaves.

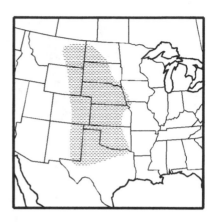

INDIAN NAMES

The Lakota name is "hupe'stola" (sharp-pointed stem) (Rogers, 1980, p. 28). The Blackfeet name is "ek-siso-ke" (sharp vine) (McClintock, 1909, p. 272). No translations were given for the following names: Kiowa, "kaw-tzee-a-tzo-tee-a," "ol-po-on-a," or "kee-aw-gee-tzot-ha'-a'h" (Vestal and Shultes, 1939, p. 17); Dakota, "hupestula"; Omaha and Ponca, "duwaduwa-hi"; and Pawnee, "chakida-kahtsu" or "chakila-kahtsu" (Gilmore, 1977, p. 19).

SCIENTIFIC NAME

Yucca glauca Nutt. is a member of the Agavaceae (Agave Family). John Gerarde, an English physician, horticulturalist, and author of a 1597 herbal, gave *Yucca* its name by mistake. He believed that a specimen imported from the West Indies was the *yuca* or "manioc" from which tapioca is made. The species name, *glauca* (whitened with a bloom), describes the leaves, which are covered with a whitish, waxy film.

DESCRIPTION

Perennials with woody root-stocks, often growing in clumps. Leaves radiating out from basal rosettes, abundant, bayonetlike, waxy green, 4–7 dm (16–28 in) long, margins whitish and fibrous. Flowers in branched groups on stout, spikelike stalks extending above leaves, from May to Jul; each one bell-shaped, with 6 separate segments, thick, oval, 3.5–5.5 cm (1⅜–2¼ in) long, greenish-white to cream. Fruits dry, woody, 6-sided, about 4.5–6 cm (1¾–2¼ in) long, opening to release numerous flat black seeds.

HABITAT

Upland prairies, plains, sandy blowouts, and hillsides (often in limestone soils).

The root.

The Lakotas pulverized the roots of the small soapweed or yucca, mixed them with tepid water, and drank the resulting tea for stomachache (Rogers, 1980, p. 28). When mixed with the roots of the prickly pear cactus (*Opuntia* species), the roots were used to help mothers give birth. However, there was the danger that this medicine would prevent birth—the Lakotas called it "hoksi'yuhapi sni peju'ta" (medicine for not give birth). They also used the root to make soap. They soaked their hair in a root solution to kill head lice, a treatment that reportedly made the hair grow. The fumes from burning roots subdued a horse so that it could be caught and haltered easily. The Omahas and Poncas also used the root as a smoke treatment for humans, but the purpose and methods of this treatment were not given (Gilmore, 1977, p. 19).

The Blackfeet boiled the small soapweed roots in water and used them as a tonic to prevent hair loss (McClintock, 1909, p. 274). They believed there was no better treatment of breaks and sprains than the boiled, grated root. Inflammation from an injury was reduced by placing the injured member in the rising steam of boiling roots. They

also placed the small soapweed roots on cuts to stop bleeding and to reduce inflammation. Besides its medicinal uses, the emerging flower stem and immature seed pods of the small soapweed and other *Yucca* species were a source of food for several tribes (Kindscher, 1987, pp. 225–27).

Michael Moore, a folk medicine practitioner, described the use of Yucca to treat arthritis in *Medicinal Plants of the Mountain West*:

At one time considered a potential source of phytosterols, a family of plant substances used in manufacturing steroidal hormones, its present use is as a sudsing agent in the cosmetic and soap industries and as a home remedy for arthritic pain. Recent clinical studies have shown it to be of some use in the treatment of joint inflammations but the function is not understood. One-fourth ounce of the inner root should be boiled in a pint of water for fifteen minutes and drunk in three or four doses during the day. Arthritis being such an idiosyncratic disorder, no single treatment will help more than a percentage of people, but if Yucca tea is effective, it can relieve pain for several days afterwards. If a strong laxative effect persists, especially if accompanied by intestinal cramping, decrease the amount next

time. *If there are no side effects,*
the quantity can be increased to
one-half ounce a day. Long-term
daily use can slow absorption in
the small intestine of fat-soluble
vitamins. The tea has some value
for urethra or prostate inflamma-
tions (Moore, 1979, pp. 169–70).

SCIENTIFIC RESEARCH

Yucca species contain large quantities of saponins. These substances are bitter, generally irritating, and characterized by their
ability to foam when shaken with
water. The saponins in yucca
are steroid derivatives and have
been extensively studied as starting materials for the synthesis of
cortisone and related corticoids
(Tyler, 1981, p. 235). The steroidal
saponins found in both the leaves
and roots of the small soapweed,
Y. glauca, include sarsapogin,
smilagenin, and tigogenin (El-
Olemy et al., 1974, p. 489). The specific identities and amounts of the
numerous saponins in yucca vary
markedly with the plant tested and
the time of collection. The maximum amount of saponins found
in the small soapweed, collected
in Kansas, was 2 percent (Beath,
1914, p. 102). In addition, the following sterols have been found
in the small soapweed: stigma-
sterol, sitosterol, campesterol,
and trace amounts of cholesterol
(Stohs, Rosenberg, and Billets,
1975, p. 257).

A water extract from the small
soapweed has shown antitumor
activity against B16 melanoma in
mice (Ali et al., 1978, pp. 213–23).
Research with a soapweed from
the Southwest, *Y. schottii* Engelm.,
has shown that the saponin-
containing fraction of the leaves
has anti-inflammatory properties
(Backer, Bianchi, and Cole, 1972,
p. 1665).

Around the turn of the century,
Yucca was reported to contain an
alkaloid useful in treating rheumatism when taken internally.
When the reports were investigated, no positive results could be
produced. Recently, a study published in the *Journal of Applied*
Nutrition re-examined this claim.
This time investigators found that
a "saponin extract" of the "desert
yucca plant," taken four times
daily, was both safe and effective
in treating various forms of arthritis (Beath, 1914, p. 102; Tyler,
1981, p. 235). The methodology
and results of this experiment
have been criticized by the Arthritis Foundation for the following
reasons: the investigators did not
differentiate between rheuma-
toid arthritis and osteoarthritis,
two very different diseases; other
medications were taken by the
patients; and although individual
dosages and lengths of treatment
varied greatly, the results were
lumped together—even though
some of the results were incon-
sistent (ibid.). There is currently
no definitive scientific evidence
for beneficial effects of yucca in
treating arthritis.

Soapweed is a robust, attractive plant that stays green throughout the winter. Its sharp spines make it an effective border plant. It has been planted in cemeteries in western Kansas because of its evergreen character and because it often blooms on Memorial Day. Several *Yucca* species are used as ornamentals. A cultivar of our native *Y. glauca* is called 'Rosea' for its flowers, which are tinted rose on the outside. Soapweed can be propagated by seed, offsets, and cutting of stems, rhizomes, or roots. Roots of mature plants can be 6 m (20 ft) long, making them difficult, if not impossible to transplant easily. Soapweed plants do well in areas with good drainage, a sandy loam soil, and full exposure to the sun.

Other Medicinal Prairie Plants

This section includes species that were less important as medicinal plants. We have less information regarding these species, and generally there has been less scientific research on their chemical constituents.

Abronia fragrans Nutt. ex Hook.

SWEET SAND VERBENA
Nyctaginaceae
Four-O'Clock Family

This low, spreading perennial herb grows on sandy prairies, dunes, and stream valleys. The stems are finely hairy, sticky, and branched. The leaves are opposite, fleshy, and lance-shaped to triangular. The flowers are white to pink, fragrant, trumpetlike, and in rounded terminal clusters above the upper leaves.

The Ute Indians in the Great Basin used the roots and flowers as

a remedy for stomach and bowel trouble (Chamberlin, 1909, p. 32). To counteract the effects of accidentally swallowing a spider, the Navahos took a medicine made from this plant (Elmore, 1944, p. 98). They also used it to treat the stings of scorpions, hornets, bees, ants, and "red bugs," and to cure stomach cramps (Wyman and Harris, 1951, p. 21).

B. B. Smythe, professor of medical botany at the Kansas Medical College in Topeka from 1891 to 1896, compiled an extensive list of medicinal plants found in Kansas. He listed the sweet sand verbena as a laxative (Smythe, 1901, p. 192).

Agastache foeniculum (Pursh) O. Ktze.

LAVENDER HYSSOP
Lamiaceae
Mint Family

Lavender hyssop is a robust perennial herb with opposite, egg-shaped, toothed leaves and small, blue to violet, tubular flowers in dense whorls around the upper stem. Lavender hyssop is found in upland woods and prairies.

The Lakota name for this plant is "wahpe' yata'pi" (leaf that is chewed) (Rogers, 1980, p. 76). The Cheyenne name for lavender hyssop is "mo e'-emohk' shin" (elk mint) (Grinnell, 1962, 2: 186).

The Cheyenne made a tea from the leaves. When cooled, it was

Amorpha canescens Pursh

LEADPLANT
Fabaceae
Bean Family

This small shrub has alternate, gray-hairy, pinnately compound leaves. Plants on hayed prairies have herbaceous stems. The flowers are bright blue to violet and in dense, elongate groups among the upper leaves. The presence of leadplant is usually indicative of a well-managed native pasture or prairie remnant.

The Omahas and Poncas call this plant "te-huntonhi" (buffalo bellow plant) because it was the dominant prairie plant in flower during the rutting season of the buffalo (Gilmore, 1977, p. 41). The plant was considered female, while round-head lespedeza (*Lespedeza capitata* Michx.) was the "male buffalo bellow plant." The Lakotas called it "zitka'tacan'"

drunk for chest pains, particularly those related to coughing, or for a weak heart. The tea was also drunk to cure "a dispirited heart," and it was one of ten ingredients used in special medicinal preparations or perfumes. It was also valued in treating colds (Hart, 1981, p. 27). The powdered leaves were rubbed on the body for a cooling effect during a fever, and the leaves were used to induce sweating in a sweat lodge. The Crees frequently included the flowers in their medicine bundles (Johnston, 1970, p. 318).

Lavender hyssop can easily be propagated by division of the rootstock, cuttings, or by seed sown in the spring or fall. It thrives in sandy, well-drained, soil that is rich and limy. It prefers full sun, but will tolerate some shade.

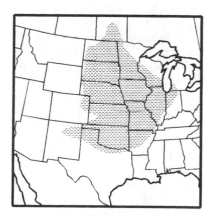

("the bird's wood" or "the bird's tree") because birds perch on it in the prairie where there are no trees (Rogers, 1980, p. 70). The Mesquakie names are "kisimitiye'on'" and "kisimitia'on," and the Potawatomi name is "kasimita'on" (Smith, 1928, p. 227). All of these names mean "something to wipe the buttocks."

The Omahas powdered the dried leaves of leadplant and blew them into cuts and open wounds. The astringent property of the leaves helped promote scab formation. Also, the very small ends, 5 or 6 mm long (less than ¼ in), of leadplant twigs were used as a moxa "applied by sticking them into the skin over a region affected with neuralgia or rheumatism and there burned" (Gilmore, 1913a, p. 334).

The leaves can be used to make a pleasant-tasting yellow-brown tea. The Lakotas drank this leaf tea and used the dried, crushed leaves mixed with a little buffalo fat as a smoking material (Gilmore, 1977, p. 41). The Potawatomis made a leaf tea to kill pinworms and other intestinal worms (Smith, 1933, p. 227). They also steeped the leaves to make a liquid to cure eczema.

Joseph N. Nicollet, a French explorer of the northern portion of the Prairie Bioregion, wrote in his 1838 journal that leadplant, along with bee spiderplant (*Cleome* species) was used by the Sioux and Assiniboins to attract buffalo. This "medicine" was prepared "by pounding up their roots, moistening them, and mixing them together." Whoever rubbed the mixture on his clothing had "the power to attract buffalo and to kill as many of them as he wants" (Bray and Bray, 1976, pp. 117, 281).

Leadplant and false indigo, *Amorpha fruticosa* L., have a cannabinoid-like substance in them called amorphastibol (Kemal, Khalis, and Raul, 1979, p. 463). Rotenoids have been extracted from different *Amorpha* species (ibid.; Ognyanov and Somleva, 1980, p. 279). Leadplant is an attractive, drought-resistant plant with deep, tenacious roots, silvery-gray foliage, and clusters of small, bright violet flowers.

Andropogon gerardii Vitman

BIG BLUESTEM
Poaceae
Grass Family

Big bluestem is the most common native grass of the tallgrass prairies. It is recognized by its 9–28 dm (3–12 ft) tall stems, which turn rust-red in the fall, and by its distinctive flower branches, which are arranged in groups of three or more along the upper stems. These flower groups bear a fanciful resemblance to the foot of a turkey, hence the common name, turkey foot bluestem. It is found in prairies, well-managed native pastures, and on roadsides.

The Kiowa-Apache name for big bluestem translates as "red grass" (Jordan, 1965, p. 98). The Omahas and Poncas called big bluestem "hade-zhide" (red hay) (Gilmore, 1977, p. 16). They used its thick, jointed stems (peska) in their earth lodge construction; boys used them to make toy arrow shafts. These tribes also made a medicine from the plant, described by ethnobotanist Melvin Gilmore:

White Horse, an old medicine-man of the Omaha, told me of a remedial use of Andropogon *which he had obtained by purchase from an Oto medicine-man. A decoction of the lower blades of this grass chopped fine was drunk in cases of general debility and languor without definitely known cause. The same decoction was used also for bathing in case of fevers, for this purpose a cut being made on the top of the head to which the decoction was applied. The people had great dread of fevers because of the evil*

effect they were supposed to have on the mind; this no doubt was because of delirium which often accompanies fever (ibid.).

The Chippewas boiled one big bluestem root in a quart of water to make a tea for stomachache and indigestion (Densmore, 1974, pp. 286, 342). The Comanches used the ashes of little bluestem, *Andropogon scoparius* Michx., to treat syphilitic sores (Carlson and Jones, 1939, p. 533). The Kiowa-Apaches used bundles of little bluestem as switches in the sweat lodge. They believed that switching one's arms, neck, and shoulders would cure aches and pains and drive away evil spirits (Jordan, 1965, p. 98).

Antennaria species

PUSSY-TOES
Asteraceae
Sunflower Family

These perennial herbs form colonies and are covered with dense, whitish hairs. The leaves are spoon-shaped and mostly basal. Flower heads are compact, fuzzy, and at the tip of short stalks. The name pussy-toes refers to the shape of these heads, which later contain small, dry fruits that are dispersed in late spring. Pussy-toes are widespread in North America.

Two Lakota names for the pussy-toes, *Antennaria parviflora* Nutt., are "canhlo'gan hu wanji'la" (weed

with one stem) and "poi'piye" (to
doctor swellings with) (Rogers,
1980, p. 35). After childbirth, Mesquakie women drank tea made
from the leaves of the pussy toes,
A. plantaginifolia (L.) Richards,
to prevent illness (Smith, 1928,
p. 210). This plant was reportedly
used by some Indians as a cure for
rattlesnake bite (Youngken, 1925,
p. 162). The leaves and stems of
A. microphylla Rydb. were chewed
as a cough remedy by the Thompson Indians of British Columbia
(Shemluck, 1982, p. 311), and the
tiny leaves were stripped and dried
as one of the ingredients in Indian
tobacco, "kinnikinnik" (Nickerson, 1966, p. 50).

Constantine Rafinesque stated
in his *Medical Flora of the United
States* that the pussy-toes,
A. neglecta Greene and *A. plantaginifolia*, are "pectoral, used in
coughs, fevers, bruises, inflammations, debility; also against
the negro poison and rattlesnake
bites: Indians will for a trifle allow
themselves to be bitten and cure

themselves at once" (Rafinesque,
1830, p. 224). Huron Smith reported that Eclectic doctors "have
recognized the volatile oils contained in this species [*A. plantaginifolia*], and have employed
them as soothing expectorants.
Also, because of their glucosides
or other bitter principles they have
used them for their stomachic
principles" (Smith, 1928, p. 210).
More recently, Michael Moore,
in *Medicinal Plants of the Mountain West*, described pussy-toes
as "an excellent remedy for liver
inflammation and mild recurrence
of former hepatitis symptoms—
a tablespoon of the chopped plant
steeped in water. It is also a good
non-irritating astringent for intestinal irritations above the ileo-
cecal valve" (Moore, 1979, p. 53).
Pussy-toes can be easily propagated by division of the rootstock
in the early spring or late fall, by
cuttings, or from seed.

Argemone polyanthemos
(Fedde) G. Ownbey

PRICKLY POPPY
Papaveraceae
Poppy Family

The prickly poppy is a stout,
spiny annual herb with distinctive
orange sap; the leaves and stems
have a blue-green color. The leaves
are alternate, deeply lobed, spiny-
toothed, and firm. The flowers are
showy, white, and near the ends of
stems; each one has a dense clus-

ter of yellow stamens at its center. Prickly poppy is usually found in the sandy soil of prairies, flood plains, and along roadsides.

The Lakota name is "to'kahu wahin'kpe on ziya'pi" (thistle used to dye arrows yellow) (Rogers, 1980, p. 53). The Comanches call the prickly poppy "pitsiteya" (no translation given); they used its sap to treat sore eyes (Carlson and Jones, 1939, p. 533). When gathering the prickly poppy, the Comanches made offerings of beads or other objects to it. John Dunbar, a Presbyterian minister who lived on the Pawnee reservation, reported in 1880 that the Pawnees were aware of the sedative property of the prickly poppy (Dunbar, 1880, p. 341).

In 1819, when the Long Expedition was in eastern Nebraska heading west along the sandy Platte River, the botanist Edwin James noted: "Here we first saw a new species of prickly poppy, with a spreading white flower, as large as that of the common poppy of the gardens. The aspect of this plant is very similar to that of the common poppy, except that the leaves are covered with innumerable large and strong prickles. When wounded it exudes a thick yellow sap, intensely bitter to the taste" (Thwaites, 1905, 15: 232).

In 1901, Professor B. B. Smythe of the Kansas Medical College listed the therapeutic properties of the prickly poppy as antihydropic, cathartic, diaphoretic, and diuretic (Smythe, 1901, p. 193). The milky exudate of the related prickly poppy, *Argemone mexicana* L., contains several alkaloids, allocryptopine, berberine, chelerythrine, coptisine, dihydrochelerythrine, dihydrosanguinarine, norargemonine, protopine (argemonine), romneine, and sanguinarine (Duke, 1985, p. 59). The latex sap of the prickly poppy does not appear to be an opium substitute, and the alkaloids in all parts of the plant are considered poisonous (Stephens, 1980, p. 149).

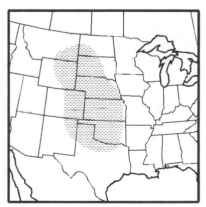

Callirhoe involucrata (T. & G.) Gray

PURPLE POPPY MALLOW
Malvaceae
Mallow Family

Purple poppy mallow is a perennial herb with numerous spreading or erect stems. The leaves are alternate and palmately lobed, with numerous linear segments. The

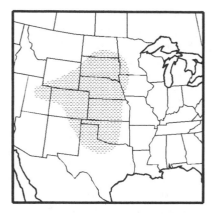

showy, 5-parted, rose to purple flowers are solitary on short stalks. Purple poppy mallow is found in the dry and often sandy soil of prairies, plains, and open woods.

The Lakota name for the purple poppy mallow is "Pezhuta nantia-zilia" (smoke treatment medicine) (Gilmore, 1977, p. 51). The dried root was used by both Lakotas and Dakotas as a smoke treatment for head colds; they inhaled the fumes from a smoldering root. The Dakotas boiled the root and drank the tea for internal pains or used it externally to bathe aching body parts.

The roots were used as food by the Osages and other tribes (Kindscher, 1987, pp. 69–72). Purple poppy mallow is a beautiful, drought-resistant wildflower. It is very easy to grow and can be propagated either by seeds or by division of a mature plant. Each division requires at least a small piece of the root and a live leaf or shoot. It has a flowering period of several weeks, and the fragrance

of its crimson-red flowers fills the air with sweet perfume on sunny, windless afternoons.

Cassia marilandica L.

SENNA
Fabaceae
Bean Family

Senna is an erect perennial herb with smooth, alternate, pinnately compound leaves. The flowers are yellow, 5-petaled, about 1.5–2 cm (⁹⁄₁₆–¹³⁄₁₆ in) wide, and in short groups among the upper leaves. The fruits are flat, black pendulous pods about 7–11 cm (2 ³⁄₄–4 ⁵⁄₁₆ in) long. Senna is found in moist prairie ravines, open woodlands, alluvial thickets, and along stream banks.

The Mesquakies called senna "neka'min" (sand) and ate the seeds, softened by soaking, as a mucilaginous medicine for sore throat (Smith, 1928, p. 228). The Cherokees used the bruised root

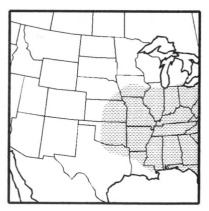

moistened with water for dressing sores. They also used it in a tea to cure fevers as well as an unspecified disease with black spots and paralysis as symptoms (Mooney, 1896, p. 325).

Charles Millspaugh, author of the 1812 *American Medicinal Plants*, called the American wild senna "a cathartic, whose action often causes severe griping" (Millspaugh, 1974, p. 182). In the U.S. Department of Agriculture's "American Medicinal Leaves and Herbs," Alice Henkel wrote:

The leaves, or rather the leaflets, are the parts employed and should be gathered at flowering time, which usually occurs during July and August. They were official in the United States Pharmacopoeia from 1820 to 1880. American senna leaves have a very slight odor and a rather disagreeable taste, somewhat like that of the foreign senna. It is used for purposes similar to the well-known senna of commerce imported from abroad, having, like that, cathartic properties. The price at present [1911] paid for American senna is about 6 to 8 cents a pound (Henkel, 1911, p. 13).

American senna contains glucosides similar to the imported sennas and probably contains saponins (Burlage, 1968, p. 99). The imported senna, particularly Indian senna, *Cassia angustifolia* Vahl, and senna products are the preferred drugs among anthraquinone cathartics and are generally recog-

nized as safe (Leung, 1980, p. 298). Three anthraquinone glycerides in the seeds of the senna, *C. obtusifolia* (L.) Endlicher, were found to be effective in blood platelet aggregation (Yun-choi and Kim, 1990, p. 630).

Ceanothus americanus L.

NEW JERSEY TEA
Rhamnaceae
Buckthorn Family

This short, much-branched shrub has egg-shaped, hairy, and finely toothed leaves. The flowers are delicate, white, 5-parted, and in elongate or rounded groups at the ends of young branches. The fruits are dry, black, 3-lobed capsules, each lobe containing a single reddish-brown seed. New Jersey tea is found on rocky prairie hillsides and roadsides, and in ravines and open woodlands.

The Indian name for this plant is the same in Mesquakie, Pota-

watomi, Menomini, and Ojibwa: "kikuki manito" (spotted snake spirit) (Smith, 1928, p. 240; Smith, 1923, p. 49). They and the above-mentioned tribes of the Great Lakes Bioregion ascribed great powers to it. They "refer to its twisted, intricately knotted roots and ascribe potency to its use in the treatment of bowel troubles" (ibid.). They also used the root to cure snakebite. When prepared by boiling and then chewed, it was considered the "premier remedy for flux" (abnormal discharge from the bowels). The Menominis made a tea from the red roots as a cure-all for stomach troubles.

The Chippewas, also from the Great Lakes Bioregion, drank a root tea for chest colds (Densmore, 1974, pp. 340–41). It was prepared by boiling five inches of root in one quart of water; the dose was one swallow. The Choctaws in Louisiana boiled the root of an unknown *Ceanothus* to make an extract that was taken in small doses for hemorrhage from the lungs (Bushnell, 1909, p. 24).

The Lakota name for the New Jersey tea, *C. herbaceous* Raf. var. *pubescens* (T. & G.) Shinners, is "upan' tawo'te" (female elk food) (Rogers, 1980, p. 87). The Dakota name is "tchanhutkansha" (red-root). The French explorer Joseph Nicollet reported in his 1838 journal that the Dakotas used the leaf as tea and the root as both a beverage and a remedy (Bray and Bray, 1976, p. 50).

The Northern Arapahos and Eastern Shoshones of the Wind River Reservation in Wyoming made a beverage tea from the mountain balm, *C. velutinous* Dougl.. It was also used for medical diagnosis as "certain results mean certain things. The patient breathes out a fresh odor" (Nickerson, 1966, p. 49).

Although New Jersey tea was never officially listed in the *U.S. Pharmacopoeia*, it was used by some physicians. In 1902 Finley Ellingwood wrote in *A Systematic Treatise on Materia Medica and Therapeutics* that the root was: "Astringent, stimulant tonic to mucous surfaces, and expectorant. It is to a certain extent mildly antiseptic." He also reported that it was useful for indigestion, syphilis, scrofula, and ovarian and uterine irregularities (Ellingwood, 1902, p. 406).

New Jersey tea root is a strong astringent (8 percent tannin) and contains an alkaloid that is mildly hypotensive (Foster and Duke, 1990, p. 248). The leaves contain the flavonols afzelin, quercitrin, and rutin (Pichon, Raynaud, and Mure et al., 1985, pp. 27–30).

New Jersey tea is an attractive shrub that can be propagated by root division in the fall, by softwood cuttings forced in a greenhouse in the spring, or by seed. Propagation by seed appears to be the most successful. Seeds should be planted immediately after scarification and soaking in hot water for 30 minutes (Smith and Smith, 1980, p. 85).

Chrysopsis villosa (Pursh) Nutt.

GOLDEN ASTER
Asteraceae
Sunflower Family

Golden aster is a rough-hairy perennial herb to 6 dm (2 ft) tall. The leaves are alternate, simple, lance-shaped to egg-shaped, and 1–3 cm (⅜–1³⁄₁₆ in) long. Numerous yellow, 2 cm (¾ in) wide flower heads are in clusters at the ends of branches. It is found growing on dry, open locations, often in sandy soil.

The Cheyennes called this plant "mis' ka tsi" or "mis ka hets'" (chickadee plant) because chickadees and titmice frequently eat its seeds (Grinnell, 1962, 2: 187). The Cheyennes made a soothing, quieting tea from the tops and stems of the golden aster. Given to a person who was "feeling generally poorly," it tended to put him or her to sleep. If a person or a house was

plagued by evil spirits, the Cheyennes burned the plant as incense. This could be done by anyone, not just the medicine men, and was done with no particular ceremony (Hart, 1981, p. 20).

Chrysothamnus nauseosus (Pall.) Britt.

RABBIT BRUSH
Asteraceae
Sunflower Family

Rabbit brush is a 3–20 dm (1–6 ½ ft) tall, much-branched shrub with feltlike hairs on the stems. The leaves are alternate, linear to narrowly lance-shaped, and smooth to hairy. Many small cylindrical heads with yellow disk flowers and no ray flowers are clustered near the ends of the branches. It is found on the open dry hills and the high plains of the western United States.

The meaning of the Cheyenne name for rabbit brush, "o' iv is se' e yo" (scabby medicine), is somehow related to itching (Grinnell, 1962, 2: 187). The Cheyennes boiled the leaves and stem and washed the itchy areas with the liquid. If relief did not occur rapidly, the fluid was firmly rubbed onto the affected parts. In severe cases, some of the tea was drunk. It was also drunk to cure smallpox. A tea made from the flower parts of rabbit brush and common sage (*Artemisia* sp.) was drunk for colds, coughs, and

tuberculosis (Hart, 1981, p. 20).
The leaves and branches were
burnt on box-elder-wood coals to
repel nightmares. The smoke was
thought to drive away the cause
of the nightmare. A Cheyenne informant reported that rabbit brush
was also part of a mixture that was
burnt as a cold remedy; the patient
inhaled the fumes.

Cirsium undulatum
(Nutt.) Spreng.

WAVY-LEAFED THISTLE
Asteraceae
Sunflower Family

This widespread thistle has erect,
white-woolly stems to 10 dm
(3 ¼ ft) tall. The basal leaves are
alternate, wavy, and lobed, the
lobes tipped with yellowish spines;
the stem leaves are gradually reduced upward. The urn-shaped
or bell-shaped flower heads are at
the ends of a short branch at the
top of stem. Bracts of the heads

each have a short, stout spine.
The small flowers are tubular and
pale purple to purple. Wavy-leafed
thistle is found growing in prairies,
pastures, and disturbed areas.

The Comanches called the
wavy-leafed thistle "tsen" (no
translation given). They boiled its
root and prepared a tea that was
drunk in cases of gonorrhea (Carlson and Jones, 1939, pp. 521, 533).
The Kiowa name for the yellow-
spined thistle, Cirsium ochrocentrum Gray, is "sengts-on" (thistle)
(Vestal and Shultes, 1939, p. 85).
The Kiowas made a tea of the blossoms which they applied to heal
burns and sores; they considered
this remedy "very effective."

The Zunis used this plant as a
cure for a venereal disease:

*The entire plant is placed over-
night in a vessel of cold water. The
water is drunk morning, noon and
at sunset as a cure for syphilis.
Immediately after taking each
dose the patient, if a man, runs
rapidly to promote perspiration
and to accelerate action of the kid-*

neys. On returning to the house he is wrapped in blankets. If the patient be a woman she does not run, but sits bundled in heavy blankets. The medicine often induces vomiting. It belongs to all the people (Stevenson, 1915, pp. 44–45).

The Zunis prepared a tea from the fresh or dried root of the yellow-spined thistle that was drunk three times a day as a remedy for diabetes (Camazine and Bye, 1980, pp. 372–74). The root tea of the thistle (*Cirsium* species) was also reported to be a Zuni contraceptive and a preintercourse drink used to insure a female child (Camazine, 1978, in Shemluck, 1982, p. 325).

The Mesquakie name for the field thistle, *C. discolor* (Muhl. ex Willd.) Spreng., is "kaa'wak" (to stick one) (Smith, 1928, p. 213). The Mesquakies made a tea from the root of this plant to cure stomachache. The Crees used it as a styptic (Beardsley, 1941, p. 484).

The field thistle contains a glucoside, cnicin, and an alkaloid. It was prescribed at one time by physicians and used in folk medicine as a diuretic, tonic, and astringent (Rogers, 1980, p. 37; Munson, 1981, p. 233).

Cleome serrulata Pursh

ROCKY MOUNTAIN BEE PLANT
Capparaceae
Capper Family

The Rocky Mountain bee plant is a smooth, acrid-smelling annual with erect, branched stems. The leaves are alternate and divided into 3 fingerlike segments. The flowers are 4-parted, bright pink to purplish, and in dense groups at ends of branches; each has 6 long, pinkish stamens. It is found on sandy and rocky prairies and disturbed sites.

The Rocky Mountain bee plant was used in the Southwest as a medicine and a semi-cultivated food plant (Kindscher, 1987, pp. 92–94). The Tewas in New Mexico drank the finely ground plant mixed with water as a remedy for stomach disorders. Sometimes they treated stomach problems by wrapping fresh plants in a cloth and applying them to the abdomen (Robbins et al., 1916, p. 59).

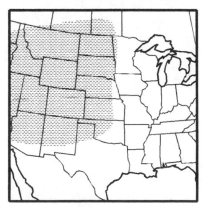

B. B. Smythe of the Kansas Medical College reported in 1901 that this plant was anthelmintic, antipyretic, and a tonic (Smythe, 1901, p. 196).

The Rocky Mountain bee plant and another (possibly lead plant, *Amorpha canescens* L.) were reported by the French explorer Joseph Nicollet in 1838 to be mysterious and valuable to the Dakotas as "a medicine to find as many Buffaloe as they want." They used a mixture of the plants in the following manner:

The performer goes on horseback near the buffaloe, which attracted by the agreeable scent, follow him in the enclosure, (put up for the purpose) through a narrow entrance, wherein they meet their death. This medicine is not very public among the Indians only few know the ingredienies [sic] and performance so that it is said, an Indian will give for the first article 5 horses & for the Second his Lodge" (Bray and Bray, 1976, pp. 93, 117, 281).

Conyza canadensis (L.) Cronq.

HORSEWEED
Asteraceae
Sunflower Family

The horseweed is a tall, weedy, erect annual herb usually with unbranched stems. The leaves are abundant, alternate, narrowly lance-shaped to linear, and gradually reduced upward. The tiny cylindrical flower heads are in open, branched groups at the ends of stems. The inconspicuous ray flowers are white or pale pink; the disk flowers are yellow. The horseweed is found in cultivated and waste ground throughout temperate North America.

The Lakota name is "canhlo'gan was'te'mna iye'ceca" (similar to sweet-smelling weed). The Lakotas made a tea from the roots and lower stalks to treat pain in the bowels and diarrhea, particularly in children (Rogers, 1980, p. 37; Munson, 1981, p. 233). The Mes-

quakie name for the horseweed is "no'sowini" (sweat). They used it in their sweat bath (Smith, 1928, p. 213).

The Zuni name for the horseweed, "ha'mo u'teawe" (leaf ball flowers), refers to the rounded appearance of the flowers among the uppermost leaves after they have lost their ray flowers (Stevenson, 1915, p. 55). The horseweed was a common Zuni medicine. They crushed the ray flowers between their fingers and inserted them into the nostrils to cure rhinitis. This treatment caused sneezing, and relief soon followed.

The ethnobotanist Huron Smith reported the Anglo folk use of the horseweed in 1928: "The white man has used the dried leaves and flowering tops, because of their astringent and styptic action. It is somewhat aromatic and has been used as a diaphoretic and expectorant. In a decoction it has been used in the treatment of dropsy and chronic bronchitis. In the country districts, its common use is as an intestinal astringent in diarrhoea" (Smith, 1928, p. 213).

Under its previous scientific name, *Erigeron canadensis* L., the horseweed was officially listed in the *U.S. Pharmacopoeia* from 1820 to 1882. The leaves and flowering tops were recommended for their stimulant and diuretic properties. A volatile oil distilled from the plant was also officially listed from 1863 to 1916. It was used to accelerate uterine contractions immediately prior to childbirth.

Coreopsis tinctoria Nutt.

PLAINS COREOPSIS
Asteraceae
Sunflower Family

The Plains coreopsis is a smooth, erect annual with a single or much-branched stem. The leaves are opposite and pinnately divided into linear segments. The flower heads are at the ends of short stalks near the ends of branches. The ray flowers are yellow, often with a reddish spot at the bases, and up to 1.3 cm (½ in) long; the disk flowers are 4-lobed, tubular, and reddish. The Plains coreopsis is found in seasonally damp, disturbed sites, especially roadside ditches and low sandy ground.

One Lakota name for the Plains coreopsis is "canhlo'gan wakal'yapi" (boiled weed) (Rogers, 1980, p. 37). Another name I learned while on the Rosebud Reservation in South Dakota is "peji' zizi" (yellow herb), in reference to its yellow flowers. When

the flowers are boiled in water for a few minutes, the water turns red and is used as a beverage. The plant tops are also harvested and dried for later use in a tea to strengthen the blood.

The Plains coreopsis is called "tza-a-gudl" (no translation given) by the Kiowas, who also used it to make a beverage tea (Vestal and Shultes, 1939, p. 59). The Mesquakie name for the tall coreopsis, *C. tripteris* L., is "no'sowini" (no translation given). The Mesquakies boiled the plant to make a drink for the cure of internal pains and bleeding (Smith, 1928, p. 213).

The tall coreopsis was used by Anglos in folk medicine as an alterative and expectorant (Burlage, 1968, p. 41). Investigations of *Coreopsis* species have shown that flavonoids, chalcones, aurones, and special acetylenic compounds, as well as a large variety of unusual and rare phenylpropane derivatives are characteristic constituents (Bohlmann et al., 1983, p. 2858; Reichling and Thron, 1989, p. 83).

The Plains coreopsis can be easily grown as an ornamental from seed. Seedlings can be grown in a greenhouse or cold frame and transplanted, or sown directly in the garden when the soil is warm in the spring. Several perennial *Coreopsis* species are also used ornamentally. The cultivar "Grandiflora" of *C. lanceolata* L. Pers. is often grown.

Delphinium virescens Nutt.

PRAIRIE LARKSPUR
Ranunculaceae
Buttercup Family

Prairie larkspur is a perennial herb 50–120 cm (20–45 in) tall, with fibrous rootstocks; stems are erect, single or clustered, sometimes branched, hairy, and often glandular. Leaves are alternate, crowded and stalked below but gradually reduced up the stem, deeply lobed; the segments are linear. The flowers are on a spikelike stalk that extends above the leaves, from May to June. Sepals and petals are white to bluishwhite; the uppermost sepal has a long curved spur, and the lower 2 petals are hairy. Fruits are erect, podlike, about 2 cm (¾ in) long, opening to release many small, brown seeds. It is found on prairies and pastures.

Prairie larkspur was named by early botanists, who thought the flower resembled the spur on the

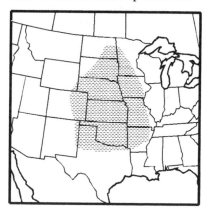

foot of a lark. The Kiowa called the prairie larkspur "toñ-a" (gourd seed) because the small seeds were used in peyote rattles (Vestal and Shultes, 1939, p. 28).

Several species of *Delphinium* have been used as a folk remedy to kill lice (Moore, 1979, p. 96). A tincture made from the seeds or flowers was mixed with soap and used as a shampoo; apparently the alkaloids in the plant kill the lice. Some people develop a skin irritation from the plant (ibid.).

Larkspurs are known to contain the glycoside delphinidin and the terpinoid alkaloids: aconitine, atisine, ajacine, and lyctonine (Trease and Evans, 1973, pp. 131, 145). All parts of the plant are considered poisonous, and cattle have been the species most commonly affected. Death from larkspur poisoning is caused by clogging or paralysis of the respiratory system (Stephens, 1980, p. 9). Larkspur can be easily propagated by seed or division of the rootstock in early spring or late fall.

Desmanthus illinoensis (Michx.) MacM.

ILLINOIS BUNDLEFLOWER
Fabaceae
Bean Family

Illinois bundleflower is a perennial herb with smooth, alternate, twice-pinnately compound leaves. The tiny, white, tubular flowers are in small, dense, spherical clus-

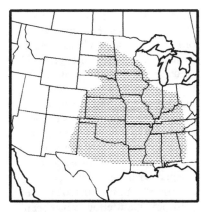

ters on short stalks that arise from the bases of the leaves. Stamens projecting from flowers give the clusters a fluffy appearance. The fruits are flat, crescent-shaped, and remain on the stems into the fall. It is found on prairies, roadsides, disturbed areas, and rocky, open, and wooded slopes.

Illinois bundleflower was a minor medicinal plant of the Indians. The Omahas and Poncas called it "pezhe gasatho" (rattle plant) because the seeds in the dried pods were "used by little boys as a rattle when in play they mimicked some of the dances of their people" (Gilmore, 1977, p. 37). The Pawnees had two names for the Illinois bundleflower: "atikatsatsiks" (spider-bean) and "kitsitsaris" (bad plant). They made a wash from the boiled leaves to apply as a remedy for the itch (ibid.).

The use of Illinois bundleflower by the Moapa Paiutes was described in "Medicinal Uses of Plants by Indian Tribes in Nevada."

239

This is surprising, because the range of this plant extends west only to Colorado and New Mexico. Either the Moapa Paiutes traveled some distance to obtain it, traded for it, or cultivated it, or the plant they used was misidentified. At any rate the plant was reportedly used to relieve trachoma by "placing five seeds of the plant in each eye at night. The eyes were washed with clear water each morning" (Train et al., 1941, p. 67).

Illinois bundleflower has been found to contain a diglucoside of kaempferol, rutin, quercitrin, myricitrin, and two gallic esters of myricitrin. One of these two esters had both antibacterial properties and restricted the larval growth of tobacco budworms (Nicollier and Thompson, 1983, pp. 112–15).

Illinois bundleflower is considered one of the most important native legumes for livestock and is being studied as a potential food crop by the Land Institute of Salina, Kansas (Jackson, 1985). It can be easily propagated by seed and is used in range revegetation programs.

Dyssodia papposa (Vent.) Hitchc.

FETID MARIGOLD
Asteraceae
Sunflower Family

This low annual herb has the pungent odor of marigolds and is covered with abundant, tiny orange oil glands. The stems typically are much-branched, and the leaves are deeply pinnately divided, with toothed margins. Small, cylindrical flower heads are near the ends of branches. The ray flowers are yellow to orange and inconspicuous; the disk flowers are brownish-yellow. The fetid marigold was originally found in prairie dog towns. Now it is also found in open fields, along roadsides, and in other disturbed habitats.

The Omaha and Ponca name for the fetid marigold, "pezhe piazhe" (bad-smelling weed), describes the unmistakable odor of the plant (Gilmore, 1977, p. 80). The Omahas pulverized the leaves and tops and used the powder as a snuff to make the nose bleed for the relief of headache. The Lakota name, "pispiza tawote," translates as "prairie dog food" (Buechel, 1983, p. 444). The Lakotas administered the powdered leaves to people with breathing difficulties. The fetid marigold plant was boiled with

the yellow blossoms of the curly-top gumweed, *Grindelia squarrosa* (Pursh) Dun., to make a tea to treat the spitting of blood (Rogers, 1980, p. 37). The Lakotas also inhaled a preparation of this plant for headache relief.

The fetid marigold also has had some Anglo folk use. A tea of the boiled fresh leaves was used to settle the stomach, stop vomiting, and treat diarrhea. The fresh leaves were chewed to relieve stomachache, and a liquid made by soaking seeds in warm water was given to babies for severe stomach pains (Krochmal and Krochmal, 1973, p. 91). This use of the plant is not entirely safe, since the "strong-smelling volatile oil and resin secretions are irritating to the mucous membranes and may cause dermatitis in susceptible persons" (Stevens, 1961, p. 393).

Equisetum hyemale L.

HORSETAIL
Equisetaceae
Horsetail Family

The horsetail is a perennial with rough, ridged, tubular, leafless stems. Green, sterile stems are slender and branched; fertile stems, distinguished by conelike structure at their tips, are stout and flesh-colored. The horsetail, a wetlands plant, grows on moist sites along rivers and streams, in meadows and wet prairies, and in disturbed sites. Also called

"scouring rush" because of its silica-laden stems, horsetail was used by both Indians and settlers for scouring and polishing. Some Indian tribes also wove the stems into mats.

The Blackfeet name for the horsetail is "sa-po-tun-a-kio-toi-yis" (jointed water grass) (McClintock, 1909, p. 226). The Mesquakies made a tea from the whole plant of the horsetail as a cure for gonorrhea (Smith, 1928, p. 220). The Crees made a medicine to correct menstrual irregularities by boiling the horsetail with two unknown roots, one of which may have been calamus, *Acorus calamus* L. (Johnston, 1970, p. 304). The Menominis also made a tea from the horsetail to cure kidney troubles. Women drank it after childbirth to "clear up the system" (Smith, 1923, p. 34).

The Blackfeet made a tea from the root of the horsetail, *E. arvense* L.,—from roots whose stems had terminal fertile cones—and drank it as a powerful diuretic to elimi-

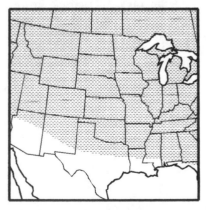

nate sickness. It was reported that "no one would disturb the place where the sickness was urinated for fear of becoming diseased." Pieces of the stem were also applied to rashes under the arm and in the groin (Hellson, 1974, pp. 69, 76). The Tewas brewed a tea from an unidentified horsetail species that was fed to babies as a cold and diarrhea remedy (Youngken, 1925, p. 172).

Although Charles F. Millspaugh discussed the horsetail, *E. hyemale*, and a tincture made from it in his 1892 *Medicinal Plants*, he suggested that the plant was never widely used (Millspaugh, 1974, pp. 724–27). However, the horsetail (*Equisetum* sp.) was used as a folk medicine in Quebec; a tea from the plant was drunk as a diuretic, hemostatic, and remineralizer. The horsetail (*E. arvense*) is particularly rich in silica and salts of potassium. It also "contains traces of a toxic alkaloid, palustrin (or equisetine), and a saponoside only slightly toxic, equisetonoside" (Mockle, 1955, in Erichsen-Brown, 1979, p. 237). Livestock are occasionally poisoned by eating horsetails; it appears that the alkaloid interferes with either the production or the use of vitamin B_1 (Frohne and Pfander, 1984, p. 104).

Eriogonum jamesii Benth.

WILD BUCKWHEAT
Polygonaceae
Buckwheat Family

Wild buckwheat is a mat-forming perennial herb with a tough, woody rootstock. The leaves are mostly basal, elliptic to spatula-shaped, and light green above but white-woolly beneath. Tiny white or greenish-white flowers are clustered at the tips of stalks, which extend above the leaves. Wild buckwheat is found on dry, sandy, and clay soils.

The name wild buckwheat describes the flowers of some species, which resemble those of buckwheat. There are many species of wild buckwheat, and they were used for a variety of ailments.

The Zunis used the root of the wild buckwheat, *E. jamesii*, to cure a sore tongue by placing a piece in the patient's mouth, where it was to remain for a day

and a night. The completed treatment was followed by a ritual disposal of the used root. The Zunis also ingested the fresh root of wild buckwheat for stomachache. They soaked a small amount of root in water and used the liquid for sore eyes (Stevenson, 1915, p. 50).

The Navahos used this wild buckwheat as a contraceptive. The root was "boiled for 30 minutes and one cupful was drunk by a woman during menstruation to prevent conception; used by both sexes [sic]" (DeLaszlo and Henshaw, 1954, p. 628). The Navahos used numerous other wild buckwheat species to treat a variety of ailments (Wyman and Harris, 1951, pp. 18–20; Elmore, 1944, p. 96).

The Comanches made a tea from the roots of the wild buckwheat, *Eriogonum longifolium* Nutt., for stomach trouble (Carlson and Jones, 1939, p. 533). The Lakotas called the annual wild buckwheat, *E. annuum* Torr., "i'hiyan peju'ta" (to make the mouth breathe better). They made a tea from this plant for children with sore mouths and "for those who cannot urinate well" (Rogers, 1980, p. 54).

George Bird Grinnell, in *The Cheyenne Indians, Their History and Ways of Life*, described their use of the wild buckwheat, *E. umbellatum* Torr. var. *subalpinum* (Green):

This is considered very scarce, and very desirable; but this ap- *plies only to the lower plains where the Cheyennes live at present. In the Big Horn Mountains it is extremely abundant, and grows everywhere in the open. When full blown, the flowers are yellow.*

If a woman's menses run too long, a strong tea made from the powdered stems and flowers will stop the trouble. A tablespoon or two of the tea drunk will act at once. The medicine is so desirable that a man of family would often give a horse for a small portion of the prepared medicine (Grinnell, 1962, 2: 172).

Eriogonum species contain saponins and cyanogenic glycosides (Camazine and Bye, 1980, p. 382). Several wild buckwheats, including *E. alatum* Torr. and *E. annuum*, are known to contain the alkaloid hordenine. These substances could have both positive and negative effects on human health.

Erysimum asperum (Nutt.) DC

WESTERN WALLFLOWER
Brassicaceae
Mustard Family

The western wallflower is a short, erect biennial or perennial with stiff, branched stems. The leaves are linear to lance-shaped, usually toothed, and numerous. The showy cluster of 4-parted, yellow or yellow-orange flowers is in terminal clusters. Western wallflower is found in prairies, on sandhills, and in open woods.

The Lakotas have two names for the western wallflower. They are "wahca'zi s'ica'man" (bad-smelling yellow flower), which refers to the disagreeable odor of the flowers as they wither, and "canhlo'gan pa" (bitter weed), which describes the bitter taste of the roots and leaves when chewed (Bray and Bray, 1976, pp. 93, 117, 281). The Lakotas made a remedy for cramps of the stomach and bowels from the western wallflower; either the entire plant was dried and then chewed, or it was prepared as a tea. Another tea for this purpose was made by mixing the crushed seeds with warm water (Rogers, 1980, p. 41; Munson, 1981, p. 234).

Dr. Edwin James, botanist for the Long expedition, reported that he collected the western wallflower on June 15 and 16, 1819, along the Platte River one hundred

miles west of the Pawnee villages in central Nebraska. He characterized it as "intensely bitter in every part, particularly the root, which is used as medicine by the Indians" (Thwaites, 1905, 15: 226, footnote).

The explorer John Bradbury, who traveled up the Missouri River only three years after Lewis and Clark, told of an Arikara medicine man who carried the western wallflower in his medicine bag. He reported from an Arikara village near present-day Campbell, South Dakota, on June 14, 1809:

I walked with Mr. Bracken-ridge to the upper village, which is separated from the lower one by a small stream. In our walk through town, I was accosted by the Medicine Man, or doctor, who was standing at the entrance of a lodge into which we went. It appeared that one of his patients, a boy, was within, for whom he was preparing some medicine. He made me understand that he had seen me collecting plants, and that he knew me to be a Medicine Man. He frequently shook hands with us, and took down his medicine bag, made of deer skin, to show me its contents. As I supposed this bag contained the whole materia medica of the nation, I examined it with some attention. There was a considerable quantity of the down of reed-mace, (typha palustris) [cattail] which I understood was used in cases of burns or scalds: there was also a quantity of a species

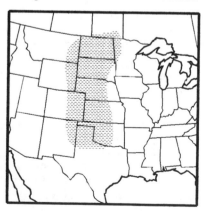

of artemisia, *common in the prairies, and known to the hunters by the name of hyssop; but the ingredient which was in the greatest abundance, was a species of wall-flower: in character it agrees with* cheiranthus erysimoides *[= western wallflower,* Erysimum asperum*]: besides these, I found two new species of* astragalus, *and some roots of* rudbeckia purpurea *[the purple coneflower,* Echinacea angustifolia*]. After examining the contents of the bag, I assured the doctor it was all very good, and we again shook hands with him, and went into several other lodges, where we were very hospitable received (Thwaites, 1905, 5: 132–33).*

In the Southwest, the Zunis used an unidentified *Erysimum* species to relieve headache caused by exposure to heat (Stevenson, 1915, p. 51). It was prepared by grinding the entire plant, mixing it with a small quantity of water, and applying the liquid to the forehead and temples. This medicine was also rubbed over the body to prevent sunburn.

Fragaria virginiana Duchesne

WILD STRAWBERRY
Rosaceae
Rose Family

The wild strawberry is a low perennial that forms colonies by spreading horizontal stems, which root and produce plantlets. The leaves are divided into 3 broadly elliptic or four-angled, toothed leaflets. The flowers are white, 5-petaled, and in clusters on short stalks. The fruits are small, dry achenes on the surface of a fleshy, red, top-shaped structure. Wild strawberries are found in prairies, old fields, and openings in woodlands, and on stream banks and roadsides.

The wild strawberry is well known for its small, tasty fruits. Various parts of the plant have been used in medicinal treatments. The Blackfeet made a tea from the wild strawberry to treat diarrhea (Hellson, 1974, p. 66). In the Great Lakes Bioregion, the Ojibwas, Chippewas, and Potawatomis all made use of wild strawberries as medicine (Smith, 1928, p. 384; Densmore, 1974, p. 347; Smith, 1933, p. 77). The Ojibwas made a tea from the root of the wild strawberry, which was primarily used to treat stomachache in babies. To treat a summer

cholera that affected young children, the Chippewas steeped two or three wild strawberry roots in a quart of boiling water. The sick child was encouraged to drink freely of this tea. The Potawatomis used the root of the woodland strawberry, *Fragaria vesca* L., to treat stomach complaints.

Constantine Rafinesque, in his 1828 *Medical Flora of the United States*, reported that the edible fruits of the wild strawberry were an effective medicine:

They are useful in fevers, Gravel, Gout, Scurvey, and Phthisis. They are cooling, promote perspiration, give relief in diseases of the bladder and kidneys, upon which they act powerfully, since they impart a violet smell and high color to urine. Hoffman and Linnaeus have long ago extolled them in gout and phthisis; persons labouring under these chronic complaints ought to eat them frequently when in season, and use at other times their Syrup. An excessive dose of either is however liable to produce emesis or a painful stricture in the bladder, with red urine, as I have experienced myself. . . . They possess also the property of curing chillblains, their water is used in France for that purpose as a wash. . . . The plant and leaves have nearly the same properties, although they are less cooling and more astringent. Both have been employed, like Cinquefoil and Agrimony for sore throat, swelled gums, bowel complaints, jaundice and fevers in infusion

and decoction (Rafinesque, 1828, p. 193).

The leaves were reportedly used in folk medicine as "an astringent and tonic for convalescents and especially for children having bowel and bladder weakness" (Smith, 1928, p. 384).

Gaillardia aristata Pursh

BLANKET FLOWER
Asteraceae
Sunflower Family

The blanket flower is known for its attractive red and yellow flowers, which sometimes cover the ground so thickly they seem to form a blanket of flowers. The blanket flower is a perennial herb 3–6 dm (1–2 ft) tall, with single or clustered stems and a stout taproot. The leaves are alternate, lance-shaped to egg-shaped, entire to toothed or lobed, and mostly basal. Flower heads are 1.5–3 cm (⁹⁄₁₆– 1³⁄₁₆ in) wide, solitary or few on long stalks. The ray flowers are yellow and somewhat purplish toward the base; the disk flowers are purplish to brownish-purple. It can be found in open plains and prairies.

The Blackfeet drank a tea of the root for gastroenteritis. The chewed, powdered root was also applied to skin disorders (Hellson, 1974, pp. 66, 71, 76, 81). They bathed the sore nipples of nursing mothers in a tea made from the plant, which they also used as

either by seed or by division of the rootstock. Most ornamental varieties available at nurseries are *G. grandiflora*, a tetraploid developed for garden use.

Gaura coccinea Pursh

SCARLET GAURA
Onagraceae
Evening Primrose Family

an eyewash or for nose drops. The Cheyennes used the flowers for a sunstroke medicine (Shemluck, 1982, p. 332).

The Kiowas picked the flowers of the blanket flower, *G. pulchella* Foug., and brought them into their houses as a "good-luck-plant" (Vestal and Shultes, 1939, p. 79). In the Southwest, the Navahos used the blanket flower, *G. pinnatifida* Torr., as an internal remedy for gout (Elmore, 1944, p. 96).

The blanket flower, *G. aristata*, contains the lactones spatulin, pulchelin C, pseudoguanolid, and three sesquiterpene ketones (Gill, Dembinska, and Zielinska, 1981, pp. 213–19). The blanket flower, *G. megapotamica*, contains helenalin, a sesquiterpene lactone (Giordano et al., 1990, p. 803–9), and *G. pulchella* contains gaillardin (Lewis and Elvin-Lewis, 1977, p. 135).

The annual blanket flower is a popular ornamental and can be propagated by seed. The perennial species can be propagated

The scarlet gaura is a low, hairy perennial herb with a spreading, woody rootstock. The leaves are alternate, linear to narrowly elliptic, and less than 5 cm (2 in) long. The flowers are in loose groups at the ends of stems, each one with 4 white to pink petals and 8 projecting stamens. The fruits are short and spindle-shaped, and they contain 1–4 brownish seeds. The scarlet gaura is found on plains and prairies and in dry, open woods of the West.

The Lakotas named the scarlet gaura "on s'unk oyu'spapi"

(they use it to catch horse with) because the plant was chewed and rubbed on the hands before horses were caught (Rogers, 1980, p. 52). The Navahos used the velvety gaura, *Gaura parviflora* Dougl., as a poultice for sore breasts after childbirth and also as a fumigant and infusion in the Nightway ceremony (Wyman and Harris, 1951, p. 33).

As a Chicano folk remedy for muscular rheumatism, scarlet gaura plants (green or dry) were ground or mashed and rubbed on the afflicted limbs (Curtin, 1976, p. 202). Scarlet gaura has also been used to treat burns, inflammations, and general body pains (Burlage, 1968, p. 128).

Gentiana puberulenta Pringle

DOWNY GENTIAN
Gentianaceae
Gentian Family

Downy gentian is an erect, slightly hairy perennial herb with stout, mostly unbranched stems. The leaves are opposite, lance-shaped, and lustrous green above. The large, azure-blue to bluish-purple flowers are bell-shaped, 5-parted, and in clusters of 3–10 at the ends of stems. Downy gentian is found in prairies and upland woods.

The Winnebago name is "makan chahiwi-cho" (blue-blossom medicine). The Dakota name, "pezhuta

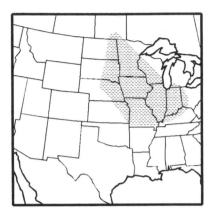

zi" (yellow medicine), refers to the color of the roots (Gilmore, 1977, p. 57). These two tribes made a root tea from downy gentian that was taken as a tonic. The Mesquakies used the root of the closed gentian, *Gentiana andrewsii* Griseb., to treat snakebite and to cure a condition called "caked breast" (Smith, 1928, p. 222).

John Woods, an Englishman who founded a colony of English expatriates at Albion, Illinois, reported in 1821 that "the following trees and herbs are used in medicine—snake-root, gentian, genseng, Columbia-root, and sumach, and sassafras tree" (Thwaites, 1905, 10: 303). After settlement, Indians probably were no longer in that part of the state, but this report indicates that Indian remedies had become a part of the frontier medical system.

The root of several species of gentian was used "as a simple bitter, exciting the flow of gastric juice, promoting the appetite, and aiding digestion. It was also used in many forms of dyspepsia, and loss of appetite following mild malaria and acute infectious diseases" (Smith, 1928, p. 222). The root of the European gentian, *G. lutea* L., was officially listed in the *U.S. Pharmacopoeia* from 1820 to 1882.

The active chemical constituents of gentians (*Gentiana* species) were enumerated by Michael Moore in his 1979 *Medicinal Plants of the Mountain West*:

> The constituents of the Gentians always vary somewhat, but nearly all contain the bitter glycoside gentiopicrin, several bitter amorphic substances, gentisic acid, several sugars peculiar to the genera, and, in perennial roots, several water insoluble sterols. Gentiopicrin [for malaria] and gentisic acid [for rheumatic inflammations] are still used in pharmacy. The Gentians are, above all, perhaps the best stomach tonics in the plant kingdom, and certainly the most specific in the West (Moore, 1979, p. 79).

Geum triflorum Pursh

TORCH FLOWER
Rosaceae
Rose Family

The torch flower is a low, colony-forming perennial with soft-hairy stems. The leaves on the lower stem are pinnately compound, with 7–19 leaflets; upper stem

leaves are much reduced. The torchlike flowers have 5 lobes, are pink to purple, and are in groups at the ends of stems. The fruits are abundant achenes, each tipped with a prominent, plumelike hair. The torch flower, or prairie smoke, is a perennial herb of northern prairies and open woodlands.

The Blackfeet, who called the torch flower "so-ya-its" (lies on his belly), had many uses for it (McClintock, 1923, p. 321; Hellson, 1974, pp. 66, 72, 76, 79, 84). They boiled the plant in water to treat sore or inflamed eyes. A root tea was used as a mouthwash for canker sores and sore throat and applied to wounds. Mixed with grease, the root was applied as a salve to sores, rashes, blisters, and flesh wounds. It was also scraped, mixed with tobacco, and smoked to "clear the head." The Blackfeet drank a tea from the entire plant as a general tonic and for a severe cough. In the Great Lakes Bioregion, the Flambeau Ojibwas used the large-leaved avens, *Geum*

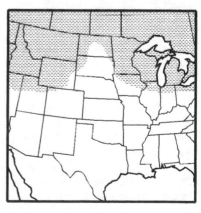

macrophyllum Willd., as "a female remedy" (Smith, 1928, p. 384).

The dried root of the water or purple avens, *G. rivale* L., was officially listed in the *U.S. Pharmacopoeia* from 1820 to 1882 as an astringent. *Geum* species contain gein, a phenolic glycoside (Trease and Evans, 1973, p. 123).

Gnaphalium obtusifolium L.

FRAGRANT EVERLASTING
Asteraceae
Sunflower Family

Fragrant everlasting is an aromatic annual 3–8 dm (1–2 ½ ft) tall. Crushed leaves and flower heads have a pleasant balsamic odor. The leaves are alternate, lance-shaped to spatula-shaped, and green above but white-woolly beneath. Abundant, short flower heads, with tubular white flowers, are arranged in a rounded cluster at the ends of stems. Fragrant everlasting, or sweet everlasting, is found in prairies, open woodlands, and along roadsides.

The Mesquakies believed that fragrant everlasting was "one of the best types of medicine [for a smoke treatment] and is sure to heal." It was burned as a smudge to restore consciousness or to treat insanity (Smith, 1928, pp. 214–15). Its characteristic smell may have been important in this remedy. This plant was used similarly by the Menominis (Smith, 1923,

p. 30). It was also used for colds, fever, and other infirmities by the Creeks, Choctaws, and Cherokees (Shemluck, 1982, p. 332).

Charles Millspaugh, in his 1892 *Medicinal Plants*, stated that the fragrant everlasting and other *Gnapthalium* species:

formed a part of aboriginal medication, and from there they descended to the white settlers, who, in conjunction with the more or less botanic physicians, used them about as follows: The herb, as a masticatory, has always been a popular remedy, on account of its astringent properties, in ulceration of the mouth and fauces, and for quinsy. A hot decoction proves pectoral and somewhat anodyne, as well as sudorific in early stages of fevers. A cold infusion has been much used in diarrhoea, dysentery, and hemorrhage of the bowels, and is somewhat vermifugal; it is also recommended in leucorrhoea. The fresh juice is considered anti-

venereal. Hot fomentations of the herb have been used like Arnica, for sprains and bruises, and form a good vulnerary for painful tumors and unhealthy ulcers. The dried flowers are recommended as a quieting filling for the pillows of consumptives (Millspaugh, 1974, pp. 89–90).

The fragrant everlasting was also used by physicians as a soothing expectorant and, because of its bitter qualities, to relieve stomachache (Smith, 1928, p. 215).

Gutierrezia sarothrae (Pursh) Britt. & Rusby

SNAKEWEED
Asteraceae
Sunflower Family

Snakeweed is a spreading or erect perennial herb or subshrub 2–10 dm (½–3 ¼ ft) tall, with a woody base. The stems usually are much-

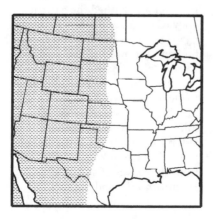

branched and resinous. The leaves are alternate, threadlike to linear, and up to 6.4 cm (2 ½ in) long. Abundant, tiny cylindrical or topshaped flower heads, with yellow ray and disk flowers, are in clusters at the ends of branches. This perennial is found in open plains and upland sites, especially in overgrazed pastures.

The Lakota name is "peji' zizi" (yellow herb) (Rogers, 1980, p. 37). The Lakotas boiled the plant to make a tea for coughs, colds, and dizziness. The Kiowa-Apaches boiled the tops of the fresh, mature snakeweed until it was strong and dark. This tea was drunk for lung trouble and colds, or applied externally for skin ailments, including heat rash, poison ivy, and athlete's foot (Jordan, 1965, p. 111).

For respiratory ailments the Blackfeet placed the root of snakeweed in boiling water and had the patient inhale the steam (McClintock, 1909, p. 276). The Comanches mixed the leaves of snakeweed with an unknown substance to make a medicine for whooping cough. They also used the stiff stems as brooms (Carlson and Jones, 1939, pp. 522, 534). The Crows made a tea of snakeweed flowers for kidney disease and sniffed the steam from the tea for sinus infections (Shemluck, 1982, p. 334). They also bathed swellings in a tea made from the leaves and flowers of snakeweed.

In the Southwest, the Navahos used the snakeweed to treat headaches and applied it to insect bites, wounds, and snakebite (Elmore, 1944, p. 97). This last use is the source of the plant's common name. The Zunis made a tea of the plant which they applied topically to aching muscles (Camazine and Bye, 1980, p. 375). Snakeweed has also been used in Mexico as a folk remedy for snakebite and by Chicanos in New Mexico to treat rheumatism, hemorrhoids, stomachache, "womb problems," and to regulate menstruation (Curtin, 1976, pp. 81–82).

Helenium autumnale L.

SNEEZEWEED
Asteraceae
Sunflower Family

Sneezeweed is a smooth or hairy perennial herb to 12 dm (4 ft) tall, with alternate, simple, lance-shaped to elliptic leaves. The flower heads are in open, leafy

clusters at the ends of branches. The ray flowers are yellow, wedge-shaped, 3-toothed at the tip, and up to 2.5 cm (1 in) long; disk flowers are yellow and in dense spherical clusters. Sneezeweed grows on low-lying, moist prairies and other open sites.

The Mesquakie name for the sneezeweed is "tcatcamo'sikani" (inhalant). The Mesquakies dried the disk flowers (probably the entire flower head) and used them as an inhalant to cure a head cold or catarrh (Smith, 1928, p. 215). The Menominis used it the same way (Smith, 1923, p. 31). The Mesquakies sometimes made the snuff from a mixture of plants, including leaves of threadleaf buttercup, *Ranunculus flabellaris* Raf., and the flowering bracts of beebalm, *Monarda punctata* L. They also drank a tea of sneezeweed flowers for "catarrh of the stomach" and used the roots for an unspecified medicine (Smith, 1928, p. 215).

To reduce a fever, the Comanches soaked sneezeweed stems in water and bathed the patient's body (Carlson and Jones, 1939, pp. 532–34). They also inhaled the broken-up flowers of the sneezeweed, *Helenium microcephalum* DC., to induce sneezing in order to clear the nasal passages. During childbirth sneezeweed was inhaled in a similar manner to aid in the expulsion of the afterbirth. The Cherokees made a tea from the leaves of sneezeweed, *H. autumnale*, and the root of the ironweed, *Vernonia noveboracensis* (L.) Michx., to prevent menstruation for two years after childbirth (Shemluck, 1982, pp. 335, 351).

Constantine Rafinesque, in his 1828 *Medical Flora of the United States*, stated that the sneezeweed "may be used in diseases of the head, deafness, . . . headache, hemicrania, rheumatism, or congestion in the head and jaws, & c. The shocks of sneezing are often useful in other cases, when other remedies can hardly avail. This plant has probably many other properties, little known as yet and deserving investigation" (Rafinesque, 1828, p. 237).

Sneezeweed is known to cause dermatitis in some individuals (Mitchell and Rook, 1979, p. 206). Many sesquiterpene lactones have been isolated from sneezeweed (Itoigawa et al., 1981, pp. 605–13). The sesquiterpene lactone helenalin has been found in sneezeweed and is an allergin (Westbrooks and Preacher, 1986, p. 169). In the cancer screening program of the National Cancer Institute this substance has also been shown to possess significant antitumor activity (Foster and Duke, 1990, p. 126). The glycoside dugaldin is found in *H. amarum* (Raf.) Rock and may be found in *H. autumnale*. This glycoside is generally considered to be the cause of sneezeweed poisoning in livestock, although other toxins may also be involved.

Helianthus annuus L.

SUNFLOWER
Asteraceae
Sunflower Family

This widespread sunflower is an erect annual with rough-hairy stems 6–30 dm (2–10 ft) tall. The leaves are mostly alternate, egg-shaped to triangular, and entire or toothed. The flower heads are 7.5–15 cm (3–6 in) wide and at the ends of branches. Ray flowers are yellow and disk flowers are reddish-brown.

The sunflower is a common roadside weed. Originally cultivated by North American Indians, it has a long and interesting history as a food plant (Kindscher, 1987, pp. 123–28). Cultivated varieties with larger seed heads and seeds are used for the production of oil, food, and birdseed.

The Teton Dakotas boiled flower heads from which the involucral bracts had been removed as

a remedy for pulmonary troubles (Gilmore, 1977, p. 78). Pawnee women who became pregnant while still nursing a child took a sunflower seed medicine to prevent sickness in the child. It was made by mixing pounded sunflower seeds with certain unidentified roots (ibid.).

The Mesquakies made a poultice from the flowers of the sawtooth sunflower, *Helianthus grosseserratus* Martens, to heal burns (Smith, 1928, p. 215). In the Southwest, Zuni medicine men cured rattlesnake bites by chewing the fresh or dried root, then sucking the snakebite wound (Camazine and Bye, 1980, p. 375).

A variety of terpenoid compounds have been found in *Helianthus* species, primarily sesquiterpene lactones and diterpenes (Gershenzon and Mabry, 1984, p. 1959). These substances probably offer sunflowers protection against some insects.

The annual sunflower and the perennial sunflowers are attractive as specimen plants or in a wild garden where they have plenty of room. They can be propagated by seed, although most of the perennials are easier to propagate by dividing the root stock when the plants are dormant.

Heracleum sphondylium L.

COW PARSNIP
Apiaceae
Parsley Family

The cow parsnip is a robust, erect perennial herb to 3 m (10 ft) tall, with a hairy, grooved stem. The leaves are hairy, up to 9 dm (3 ft) long, and lobed and coarsely toothed. Small white or light purple flowers are in broad, flat-topped groups at the ends of stems. It is found in moist, rich woods, along streams, and in thickets.

The Omaha and Ponca name for the cow parsnip is "zhaba-makan" (beaver medicine) (Gilmore, 1977, p. 55). The Omahas boiled the root to make a tea for intestinal pains. They mixed the dried, pounded roots with beaver dung and placed them in the hole in which the ceremonial sacred pole was planted. The Pawnees scraped or pounded the root, boiled it, then applied it as a poultice for boils.

The Blackfeet brewed a tea from the fresh, young stems to treat diarrhea (Hellson, 1974, pp. 67, 76; McClintock, 1923, p. 324). They removed warts with a tea made from the stems. The young, peeled stalks were roasted and eaten for food in the spring. The stalks were also used in the Sun Dance ceremony.

The Mesquakies used most parts of the cow parsnip. They used the root for treating stomach cramps and, apparently, for erysipelas (Smith, 1928, pp. 249, 365). They also ate the roots (probably cooked) for food. The seeds were used to relieve severe headache, and the stem was used as a poultice for wounds.

In the Great Lakes Bioregion, the Pillager Ojibwas macerated the fresh root of the cow parsnip and used it as a poultice to cure sores (Smith, 1928, p. 390). To the Menominis, the cow parsnip was an evil medicine used by sorcerers. Both the Pillager Ojibwas and the Menominis used a smudge from the cow parsnip to drive away evil spirits (Smith, 1923, pp. 55, 82; Smith, 1928, p. 432). The Crees living in the Northwest Territories used a small piece (about one inch square) of the root to relieve toothache by placing it on the sore tooth (Beardsley, 1941, p. 491). They spit out the saliva as it collected in the mouth, since the plant was known to be poisonous.

The fresh leaves and roots were used in early American medicine to produce a blister to counter other pain (Millspaugh, 1974, p. 242). The root was used by Eclectic practitioners to cure epilepsy and in a tea to cure dyspeptic disorders (Smith, 1928, p. 390). Only the root was officially listed in the *U.S. Pharmacopoeia* from 1820 to 1863, although the leaves and fruit were also used medicinally.

The cow parsnip contains furanocoumarin, and the fruits contain 5-methoxypsoralen (Mitchell and Rook, 1979, p. 692). The leaves, roots, and stems of the American subspecies, *H. sphondylium* L. subsp. *montanum* (Schleich.) Briq., are phototoxic and have been found to cause skin reactions, including reddening of the skin, swelling, formation of vesicles, lesions, and increased pigmentation (Frohne and Pfander, 1984, pp. 45–46). Strong light and high humidity intensify the reaction of the skin.

Hierochloë odorata (L.) Beauv.

SWEETGRASS
Poaceae
Grass Family

Sweetgrass is a fragrant rhizomatous perennial grass that grows in wet meadows, marshes, and wet prairies. It has flat leaves and smooth stems and reaches a height of 7 dm (30 in).

Sweetgrass was widely used

as incense, perfume, and medicine and for purification. It was used ceremonially by many tribes, including the Omahas, Poncas, Kiowas, Dakotas, and Lakotas (Jordan, 1965, p. 98). These tribes burned it "as an incense in any ceremony or ritual to induce the presence of good influences or benevolent powers" (Gilmore, 1977, p. 14).

The Cheyennes also used sweetgrass in many of their ceremonies, including the Sun Dance. In the Sacred Arrow ceremony, the life of the Cheyenne people is renewed through the burning of sweetgrass, which symbolizes life's growth. During healing ceremonies, the rattle was frequently passed through the smoke of burning sweetgrass to purify it. The Cheyennes have observed that sweetgrass is not as abundant as it was previously. The reason, a Cheyenne informant stated, is that the Cheyennes are losing their old ways (Hart, 1981, pp. 9–10).

Sweetgrass was the most popular perfumery of the Blackfeet, who braided it and kept it with their clothes like a sachet or carried it in small bags (McClintock, 1923, p. 325). The Blackfeet also used the sweetgrass for ceremonial smoking and in the Sun Dance (Johnston, 1970, p. 307). Blackfeet women made a tea from sweetgrass that was drunk to stop vaginal bleeding after birth and to help expel the afterbirth (Hellson, 1974, pp. 69, 76, 77, 81). Blackfeet men drank sweetgrass tea to treat venereal infections. Both sexes drank a tea from this plant to treat coughs and sore throats. Sweetgrass stems were soaked in water which was then used as an eyewash. Windburn and chapping were also treated with the same liquid or with a salve made by mixing this sweetgrass water with grease. Blackfeet and Flathead women also decorated their hair with braids of sweetgrass (Hart, 1976, pp. 28–29). The Flatheads made a sweetgrass tea that was used to cure colds and fevers and to alleviate "sharp pains inside." They also mixed it with seeds of meadow rue, *Thalictrum occidentale* Gray, to make another tea that they used to clear congested nasal passages (ibid.).

Prince Maximilian of Wied reported in 1833, while on the upper Missouri River, that the Hidatsas used the sweetgrass as a remedy for wounds. First they held their hands over the smoke of the burning plant, then placed them over the wound without touching it.

Then they laid tallow upon the wound (Thwaites, 1905, 23: 384).

Coumarin is the substance which gives sweetgrass its characteristic sweet smell. It has potentially toxic properties and can cause liver injury and hemorrhages. Research has shown coumarin and related compounds to be effective in reducing high-protein edemas, especially lymphodema (Leung, 1980, p. 155).

Lespedeza capitata Michx.

ROUND-HEAD LESPEDEZA
Fabaceae
Bean Family

This common prairie plant is a perennial herb with alternate, compound leaves, each with 3 elliptic leaflets. The flowers are small, white to reddish-purple, and arranged in round clusters among the upper leaves. The clusters of dry brown fruits that develop in the fall resemble rabbit feet. It also grows in old fields and along roadsides.

The Pawnee name for this plant is "parus-as" (rabbit foot) (Gilmore, 1977, p. 45). The Omaha and Ponca name is "te-hunton-hi nuga" (male buffalo bellow plant). The Omahas and Poncas usually gathered this plant on the hills of the loess plain, whereas the "female buffalo bellow plant," the leadplant (*Amorpha canescens* Pursh), was gathered from the sandy loam soils of valleys. Both of these plants bloomed in the buffalo rutting season—when the bulls bellow. The Mesquakie medicine man John McIntosh noted the strong odor of the round-head lespedeza and its use as an antidote for poison (Smith, 1928, p. 229). The Kiowa-Apaches made a beverage tea from the leaves that was thought to be beneficial to sick people (Jordan, 1965, p. 118).

The Omahas and Poncas used the round-head lespedeza as a moxa for neuralgia or for rheumatism. For this treatment, they moistened one end of a short piece of stem so it would stick to the skin, then lit the other end and allowed it to burn down to the skin (Gilmore, 1977, p. 45). Similar treatments are often used in traditional Chinese medicine with other plants.

Although the round-head lespedeza was not generally used in Anglo medicine, it was listed as a diuretic and emetic by B. B. Smythe in his 1901 "Preliminary List of Medicinal and Economic

Kansas Plants" (Smythe, 1901, p. 201).

Round-head lespedeza appears to lower blood cholesterol levels and remove nitrogenous compounds from the blood of people with hyperazotemia (Tin-Wa, Farnsworth, and Fong, 1969, p. 509). The round-head lespedeza contains the flavinoids lespecapitoside, kampferitrin, and derivatives of the flavinoids apigenin and luteolin (ibid.; Linard, Delaveau, and Paris, 1978, p. 144). Because of its tannins, it acts as an antitumor agent against the Walker 256 carcinosarcoma (Fong, Bhatti, and Farnsworth, et al., 1972, p. 1818).

The round-head lespedeza can be easily grown from seed. Its seed provides food for game birds and other wildlife, so it should be considered for use in prairie restorations. It is also a valuable forage plant in pastures. Its seedheads, attractive in the wildflower garden, can also be picked for bouquets and dried wreaths.

Lilium philadelphicum L.

WILD LILY
Liliaceae
Lily Family

The wild lily is a smooth perennial herb 3–9 dm (1–3 ft) tall. The leaves are whorled, 3–6 per node, linear to lance-shaped, and up to 7.5 cm (3 in) long and 1 cm (3/8 in) wide. The flowers are terminal, erect, and open bell-shaped,

with 6 deep red to reddish-orange segments. The wild lily is striking when in bloom, similar to a domesticated tiger lily. It is found in moist prairies and moist-to-dry open woods.

The Lakota name for the wild lily is "mnahca' hca" (very smelly flower) (Rogers, 1980, p. 27). The Dakota pulverized or chewed the flowers and applied them as an antidote for the poisonous bites of the brown spider. They were said to relieve the inflammation and swelling immediately (Gilmore, 1977, p. 19). Charles Millspaugh, in his 1892 *Medicinal Plants*, reported that a tincture made from the fresh bulb and flowers of the Turk's cap lily, *Lilium canadense* L., had therapeutic usefulness (Millspaugh, 1974, p. 721–22).

Both of these wild lilies are best propagated by planting scales separated from the central core of the bulb as soon as the tops die back in the fall. However, it may take several years before these scales will produce flowers. They should

be planted 2.5 cm (1 in) deep and transplanted deeper when larger. Much of the early growth occurs underground, and very little stalk development will occur while the plants are young. Mature bulbs can then be transplanted 5–12 cm (2–5 in) deep. Wild lilies grown from seed will only produce one leaf their first year and will take an additional year to bloom.

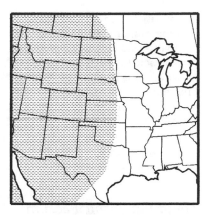

Linum perenne L.

BLUE FLAX
Linaceae
Flax Family

Blue flax is a perennial herb with narrow, alternate leaves. The flowers have 5 separate blue petals. The fruits are dry and egg-shaped; they separate into 10 segments to release flattened and slimy seeds. Blue flax is found in prairies and rocky, open woods.

In the Great Basin, the Paiutes and the Shoshones used blue flax as an eyewash. They used the whole plants, the tops, or in some cases even the roots soaked in cold water or boiled, in numerous preparations (Train et al., 1941, p. 101).

The blue flax was also used as a Chicano folk medicine in New Mexico. A poultice made from the seeds was considered good for most types of inflammation (Curtin, 1976, pp. 114–15). Chicanos also made a paste from the dry seeds by mixing one teaspoon of ground seeds with two teaspoons of cornmeal and enough boiling water to bring it to the right consistency. This paste was bandaged on infected wounds or applied to swellings or lumps two or three times a day. A similar treatment was used for boils or sore throat.

B. B. Smythe, in his 1901 list of Kansas medicinal plants, reported that all flax (*Linum*) species found in Kansas could be used as a demulcent, an emollient, and a tonic (Smythe, 1901, p. 201). The seed of the blue flax was also used as food by some Indian tribes of the Missouri River region (Kindscher, 1987, p. 244).

The seeds of the cultivated common flax, *L. usitatissimum* L., are commonly used as a folk remedy for coughs and gallstones, for treatment of digestive, urinary, and lung disorders, and as a laxative (Westbrooks and Preacher, 1986, p. 91). The common flax (and possibly its wild relatives) contains the cyanogenetic glycoside

259

linamarin, which is composed of acetone-cyanohydrin-glucoside. On hydrolysis, linamarin produces prussic acid (hydrogen cyanide). However, this is not considered a problem for humans since the concentration of linamarin is low, and the prussic acid is detoxified in the body (Frohne and Pfander, 1984, p. 187). In cattle, however, this prussic acid can cause poisoning.

Lomatium foeniculaceum (Nutt.) Coult. & Rose

PRAIRIE PARSLEY
Apiaceae
Parsley Family

The prairie parsley is a short perennial herb without a stem. The leaves are clustered at the base and divided into 2 or 3 segments, each of them dissected into many linear segments. Small yellow flowers are in flat-topped clusters on short stalks rising above the leaves. The prairie parsley is found

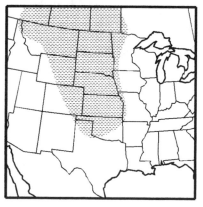

on prairie hillsides and in rocky limestone soils.

The Pawnee name for the prairie parsley is "pezhe bthaska" (flat herb) (Gilmore, 1977, p. 55). Pawnee men and those of other Plains Indian tribes used the seeds and other parts as love charms. The Pawnees believed that the seeds of the prairie parsley "rendered the possessor attractive to all persons, so he would have many friends, all people would serve him well, and if used in connection with certain other plants would make him winning to women, so he might win any woman he might desire" (ibid.). For its use as a love charm when mixed with other plants, see lobelia, *Lobelia cardinalis*.

On the Wind River Reservation in Wyoming, the wild parsley, *Lomatium dissectum* (Nutt.) Mathias & Constance, was an important medicinal plant used for several types of ailments (Nickerson, 1966, p. 49). Colds and flu were treated by drinking a tea made by boiling the root, by sponging the tea on the body, or by inhaling the steam from this tea. In addition, the pounded dry root was mixed with grease and massaged on affected parts. In the Great Basin and Pacific Northwest, wild parsley was used similarly and considered to be "the Big Medicine" (Murphey, 1959, p. 37).

The Blackfeet gathered the root of wild parsley in the fall to make a tea which was drunk as a hot tonic by people who were weak to help them gain weight (McClintock, 1923, p. 320). They also pounded the root and burned it as incense.

The Blackfeet made a tea from the roots of the wild parsley, *L. triternatum* (Pursh) Coult. and Rose, to relieve sore throats and coughs (Hellson, 1974, pp. 67, 72, 83). Long-distance runners from the Blackfeet tribe would chew the fruit to avoid sideaches. Blackfeet diviners chewed the root of this wild parsley and blew it through an eagle bone tube onto the injured or diseased part of a patient's body. The healing properties of the spray were believed to penetrate the body at that place. The roots of several species of wild parsley, often called biscuit root, were also used as food by some Indian tribes (Kindscher, 1987, pp. 147–48).

Lygodesmia juncea (Pursh) Hook.

SKELETON WEED
Asteraceae
Sunflower Family

The skeleton weed is a smooth, wiry-stemmed perennial herb with yellow milky sap. The leaves are few and greatly reduced. Solitary flower heads are at the ends of branches, each one with 5 lavender to pink, 1.3 cm (½ in) long ray flowers. The plant is found on open high plains and prairies, often in barren alkaline sites.

The Lakota name for the skele-

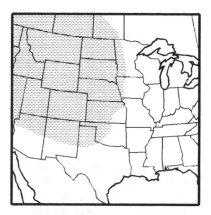

ton weed is "maka' cans'inhu" (earth sappy-wood stem or skunk resin plant) (Rogers, 1980, p. 38; Munson, 1981, p. 236). It was chewed like gum, and a tea made from the whole plant was used to cure diarrhea in children.

The Cheyenne names for this plant are "tatawisse'heyo" (blue medicine) and "matana'his-se'heyo" (milk medicine). A bluish tea made from the stems was drunk every morning and evening by nursing mothers with an insufficient supply of milk to increase the flow (Grinnell, 1905, p. 41; Hart, 1981, p. 22; Grinnell, 1962, 2: 184–85). It reportedly had an "inner power" and imparted a feeling of contentment to the mother. The child whose mother drank skeleton weed tea became healthy (ibid.).

The Blackfeet name for skeleton weed is "oot-squeeks-see" (blue sticks) (Hellson, 1974, pp. 61, 67, 70, 72), and they had many medicinal uses for the plant. Pregnant Blackfeet women drank a tea made from the entire plant for symptoms resembling heartburn. It was also used for kidney trouble and as a general tonic for children. The galls on the stems were pulverized in a soft hide bag, and the powder was used to make a diuretic tea. A stem tea was drunk for a burning cough.

The Omahas, Poncas, and Kiowa-Apaches made a tea from the plant that was used for sore eyes (Gilmore, 1977, p. 84; Jordan, 1965, p. 124). The Omahas and Poncas also used the plant to increase a mother's milk flow. This use is an example of the Doctrine of Signatures—the milky sap was probably interpreted as a signature or sign that the plant would help with a "milk problem."

Chicano children in New Mexico picked the small, round, yellow galls in May to chew as gum. When chewed, these galls turn a surprisingly bright blue, and small boys were reported to "spit a nice long blue streamer at the family cat, or sister's clean dress, or perhaps . . . scare mother a little into thinking they have been eating something perfectly horrible" (Curtin, 1976, p. 61). The tops of the skeleton weed may be poisonous to livestock and humans, as they can accumulate toxic quantities of nitrates (Stephens, 1980, p. 152).

Madia glomerata Hook.

TARWEED
Asteraceae
Sunflower Family

Tarweed is a strong-scented, weedy annual, usually less than 5 dm (1½ ft) tall. The leaves are opposite below but alternate above, linear to narrowly lance-shaped, up to 7 cm (2¾ in) long, and entire. The flower heads are in small clusters at the ends of branches. The inconspicuous ray flowers are yellow, but sometimes absent. It is usually found growing in disturbed areas.

Tarweed had only limited use as a medicinal plant. The Cheyennes boiled the plant and inhaled the vapors to cure love sickness. They also used it ceremonially in sweat baths and carried the dried plant in their pockets as a charm to attract women (Shemluck, 1982, p. 341). The Crows made a tea containing tarweed and mint, *Mentha arvensis* L., to cleanse snakebite

wounds. They also applied tarweed as a poultice and used it in some of their ceremonies. The Crow and Klamath Indians ate the flowers and seeds as food (ibid.).

Mentzelia nuda (Pursh) T. & G.

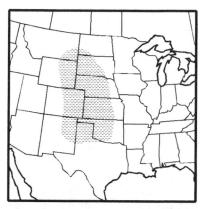

SAND LILY
Loasaceae
Stickleaf Family

The sand lily is a stiffly erect, coarse biennial or perennial herb with alternate, lance-shaped leaves. Flowers near the tips of branches are white and open in the late afternoon but close before sunset. The sand lily is found on sandy or gravelly hillsides, roadsides, and stream banks.

The Dakotas stripped sand lily stems of their leaves and pounded the stems to extract a gummy yellow juice that was boiled, strained, and applied externally as a remedy for fever (Gilmore, 1977, p. 51).

The Cheyenne name for the sand lily, *Mentzelia laevicaulis* (Dougl.) T. & G., is "vo'?ome-hese'eo?otse" (white medicine) (Hart, 1981, p. 30). It is one of the Cheyennes' oldest medicines, held in high esteem because of its power. It was used only as an ingredient in medicines, never by itself. The root was dug before the plant had flowered. It was considered particularly beneficial for fevers and complicated illnesses, but was also used

to treat earache, rheumatism, and arthritis.

The Cheyennes' medicinal uses of the sand lily were similar to their uses of the purple coneflower, *Echinacea angustifolia* DC. Both plants were used in a root tea for mumps, measles, and smallpox; a salve was also made and applied to the affected area. These two roots were also chewed for thirst prevention.

In the Southwest, the Zunis used the powdered root of the sand lily, *M. pumila* T. & G., to relieve constipation by inserting the medicine into the rectum (Stevenson, 1915, p. 57).

Mirabilis nyctaginea (Michx.) MacM.

WILD FOUR-O'CLOCK
Nyctaginaceae
Four-O'Clock Family

The wild four-o'clock is a smooth, erect perennial herb with a thick,

263

fleshy taproot. The leaves are opposite, entire, mostly smooth, and lance-shaped to heart-shaped or triangular. The flowers are pink to reddish-purple, funnel-shaped, and in branched clusters at the ends of branches. Wild four-o'clock is found in prairies and pastures, on plains or hillsides, and along streamsides and roadsides.

The Omaha and Ponca name for the wild four-o'clock is "makan-wasek" (strong medicine); the Pawnee name is "kahtstakat" (yellow medicine); and the Dakota name is "poi'pie" (no translation given) (Gilmore, 1977, p. 26). The Poncas chewed the root and blew it into wounds to heal them. The Pawnees ground the dried root and applied it as a remedy for sore mouth in babies. After childbirth women drank a tea to reduce abdominal swelling.

The Teton Dakotas boiled the root to make a tea used for fever. A Lakota informant reported that the roots of the four-o'clock and the purple coneflower, *Echinacea angustifolia* DC., were used to treat intestinal worms (ibid.). A tea made of the two roots was drunk every night at bedtime for four nights, then with the next evacuation of the bowels, the worms were eliminated. This medicine was effective even with very large tapeworms. Another medicine made from the roots of the same two plants was rubbed downward on swollen arms or legs to reduce the swelling.

The Lakotas grated and moist-

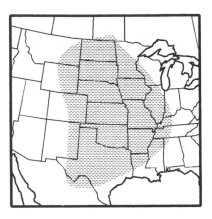

ened the roots of the wild four-o'clock as an external treatment for broken bones (Munson, 1981, p. 237). They also treated difficulty in urinating with a tea made from the roots of the narrowleaf four-o'clock, *Mirabilis linearis* (Pursh) Heimerl., (Rogers, 1980, p. 52). The Lakota name for this plant is "huo'kihe hanskaska" (tall jointed stem) (ibid.).

The wild four-o'clock is considered poisonous (Foster and Duke, 1990, p. 152). The four-o'clock, *M. jalapa* L., commonly cultivated for its flowers in the garden, contains the alkaloid trigonelline in its roots and seeds (Mitchell and Rook, 1979, p. 491). This alkaloid is an irritant to the skin and mucous membranes.

Onosmodium molle Michx.

FALSE GROMWELL
Boraginaceae
Borage Family

False gromwell is a coarse, stiffly erect perennial herb with few to many stems arising from a woody rootstock. The leaves are alternate, simple, lance-shaped to egg-shaped, and rough-hairy. The flowers are white, tubular, 5-lobed, and in coiled clusters at the ends of stems. False gromwell is found on the dry, rocky or sandy hillsides of prairies, pastures, and open woods.

The Lakota names for the false gromwell are "poi'piye" (something to fix swelling with) and "sunkcan'kanhuipije" (horse spine cure) (Rogers, 1980, p. 41; Buechel, 1983, p. 469). These Indians made both a tea and a salve from the root and seeds, which were administered internally for the treatment of swellings in horses and exter-

nally for the treatment of swellings in humans.

The Cheyenne name is "mak esk o wa ni'a" (big rough medicine) (Grinnell, 1962, 2: 185). The leaves and stems of this plant were pulverized, mixed with a little grease, and rubbed on a patient's skin to restore feeling to a numb area. This medicine was also used for lumbago.

This plant was not commonly prescribed by doctors. B. B. Smythe provided one of the few references to its medical use in his 1901 "Preliminary List of Medicinal and Economic Kansas Plants." He described the false gromwell as a "demulcent, diuretic, and emollient" (Smythe, 1901, p. 202).

Oxytropis species

LOCOWEED
Fabaceae
Bean Family

The locoweeds are perennial herbs with short stems and woody rootstocks. The leaves are pinnately compound and clustered at the base of the plant. Flowers are yellowish-white to bright pink or purple and are typical of the pea family. They are similar to the milkvetches (*Astragalus*); however, the two united petals (keel) in *Oxytropis* are pointed, whereas in *Astragalus* they are blunt. The fruits are often woody and several-seeded. The locoweeds grow in a variety of habitats, often

in rocky or sandy and sparsely vegetated areas.

The use of locoweeds by the Indians shows a considerable breadth of knowledge concerning the use and effects of native plants because the locoweeds are known to be poisonous and their use can produce deleterious side effects. The Blackfeet name for hare's locoweed, *Oxytropis lagopus* Nutt. var. *atropurpurea* (Rydb.) Barneby, is "a-sat-chiot-ake" (rattle-weed) (McClintock, 1923, p. 320; Murphey, 1959, p. 38). The name rattleweed refers to the seeds rattling in the large, dried seed pods. The Blackfeet chewed the leaves to alleviate sore throats (Johnston, 1970, p. 314). Blackfeet children with asthma were fed unspecified parts of the showy locoweed, *O. splendens* Dougl. ex Hook., especially when their breathing "rattled" (Hellson, 1974, pp. 73, 77, and 81). The Blackfeet also made a leaf tea from the white locoweed, *O. sericea* Nutt., to apply to sores and to treat ear troubles.

The Cheyenne name for an unspecified *Oxytropis* species is "wi' ke isse e yo" (sweet medicine or bitter medicine) (Grinnell, 1962, 2: p. 179). They mixed the powdered root of this plant with another poisonous plant, baneberry, *Actea rubra* (Ait.) Willd., From this mixture they made a tea that helped mothers increase their milk flow and made their milk more agreeable to the infant. If baneberry was not available, they mixed the locoweed with bluebell, *Mertensia cilata* (Torr.) G. Don.

In the Southwest, the Navahos used unspecified parts of the purple locoweed, *Oxytropis lambertii* Pursh, to make a tea for constipation. They also ate it, parched or as a mush, for food (Wyman and Harris, 1951, p. 28). The Navahos also used an unidentified locoweed species to treat bronchial and esophageal ailments (Elmore, 1944, p. 96).

The poisonous substances in locoweed have not been completely identified. Feeding experiments with the purple locoweed have shown that its poisonous effects on livestock are cumulative; the animal must eat large amounts of the plant over a period of time to become poisoned. Horses are more susceptible than cattle or sheep and will even develop a craving for the plant. In *Poisonous Plants of the Central United States*, H. A. Stephens described the symptoms of purple locoweed poisoning in livestock:

Lack of coordination, trembling, vision trouble, inability to eat or drink, paralysis, listlessness, lack of interest unless startled— and then the animal becomes unruly. During these activities the back legs often buckle and the horse goes down on its haunches or even becomes completely prostrate. Death usually comes about a month after the first ingestion of the material (Stephens, 1980, p. 60).

Most of the numerous species of locoweed have showy, colorful flowers and are well suited to rock gardens in drier portions of the country. In his 1983 *Jewels of the Plains*, Claude Barr gives a thorough account of the adaptability of various Great Plains species of locoweed to the rock garden (Barr, 1983, pp. 126–30).

Penstemon grandiflorus Nutt.

LARGE BEARDTONGUE
Scrophulariaceae
Figwort Family

The large beardtongue is a showy, stout, erect, perennial herb. The leaves are opposite, fleshy, waxy, spatula-shaped to egg-shaped or oval, and entire. The trumpet-like flowers are inflated, 5-lobed, bluish-lavender to pale blue, and in open groups along the upper stem. The fruits are small, woody capsules that split open to release

numerous brown seeds. Large beardtongue is found in sandy to loamy soil of prairies.

For chills and fever, some Pawnees drank a tea made from the leaves of the large beardtongue, but this use was not common knowledge among tribe members (Gilmore, 1977, p. 62). The Kiowas made a tea from the boiled roots as a cure for stomachache (Vestal and Shultes, 1939, p. 51). The Lakota name for the large beardtongue is "kimi'mila tawana'hca" (butterfly flower) (Rogers, 1980, p. 59). The Dakotas boiled the root and used it for pains in the chest.

The Lakota name for the slender beardtongue, *Penstemon gracilis* Nutt., is "zuze'ca tapeju'ta" (snake's medicine). Its roots were used to treat snakebite (ibid.). The Blackfeet name for the beardtongue, *Penstemon acuminatus* Dougl. ex. Lindl., is "at-si-pl-koa" (fire taste), in reference to its biting flavor (McClintock, 1909, p. 276; Johnston, 1970, p. 319). It was boiled in water and taken internally for cramps and stomach pains. A tea from the leaves was used to stop vomiting.

In the Southwest, the Navahos used various species of beardtongue as a cathartic, diuretic, hemostatic, and poultice for wounds. Beardtongue was also used to treat burns, toothache, snakebite, eagle bite, stomachache, backache, and for some aspect of childbirth (Hocking, 1956, p. 162; Wyman and Harris, 1951, pp. 42–43).

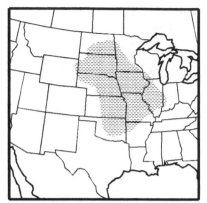

In New Mexico, the red-flowered beardtongue, *Penstemon torreyi* Benth., is called "varas de San José." The Spanish name "varas" translates as "staff" or "wand." Its use was reported by Lenora Curtin in her 1976 *Healing Herbs of the Upper Rio Grande*:

Spanish New Mexicans boil the flowering top of the varas de San José *in cold water, strain the liquid, and drink it for kidney trouble and for a cold in the chest. The boiled dry or fresh flowers, with the addition of enough sugar to make a syrup, are given to babies with whooping-cough when they have paroxysms. Infants under six months of age are treated with one-half teaspoonful, but those who are older take an entire teaspoonful.*

In cases of excessive menses, the whole plant is broken into small pieces, and boiled in water. The patient must drink three swallows of the decoction, and bathe the lower portions of the body with this liquid. This may be another

indication of the Doctrine of Signatures in the utilization of plants (Curtin, 1976, pp. 194–95).

A salve of beardtongue and oil was also used as a dressing for skin irritations (Moore, 1979, p. 125).

Recently the chemical constituents of beardtongue, *Penstemon* species, have been analyzed by researchers. The large beardtongue was found to contain lanatoside B, gitoxin, and acetyl digitoxin-like cardiac glycosides (Chang et al., 1970, p. 324). The smooth beardtongue, *P. digitalis* Nutt. ex Sims, contains stansioside (an iridoid glycoside), orobanchoside and martynoside (phenyl propanoid glycosides), and a novel compound diginpenstroside (a glycoside) (Teborg and Junior, 1989, p. 474).

Although the large beardtongue is an attractive ornamental, it is difficult to propagate and often does not survive outside its native habitat. It can be propagated by seed, division of the root stalk, and summer cuttings. Other *Penstemon* species are more easily propagated by seed, especially within their native ranges.

Physalis heterophylla Nees.

CLAMMY GROUND CHERRY
Solanaceae
Nightshade Family

Clammy ground cherry is a low, sticky-hairy perennial herb. The leaves are alternate and egg-

268

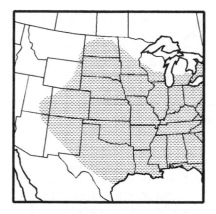

shaped, with entire to irregularly
wavy or toothed margins. The
flowers are solitary among the
leaves, nodding, funnel-shaped,
5-angled, and pale yellow with
brownish spots at the base. The
fruits are yellow, many-seeded berries enclosed by papery, lantern-
like sepals. Clammy ground cherry
is found in the sandy soil of prairies, pastures, roadsides, and
disturbed areas.

Melvin Gilmore reported that
the Indians of the Upper Missouri
River made a tea from the root
of the clammy ground cherry for
stomach trouble and headache
(Gilmore, 1977, p. 61). They also
inhaled the smoke of the burning root (probably for headache or
nerve problems) and applied the
root as a dressing for wounds.

In the Omaha tribe, individuals
of either sex to whom the buffalo
appeared in dreams could become
buffalo doctors, "Te' ithaethe"
(those to whom the buffalo has
shown compassion). This society
was dedicated to the knowledge of

medicines for healing of wounds. A
buffalo doctor would make a dressing for a wound in the following
manner: first he would chew the
roots of the clammy ground cherry,
hops, *Humulus lupulus* L., and the
wild anise, *Osmorhiza longistylis*
(Torr.) DC.; then he would take
water into his mouth and blowing
this medicated liquid with force
into the wound (ibid.; Fletcher and
La Flesche, 1911, p. 487).

The Lakotas used the clammy
ground cherry to stimulate appetite (Munson, 1981, p. 237); one
dose was three-to-five fruits. The
Mesquakie names for the clammy
ground cherry are "tcekwakwote"
("twisted," probably in reference
to the root) and "dumwo'sa" (old
woman berries) (Smith, 1928,
p. 246). The Mesquakies used the
root as an unspecified medicine.
They and several other tribes also
ate the ripe fruits of the clammy
ground cherry as food (Kindscher,
1987, pp. 161–64).

The Mesquakies made a tea
from the entire plant of the Virginia ground cherry, *Physalis virginiana* P. Mill., to cure dizziness
(Smith, 1928, p. 248). The Kiowas
pounded the roots of the closely related purple ground cherry, *Quincula lobata* (Torr.) Raf. (formerly
in the genus *Physalis*), and applied
them as a poultice or made a tea
to treat grippe (Vestal and Shultes,
1939, p. 50).

The roots, foliage, and unripe
fruits of the ground cherry, *Physalis* species, contain the glyco-
alkaloid solanine. Children have

been poisoned by eating the unripe fruits. The symptoms of poisoning in livestock and humans are stomach and intestinal irritation and inflammation, troubled breathing, trembling, weakness, and paralysis (Stephens, 1980, p. 93).

Populus deltoides Marsh

COTTONWOOD
Salicaceae
Willow Family

The cottonwood is a common tree along rivers and streams. The bark of the trunk is tan and deeply furrowed; young twigs are brown to gray and flexible. The leaves are light green, fan-shaped or heart-shaped, and toothed. Tiny male and female flowers are in separate clusters on different trees. The fruits are small capsules that open to release abundant tiny seeds, each with a dense tuft of silky hairs at the base.

The Blackfeet scraped the bark

of the cottonwood and brewed the scrapings to make a tea for women about to give birth (Hellson, 1974, p. 61). They also made a bark tea for symptoms resembling heartburn or for general discomfort. In 1877 Valery Havard, the Assistant Surgeon and Botanist for the Seventh Cavalry, reported from an area that is in present-day Montana that "whole groves of Cottonwood were seen with their trunks stripped by the Indians, who use the inner layers of the bark as a mucilaginous and anti-scorbutic food" (Havard, 1877, p. 1682). The Lakota names for the cottonwood, "canya'hu" (peel off wood) and "wa'ga can" (take off wood), in reference to their use of the bark as feed for horses (Rogers, 1980, p. 57).

Writing in 1918, Melvin Gilmore described the "mystic character" that the tribes of the Upper Missouri River attributed to the cottonwood:

The cottonwood they found in such diverse situations, appearing always so self-reliant, showing such prodigious fecundity, its lustrous young leaves in springtime by their sheen and by their restlessness reflecting the splendor of the sun like the dancing ripples of a lake, that to this tree also they ascribed mystery. This peculiarity of the foliage of the cottonwood is quite remarkable, so that it is said the air is never so still that there is not motion of cottonwood leaves. Even in still summer after-

noons, *and at night when all else* *was still, they could ever hear* *the rustling of cottonwood leaves* *by the passage of little vagrant* *currents of air. And the winds* *themselves were the paths of the* *Higher Powers, so they were con-* *stantly reminded of the mystic* *character of this tree (Gilmore,* *1977, pp. 3–4).*

The cottonwood has been used in folk medicine as a tonic and febrifuge (Burlage, 1968, p. 161). All of the *Populus* species contain varying amounts of salicin and populin, the precursors to aspirin (Moore, 1979, p. 133). The bark is the most effective part, but quite bitter, so a leaf tea was often used for reducing fever or inflammation. The bark tea was also used for diarrhea. Cottonwood buds were made into a salve by soaking them in olive or almond oil for a week, then adding a little melted beeswax as a thickener.

foil is found in meadows and on rocky slopes.

The Cheyenne, who called the shrubby cinquefoil "o nuhk'is e' e yo" (contrary medicine), used it in the contrary dance:

During the Contrary dance this *plant is used to protect the hands* *from injury when they are thrust* *into the kettle of boiling soup. The* *leaves, after having been dried,* *are ground to a fine powder, which* *may be rubbed over the hands,* *arms, and body; or an infusion of* *the powder may be made by soak-* *ing it for a time in cold water, and* *the infusion may be rubbed over* *the whole body. It is said perfectly* *to protect the parts exposed to a* *severe temporary heat (Grinnell,* *1962, 2: 176–77).*

The Cheyennes used the leaves to make a beverage tea, and the plant was also regarded as medicine against the enemy (Hart, 1981, p. 35). It was considered a deadly arrow poison, but could only

Potentilla fruticosa L.

SHRUBBY CINQUEFOIL
Rosaceae
Rose Family

The shrubby cinquefoil is a low, spreading shrub with many slender branches. The leaves are pinnately compound, with 5–7 linear to lance-shaped leaflets. The flowers are 2.5 cm (1 in) wide, yellow, and solitary or in small clusters along the branches. The shrubby cinque-

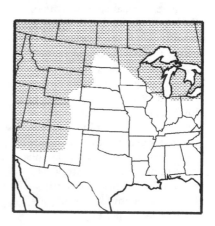

be used by holy people. For this purpose, arrow tips were dipped into a concoction made from the leaves. The poison was thought to go directly to the heart. "At the time of Custer's battle with the Cheyenne and Sioux, a holy person, who was also Keeper of the Sacred Hat, wished to use it against Custer, but the plant could not be found" (ibid.).

The Blackfeet made an emetic for stomach disorders from the silverweed, *Potentilla anserina* L., by soaking it in water and drinking the solution (Hellson, 1974, p. 68). They also chewed the root and applied it to sores and scrapes.

In the Great Basin, the Paiutes cooked the whole plant of a *Potentilla* species and ate it as a laxative (Murphey, 1959, p. 42). In the Great Lakes Bioregion, the Chippewas made a tea from the purple cinquefoil, *P. palustris* (L.) Scop., by decocting half of a root in a quart of water. The tea was drunk for dysentery.

The chemical constituents of this species contain mucilage and tannins. They were described as bitter and astringent (Densmore, 1974, pp. 302–04, 344).

In folk medicine, a tea made from the various species of cinquefoil was recommended as a treatment for a variety of inflammations, for esophagus and stomach ulcers, and for fever and diarrhea. As a mouthwash and gargle, the tea was used to treat sore throat, tonsil, and gum inflammations (Moore, 1979, p. 132).

The shrubby cinquefoil has been commonly used as an ornamental or border plant because of its attractive foliage, its yellow flowers, its long blooming period during the heat of summer, and its low growth habit. Several named cultivars are available. This species can be propagated by seed, but is most easily propagated by layering or cuttings.

Prenanthes aspera Michx.

RATTLESNAKE ROOT
Asteraceae
Sunflower Family

The rattlesnake root is a coarse, erect, rough-hairy perennial herb to 15 dm (5 ft) tall, with milky juice. The leaves are egg-shaped to lance-shaped, entire to toothed, and gradually reduced up the stem. Numerous hairy, cylindrical flower heads are in groups along the elongate stem. The flowers are all raylike, creamy white, and

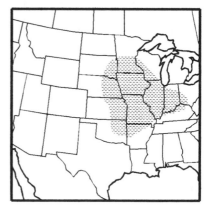

scented. The plant is found on open prairies and at the edges of wooded areas.

The Choctaws made a tea of the roots and tops that they used as a stimulating diuretic and anodyne (Campbell, 1951, p. 288). The Chippewas made a broth from the root of the rattlesnake root, *Prenanthes alba* L., that was used by women who drank it after childbirth to promote the flow of milk (Densmore, 1974, pp. 360–61). Since the plant has milky sap, this use apparently relates to the Doctrine of Signatures. The Flambeau Ojibwas used the milk of the rattlesnake root (also called white lettuce and gall-of-the-earth) as a diuretic, especially in "female diseases" (Smith, 1928, p. 365).

Prunus americana Marsh.

WILD PLUM
Rosaceae
Rose Family

The wild plum is a thicket-forming shrub or small tree. Small branches sometimes are spiny. The leaves are lance-shaped to egg-shaped and toothed. The flowers are white, in groups of 2–5 at the ends of branches, and they usually appear before the leaves. The fruits are fleshy, red to orange, and about 2.5 cm (1 in) in diameter. Wild plums are found in prairies and pastures, on the edges of woodlands, and along roadsides and stream banks.

The Omahas scraped and boiled the bark from the roots of the wild plum (*Prunus americana*) and applied it to abrasions (Gilmore, 1977, p. 35). They also used the wild plum as a seasonal indicator: when the wild plums came into bloom, they knew it was time to plant their corn, beans, and squash. They also bound together the tough, elastic twigs of the wild plums and used them as brooms.

The Dakotas used the sprouts of the wild plum as an offering for the sick.

Sprouts or young growths of the wild plum are used by the Teton Dakota in making waunyanpi. *This is an offering or form of prayer, consisting of a wand, made preferably from a wild-plum sprout peeled and painted. If painted, the design and color are emblematic. Near the top of the wand is fastened the offering proper, which may take the form of anything acceptable to the higher powers. A small quantity of*

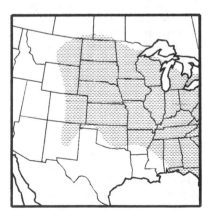

*smoking tobacco is an article very
frequently used for this purpose.
No matter how small a portion of
the thing offered is used, the im-
material self of the substance is in
it. Such offerings are usually made
for the benefit of the sick. Waunyanpi may be made by anyone at
any place if done with appropriate
ceremony, but the most efficient
procedure is to prepare an altar
with due ceremony and there set
the wand upright with the offering
fastened near the top (ibid.).*

The Cheyennes mixed the
crushed fruits of this wild plum
with salt to treat a mouth disease (Hart, 1981, p. 35). They also
crushed and boiled the small rootlets and the bark of older wild
plums with the roots of the scarlet thorn, *Crataegus chrysocarpa*
Ashe. This mixture served as a
diarrhea remedy (Youngken, 1925,
p. 260). The Mesquakies also used
the root bark of the wild plum
to cure canker sores around the
mouth. They used a bark tea made
from Canada plum, *Prunus nigra*
Ait., to settle the stomach and stop
vomiting (Smith, 1928, p. 242).

The wild plum had only limited
use in folk medicine and apparently was not used by medical
doctors. Pioneers and settlers used
it primarily as an edible fruit,
especially prized for making jelly
(Kindscher, 1987, pp. 172–75). The
wild plum was used in Kentucky
as a folk remedy to cure asthma
(Bolyard et al., 1981, p. 123). In this
remedy, a bark tea, with brown

sugar and honey added, was drunk.
B. B. Smythe of the Kansas Medical College reported in 1901 that
the various species of wild plum
were astringent and sedative, and
that the bark was tonic (Smythe,
1901, p. 204). The roots and bark
contain a bitter substance as well
as a substance called phloretin,
which is an active agent against
gram positive and negative bacteria (Lewis and Elvin-Lewis, 1977,
pp. 95, 362).

*Pycnanthemum
virginianum* Robins & Fern.

MOUNTAIN MINT
Lamiaceae
Mint Family

The mountain mint is an aromatic
perennial herb with square stems,
which are branched above, and
opposite, linear to lance-shaped,
entire leaves. The flowers are 2-
lipped and crowded in clusters at
the ends of stems. The mountain
mint is found in prairie sloughs,
meadows, and moist woodlands.

The Mesquakie name for the
mountain mint, "koki'sikani" (no
translation given) refers to its use
as a luring scent on mink traps
(Smith, 1928, p. 226). The roots,
leaves, and flowers were all used
as medicine. A tea from the leaves
was considered one of the "best
medicines"; it was drunk as an
alterative by a person who was
"all run down." The Mesquakies

274

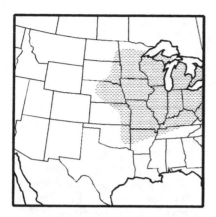

Ribes americanum P. Mill.

WILD BLACK CURRANT
Grossulariaceae
Currant Family

This small, spineless shrub grows in moist thickets, edges of woods, and along ravines and streams. The leaves are alternate, stalked, 3-lobed and toothed, with the lower surfaces glandular-dotted. The flowers are in elongate groups from leaf bases, 5-parted, and greenish-white to cream colored. The fruits are reddish-purple to black, juicy, pea-sized berries. The wild black currant is found in moist thickets and ravines, on the edges of woods, and along streams.

The Dakota name for this plant is "chap-ta-haza" (beaver berries). The Omaha and Ponca name is "pezi nuga" (male gooseberry) (Gilmore, 1977, p. 32). The Omahas made a strong tea from the root as remedy for kidney trouble. The Winnebagos used the root to treat women with "uterine trouble." The Mesquakies called it "kasoo'soana kuko ke'shikeki" (tail-like) (Smith, 1928, p. 246). They made a medicine from the root bark to expel intestinal worms. The Blackfeet ate the berries of an unknown Ribes species as a mild laxative (Hellson, 1974, p. 68).

In the Great Basin, the Shoshones ground the internal bark of the wild currant, Ribes aureum Pursh, to make a poultice (Murphey, 1959,

made an inhalant from a mixture of mountain mint flowers (and probably the leaves), the flowers of the dotted bee balm, Monarda punctata L., and snake bones. It is applied at the nostrils to rally a patient near death. A tea was also made from this mixture to cure chills and ague.

The Lakotas call the mountain mint "wahpe'ceyaka" (mint leaf) and "wahpe' i'cikoyagyaka" (leaves fastened together like a chain) (Rogers, 1980, p. 50). They made a tea from the plant to stop coughing.

The mountain mints were used in folk medicine and by medical doctors as well. They were considered tonic, diaphoretic, and sedative and were used as both an emmenagogue and a stimulant (Smythe, 1901, p. 204; Burlage, 1968, p. 94).

Rubus occidentalis L.

BLACK RASPBERRY
Rosaceae
Rose Family

p. 43). When it caused the skin to turn yellow, they judged the poultice strong enough.

In his 1830 *Medical Flora* Constantine Rafinesque reported the following uses for the wild currant: "Roots in infusion, bark in gargles used for eruptive fevers, dysentery of cattle, fruits and jelly for sore throat. Anodyne, diuretic, pellent, depurative, used in angina, ezanthems, dysentery, hydrophobia, scabs, and ictus. A fine cordial made of black currants. . . . Wine made with currants and gooseberries" (Rafinesque, 1830, p. 257).

An extract of the leaves of the European black currant, *R. nigrum* L., has shown enough anti-inflammatory activity to compare favorably with reference drugs (Declume, 1989, pp. 91–98).

The buffalo currant, *R. odoratum* Wendl., was an important food source for the Plains Indians (Kindscher, 1987, pp. 196–98). Wild currants were eaten fresh, dried, or made into jelly. Some species and varieties are still cultivated today.

The black raspberry is a woody perennial with waxy, arched stems that bear hooked prickles. The leaves are alternate, compound, with 3 or 5 toothed and egg-shaped leaflets, green above, and densely white-hairy beneath. The flowers are white and in flat-topped or elongate groups on short branches. Fruits are black, juicy, and sweet. The black raspberry is found in woods, thickets, and pastures, on hillsides and roadsides, and often in dry, rocky sites.

Raspberries, blackberries, and dewberries were commonly used by the Indians for both food (Kindscher, 1987, pp. 206–08) and medicine. The Omaha name for the raspberry bush is "takan hecha" (no translation given). The Omahas scraped and boiled the root of the black raspberry and fed it to children with bowel trouble (Gilmore, 1977, p. 33). John Dunn Hunter described the same use for the dewberry, *Rubus flagellaris* L., apparently by the Osages (Hunter, 1957, p. 376). It was considered a weak remedy.

The Mesquakies made a beverage tea called *atetaa* (red root) from the roots of the black raspberry and the red raspberry, *R. idaeus* L. subsp. *sachalinensis* (Levl.) Focke. This tea was also mixed with other medicines as a "seasoner" (Smith,

In 1830 Constantine Rafinesque
reported these uses of wild raspberries and blackberries, *Rubus*
species:

*Nearly 30 wild species. . . . Roots
of all more or less astringent,
subtonic, much used in cholera
infantum, chronic dysentery, diarrhea, &c. The Cherokis chew them
for cough; a cold poultice useful
in piles; used with Lobelia in gonorrhea. . . . Ripe fruits, preserves,
jam, jelly or syrup, grateful and
beneficial in diarrhea, gravel, hemoptysis, phthisis, sorethroat,
putrid and malignant fevers,
scurvy. . . . Raspberries afford de-
licious distilled water, beer, mead
and wine. Said to dissolve tartar
of teeth (Rafinesque, 1830, p. 258).*

1928, p. 243). (The red raspberry is
native to Europe, but has become
established in many parts of North
America.) The Kiowa-Apaches
used the root of the blackberry
(*Rubus* species) to make a tea for
diarrhea and stomachache. For
this purpose, the root was dug in
summer and either used fresh or
dried. The medicine was very bitter, causing the mouth to pucker
(Jordan, 1965, p. 129).

In Appalachia the roots of various *Rubus* species were used in a
number of folk remedies (Bolyard
et al., 1981, p. 128). Blackberry root
tea was drunk for hemorrhaging
and hemophilia. When taken every
three hours it was used for summer
sickness and diarrhea. It was also
drunk during childbirth to speed
delivery. Raspberry root tea was
also used for this purpose.

Dewberry and blackberry roots
were boiled together to make a
strong tea used to relieve abdominal pains. The pain of a beesting
was also relieved by rubbing a
raspberry leaf on the sting.

The juice of the blackberry fruit,
spiced and mixed with whiskey,
was a valued carminative in Kentucky and other southern states. It
is the flavoring ingredient in the
well-known Blackberry Cordial
(Lloyd, 1921, p. 277).

Nineteenth-century physicians
used the root of the raspberry or
blackberry, *Rubus* species, as an
astringent in diarrhea, cholera infantum, and chronic dysentery.
The root, combined with gold-
thread, *Coptis trifolia* (L.) Salisb.,
and boiled into a strong tea, was
a "remedy for throat, mouth, and
stomach cankers, and provided
relief from gravel and dysentery"
(Bolyard et al., 1981, p. 129).

The fruit of the red raspberry
was officially listed in the *U.S.
Pharmacopoeia* from 1882 to 1905

and in the *National Formulary*
from 1916 to 1942. The juice was
officially listed in the *National
Formulary* from 1942 to 1950 and
has been listed in the *U.S. Pharmacopoeia* since 1950. It is used in
the preparation of raspberry syrup,
a pharmaceutical aid used to dis-
guise the unpleasant taste of other
medicines.

The astringent property of the
raspberry comes from the hydro-
lyzable tannin, containing both
gallic and ellagic acids, and fil-
losin (ibid., p. 130). Leaves of the
red raspberry contain higher levels
of vitamin C than do the fruits.
Aqueous extracts of red raspberry
leaves contain a smooth muscle
stimulant, an anticholinesterase, and a spasmolytic (Trease and
Evans, 1973, p. 431). The American
wild blackberry is more biologically active than the red raspberry
cultivated in England.

Rumex venosus Pursh

WILD BEGONIA
Polygonaceae
Buckwheat Family

The wild begonia is a perennial
herb with spreading rhizomes.
The stems are solitary to many
and frequently reddish. The leaves
are alternate, lance-shaped, and
thickish. The flowers are tiny and
in clusters above the leaves. The
fruits are brown achenes, 0.6 cm
(¼ in) long and borne at the base
of the enlarged pinkish sepals.

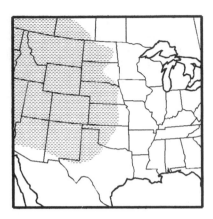

The wild begonia grows on sandy
dunes and along stream banks.

The Cheyennes call the wild
begonia "ma'i tuk ohe'" (red
maker) because the water in which
it is steeped turns red (Grinnell,
1962, 2: 172). They used it to make
a red and a yellow dye to color
feathers, quills, or hair. The Arapahos used the wild begonia to make
a burnt-orange dye. They also used
the stems and leaves as a wash for
sores (Nickerson, 1966, p. 47).

The Lakota name for the wild
begonia is "wahpe' sku'ya" (sweet
leaf) (Rogers, 1980, p. 55). They
made a tea from the roots for
women who did not expel the
afterbirth promptly after childbirth. They also used the pale
dock, *Rumex altissimus* Wood., as
a remedy (neither parts nor method
given) for stomach cramps, diarrhea, or hemorrhage. The Omahas
also used the pale dock for drawing
out the liquid in boils (Gilmore,
1913b, p. 361). For this purpose,
either green leaves or green leaves

278

mixed with dried crushed leaves were applied to the boil.

The Blackfeet boiled the willow-leaved dock, R. mexicanus Meisn., to make a tea used for swellings and a variety of complaints (McClintock, 1923, p. 320). Their name for this plant is "matoa-koa-ksi" (yellow-root). The Pawnees used the root of the wild rhubarb or canaigre, R. hymenosepalus Torr., to cure diarrhea (Gilmore, 1977, p. 25). In 1919 ethnobotanist Melvin Gilmore reported that the Pawnees and the Wichitas had begun to cultivate this plant in Oklahoma (ibid.).

The roots of the wild rhubarb have been used by Indians of the Southwest as food. The leaf stems make an acceptable rhubarb substitute. The Hopis and Papagos used the roots to treat colds and sore throat (Kearney and Peebles, 1951, p. 245).

Because the roots of the wild rhubarb (R. hymenosepalus) contain 25 percent tannin, it has been proposed as a crop for the desert Southwest (Krochmal et al., 1954, p. 8; Krochmal and Paur, 1951, pp. 367–77). More recently, it has been marketed as wild red American ginseng or wild red desert ginseng. However, it does not contain any of the active panaxoside-like saponin glycosides responsible for ginseng's physiological activities, and they are not botanically related (Tyler, 1981, p. 62). A policy adopted by the Herb Trade Association in 1979 stated that the wild rhubarb or canaigre should not be labeled "ginseng." In addition to tannin, wild rhubarb roots contain starch and a small amount of anthraquinones. When hydrolyzed, the tannin yields leucodelphinidin and leucopelargonidin (Lewis and Elvin-Lewis, 1977, p. 135).

The wild docks all contain tannin. Although this component is probably responsible for several of their uses, tannins are not always healthful. In fact, consumption of tannins in large quantities can cause liver damage. Both the curly dock, R. crispus L., and the bitter dock, R. obtusifolius L., are native to Europe, but have become naturalized throughout much of the world. The root of the bitter dock was officially listed in the U.S. Pharmacopoeia from 1820 to 1905. The curly dock root was listed in the U.S. Pharmacopoeia from 1863 to 1905 and in the National Formulary from 1916 to 1936. At one time they were used in the treatment of skin diseases and for alterative and depurative purposes; later they were used as a laxative and a tonic (Vogel, 1970, p. 398).

Scutellaria lateriflora L.

MAD-DOG SKULLCAP
Lamiaceae
Mint Family

Mad-dog skullcap is a delicate, erect, perennial herb with smooth, square stems that often are branched above. The leaves are opposite, thin, and egg-shaped, with toothed margins. The flowers are blue, 2-lipped, and in elongate groups on stalks in the upper half of the plant. The plants are found in riparian habitats, usually on stream banks.

Mad-dog skullcap was named for its use in the treatment of rabies by doctors in colonial America.

There are eight species of skullcap found throughout the Prairie Bioregion (Great Plains Flora Association, 1986, pp. 734–37). The Mesquakies used the small skullcap, *Scutellaria parvula* Michx., in the treatment of diarrhea (Smith, 1928, p. 227). This is the only reference I found to medicinal use of skullcap by the Indians of the region, indicating that for the Indians, it was probably of little importance.

The debate among doctors over the usefulness of skullcaps, on the other hand, has been long and even continues today. In his 1830 *Medical Flora*, Constantine Rafinesque chronicled the medicinal use of

the skullcap and the controversy that surrounded it:

[S. lateriflora] is lately become famous as a cure and prophylactic against hydrophobia. This property was discovered by Dr. Vandesveer, towards 1772, who has used it with the utmost success, and is said to have till 1815, prevented 400 persons and 1000 cattle from becoming hydrophobus, after being bitten by mad dogs. . . . Many empirics, and some enlightened physicians have employed it also successfully. But several sceptical physicians have since denied altogether these facts, and pronounced the plant totally inert, because it has no strong action on the system, and has failed in their hands. . . . This plant has since been carefully analyzed by Cadet, in Paris, and found to contain many powerful chemical principals, which evince active properties. . . . It has been used chiefly of late in all nervous diseases, convulsions, tetanus, St. Vitus' dance, tremors, &c. . . . We lack, however a series of scientific and conclusive experiments made by well informed men; they have been discouraged by the ridiculous denial of sceptics (Rafinesque, 1830, pp. 82–83).

One reason for skepticism about the use of the skullcap was that "it was adopted by quacks who promoted it by advertising" (Vogel, 1970, p. 367).

The dried, above-ground part of the mad-dog skullcap was officially listed in the *U.S. Pharma-copoeia* from 1863 to 1916 and in the *National Formulary* from 1916 to 1947. On the other hand, the *U.S. Dispensatory* states in its 21st–23rd editions (1926–1944): "Skullcap is as destitute of medicinal properties as a plant may well be, not even being aromatic. When taken internally, it produces no very obvious effects, and probably is of no remedial value, although at one time it was esteemed as a remedy in hydrophobia. It was formerly also used in neuralgia, epilepsy, chorea and other nervous diseases from fatigue or over-excitement" (Stimson, 1946, p. 35).

Various species of skullcap are still recommended today in folk medicine for nervous system disorders and as a tranquilizing herb (Moore, 1979, p. 147). Research has shown that skullcap species contain several flavonoid pigments, including baicalein, scultellarein, and wogonin. These compounds are probably responsible for the antispasmodic properties attributed to the drug (Tyler, 1981, p. 209).

Shepherdia argentea (Pursh) Nutt.

BUFFALO BERRY
Eleagnaceae
Oleaster Family

The buffalo berry is a shrub whose tart, red fruits were commonly used as a food by the Indians of the northern Plains (Kindscher, 1987, pp. 210–13). It also had some minor medicinal use. The buffalo berry is a shrub or small tree with dark gray, sometimes spiny branches. The leaves are opposite, oblong, gray-green, and covered with silvery scales. Small, yellowish male and female flowers are produced on separate plants. The fruits are fleshy, red, egg-shaped, and berrylike. Buffalo berry is found on hillsides and along stream banks and ravines with rocky, sandy, and clayey soils.

The Blackfeet names are "me-e-nixen" and "miksinitisim" (bull berry). The Blackfeet ate the berries for stomach trouble and as a mild laxative (Hellson, 1974, p. 67; Johnston, 1970, p. 316). The Cheyenne name is "mat'si ta si' mins" (red hearted). The Cheyennes generally collected the fruits after the first freeze, which was believed to sweeten them for eating. They also dried and ground the berries for later use in medicinal mixtures

(Grinnell, 1962, 2: 181; Hart, 1981, p. 25).

The buffalo berry contains several simple amines and the harmol alkaloid, tetrahydroharmol. The closely related rabbit bush, *Shepherdia canadensis* (L.) Nutt., contains tetrahydroharmol, serotonin, and an alkaloid named shepherdine (Brown, 1968, pp. iii, 1, 4–7). Although harmol and its derivatives can have toxic effects, they seem to have therapeutic value as an anthelmintic, and in treating amoebic dysentery, angina pectoris, and malaria.

Smilacina stellata (L.) Desf.

SPIKENARD
Liliaceae
Lily Family

The spikenard is a perennial herb to 7 dm (2 ½ ft) tall. The leaves are alternate, lance-shaped, and slightly folded. The flowers, up to 15, are creamy white to greenish-white, about 1 cm (⅜ in) wide, 6-parted, 15 or less, and in open groups at the ends of stems. The foliage of the plant is similar to that of Solomon's seal, *Polygonatum biflorum* (Walt.) Ell., but the location of flowers and fruits is different: Solomon's seal has flowers and fruit along the stem in leaf axils. The spikenard is found in moist-to-dry coniferous or deciduous woods and in meadows, frequently along streams and rivers.

In the Great Basin, the Paiutes gathered the slender round root of the spikenard in the fall and cut it transversely into small rings, which were threaded and hung to dry for later use. When the root was pounded into a powder and thrown into a wound, the blood would clot almost immediately (Murphey, 1959, p. 39).

The Mesquakie name for the false Solomon's seal, *Smilacina racemosa* (L.) Desf., is "peshekisimini" (deer berries). They were eaten by deer (Smith, 1928, pp. 230–31). The Mesquakies burned the root as a smudge to quiet a crying child and to return someone to normal after temporary insanity. The Mesquakies also used the root with food "during the time of plague to prevent sickness." When mixed with the wood of black ash, *Fraxinus nigra* Marsh., it was used to loosen the bowels; when mixed with calamus, *Acorus calamus* L., it was used as a conjurer's root to perform tricks or to cast spells (ibid.).

In the Great Lakes Bioregion, the Menominis ground the root of the false Solomon's seal and soaked it in water. This liquid was then heated, and the steam was inhaled to treat catarrh (Smith, 1923, p. 41). The Flambeau Ojibwas used the root of the false Solomon's seal in combination with the spreading dogbane, *Apocynum androsaemifolium* L., "to keep the kidneys open during pregnancy, to cure sore throat, headache, and it was also used as a reviver" (Smith, 1928, p. 374).

The false Solomon's seal was used earlier in the century as a substitute for drugs containing convallarin, which is found in digitalis. False Solomon's seal is less powerful and was thought more efficient in treating dropsy. It was also reported to strengthen contractions of the heart, slow the pulse, increase blood pressure, stimulate respiration, and frequently to increase the appetite and rate of digestion (Smith, 1928, p. 231).

tic, and often whitish beneath. Small white to pink, bell-shaped flowers are in clusters at the bases of leaves on younger branches. The fruits are fleshy and white, drying bluish to black. It is found on gravelly hillsides and in ravines, open woods, pastures, and prairies.

The Omaha and Ponca name for this plant is "inshtogahte-hi" (eye lotion plant) (Gilmore, 1977, p. 64). The Omahas and Poncas made a tea from the leaves for weak or inflamed eyes. The Dakotas called this plant "zuzecha-ta-wote sapsapa" (black snake food). They used the leaves in a tea for sore eyes (Gilmore, 1913b, p. 367). They also mixed the western snowberry with the purple coneflower, *Echinacea pallida* Nutt., for the same purpose. The Mesquakies called the western snowberry "tatepa'siki" (twisted) (Smith, 1928, p. 207). They made a tea from the root "which is drunk to cleanse the afterbirth and to enable quicker convalescence."

In the northern Rocky Moun-

Symphoricarpos occidentalis Hook.

WESTERN SNOWBERRY
Caprifoliaceae
Honeysuckle Family

The western snowberry is a 1–1.5 m (3 ¼–5 ft) tall shrub, often forming large colonies. The leaves are opposite, egg-shaped to ellip-

tains, the Flatheads, Nez Perces, and Kutenais used the western snowberry as medicine (Hart, 1976, p. 59). The Flatheads applied the crushed leaves, fruits, and bark as a poultice for sores, cuts, chapped or injured skin, or used it to cover scabs and burns to promote rapid healing without scarring. They also made an eyewash from the bark of the western snowberry and the wild rose. For emergency application after an accident, such as having an eye poked, the Flatheads chewed the fruit, then poured the resulting juice in the eye. At first the eye muscles tightened up, but they soon felt better.

The Nez Perces boiled the western snowberry twigs to make a brown tea to reduce a fever. For a high fever, the medicine was taken frequently. While adults could drink as much as they liked, children were instructed to take only small doses. Kutenai women chopped the branches and brewed a tea for menstrual disorders.

family; the upper petal is erect and yellow to lemon-yellow and the remaining petals are pink to rose. The fruits are flattened, hairy legumes 2.5–5 cm (1–2 in) long, each containing 3–8 dark seeds. Goat's rue is found in sandy soils of open woodlands, prairies, sand dunes, and roadsides.

John Dunn Hunter, who lived among several tribes, reported in 1823 that the Osage, Kansas, and Pawnee Indians made a tea from the roots of goat's rue "principally with a view to destroy worms" (Hunter, 1957, p. 205). He also reported that they called the plant "soo-ke-he-ah" (young turkey's feed) because its seeds were a favorite food of wild turkeys. Rafinesque reported that the Osage name was "suckehihaw" (Rafinesque, 1830, p. 267).

The Creek Indians made a cold tea from this plant for bladder trouble and boiled it with sassafras, *Sassafras albidum* (Nutt.) Nees., to cure the "perch disease" (a chronic coughing) (Swanton,

Tephrosia virginiana (L.) Pers.

GOAT'S RUE
Fabaceae
Bean Family

Goat's rue or devil's shoe string is a hairy perennial herb with branched stems and pinnately compound leaves. The flowers are showy and typical of the pea

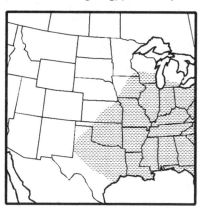

1928, p. 647). A dose was one tablespoon of the liquid—they considered it a strong medicine. Its roots were also used in fishing to stupefy fish. For lassitude the Cherokees drank a tea made from the plant. Women rinsed their hair in a tea reputed to keep the hair from breaking or falling out. They believed the toughness of the goat's rue root would be transferred to their hair (Mooney, 1896, p. 325).

Goat's rue has been used in folk medicine to treat baldness, gall bladder complications, cough, syphilis, and worms. The roots specifically have been considered anthelmintic, cathartic, diaphoretic, fortificant, laxative, piscicidal, stimulant, and tonic (Duke, 1985, p. 478). The 1885 *U.S. Dispensatory* described goat's rue as cathartic and the roots as tonic and aperient (Vogel, 1970, p. 299).

Goat's rue contains rotenoids and flavonoids, including rotenone, dehydrorotenone, tephrosin, and deguelin (Duke, 1985, p. 478; Menichini, Monache, and Marini Bettolo, 1982, p. 243). Rotenone (usually obtained from the African *Derris* species) is commonly used as an insecticide and fish poison. This substance has shown anticancer activity in lymphocytic leukemia and nasopharyngeal tumor systems. Like many other antitumor agents, rotenone is also described as carcinogenic. The wood and seed of the plant are also toxic. Duguelin, rotenone, and tephrosin can cause paralysis and

death, but they are not as toxic to man as they are to fish and insects. In addition, the crude plant preparation, or rotenone derived from it, may cause dermatitis, conjunctivitis, and rhinitis (Mitchell and Rook, 1979, p. 429).

Goat's rue is a legume and "is nutritious, palatable and relished by all classes of livestock. It is a sensitive decreaser on native ranges and has been practically eliminated by over-use on much of our grassland" (Phillips Petroleum Company, 1959, p. 101). Goat's rue, with its pink- and yellow-colored flowers, is also an attractive ornamental plant. It does well on dry, sandy sites and is most easily propagated by seed.

Zanthoxylum americanum P. Mill.

PRICKLY ASH
Rutaceae
Caltrop Family

The prickly ash is a thorny, thicket-forming shrub with alternate, pinnately compound leaves. The flowers are small, greenish, and in clusters on younger branches; male and female flowers are on separate plants. The fruits are small, rounded, reddish-brown, aromatic pods containing black, pitted seeds. Prickly ash is found in open, rocky woodlands, thickets in prairie ravines, fence rows, and roadsides. It is usually found on limestone soil.

285

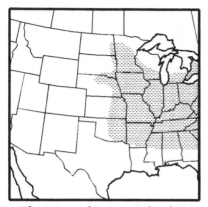

The Mesquakie names for the prickly ash are "kawakomi'shi" and "kawishi ke'koteki" (tree berries) (Smith, 1928, p. 224). The Mesquakie used four distinct parts of the plant: the bark of the trunk, the bark of the root, the berries, and the leaves. The bark and the berries, a strong expectorant, were used to make cough syrup, stop hemorrhages, and treat tuberculosis. The inner bark of prickly ash was also boiled with the root of wild sarsaparilla, *Aralia nudicaulis* L., and another undetermined root to make a tea that was drunk to gain strength during an illness. The berries were mixed with the insect gall of a plant, probably goldenrod, *Solidago canadensis* L., and a tea was made to cure kidney trouble. The powdered inner bark of the prickly ash was used to treat toothache.

In 1778 an English traveler, J. Carver, reported Winnebago use of the prickly ash:

> Soon after I set out on my travels, one of the traders whom I accompanied, complained of a violent gonorrhoea with all its alarming symptoms: this increased to such a degree, that by the time we had reached the town of the Winnebagoes, he was unable to travel. Having made his complaint known to one of the chiefs of that tribe, he told him not to be uneasy, for he would engage that by following his advice, he should be able in a few days to pursue his journey, and in a little longer time be entirely free from his disorder. The chief . . . prepared him a decoction of the bark of the roots of the prickly ash, a tree scarcely known in England . . . by the use of which, in a few days he was greatly recovered, and having received directions how to prepare it, in a fortnight after his departure from this place perceived that he was radically cured (Erichsen-Brown, 1979, p. 155–56).

The Comanches used the bark as a medicine for fever, sore throat, and toothache (Carlson and Jones, 1939, p. 524). Young Omaha men used the fruits of this shrub as a perfume and the ethnobotanist Melvin Gilmore believed that they planted them for this purpose (Gilmore, 1977, pp. 7, 46). The Illinois and Miamis used the prickly ash bark to "draw off pus" (Erichsen-Brown, 1979, p. 155).

Constantine Rafinesque reported in his 1830 *Medical Flora of the United States*:

> The whole shrub is possessed of active properties; the leaves

and fruit smell and taste like the rind of lemons, and afford a similar volatile oil. The smell of the leaves is more like orange leaves. The bark is the official part, the smell and taste are acrid, pungent, aromatic. . . . The acrimony is not felt at first when the bark or liquid is taken in the mouth, but unfolds itself gradually by a burning sensation on the tongue and palate. . . . This is a great article of the Materia Medica of our Indians; it is called Hantola by the western tribes; they prefer the bark of the root, and use it in decoction for cholics, gonorrhea, syphilis, rheumatism, inward pains, chewed for tooth-ache, and applied externally in poultice, with bear grease for ulcers and sores, it is a great topical stimulant, changing the nature of malignant ulcers. In tooth-ache it is only a palliative, as I have ascertained on myself, the burning sensation which it produces on the mouth, merely mitigating the other pain, which returns afterwards. Some herbalists employ the bark and seeds in powder to cure intermittent fevers. A tincture of the berries has been used for violent cholics in Virginia. It is very good in diseases connected with syphilitic taint (Rafinesque, 1830, p. 115).

The dried bark of the prickly ash was officially listed in the U.S. Pharmacopoeia from 1820 to 1926 and in the National Formulary from 1926 to 1947. The dried berries were officially listed in the National Formulary from 1916 to 1947. In addition to the above uses, the prickly ash was used as a tonic, mild stimulant, antirheumatic, carminative, and antispasmodic (Vogel, 1970, p. 354). It contains volatile oils, resin, gum, and coloring matter (Tehon, 1951, p. 120). In addition, the stem and root bark contains pyrocoumarins, xanthyletin, xanthoxyletin, and the alkaloids nitidine and laurifoline, and trace amounts of four other alkaloids: chelerthrine, tembetarine, magnoflorine, and candicine (Fish et al., 1975, p. 268).

Zigadenus venenosus
S. Wats.

DEATH CAMASS
Liliaceae
Lily Family

The death camass is an erect perennial herb to 4 dm (1 ¼ ft) tall with a fibrous bulb. The leaves are linear, up to 3 dm (1 ft) long and 6 mm (¼ in) wide, folded, and mostly basal. Flowers are creamy white, about 1.5 cm (9/16 in) wide, and in dense clusters at the ends of stems. Death camass is found growing in dry plains, prairies, and open coniferous woods.

The Blackfeet name for the death camass is "e cramps." The Blackfeet and Shoshones applied the mashed raw roots to leg aches or a swollen knee; the poultice adhered without a bandage (Mur-

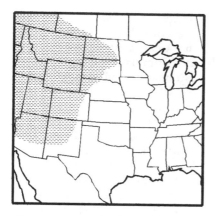

that the alkaloid content of the plant varies in direct proportion to the average daily temperature (Fluck, 1955, p. 370).

Zizia aurea (L.) Koch

GOLDEN ALEXANDERS
Apiaceae
Parsley Family

Golden alexanders is a smooth, erect perennial herb with stems branched above. The lower leaves are pinnately compound, with egg-shaped and toothed leaflets. Small yellow flowers are in flat-topped clusters at the ends of branches. Golden alexanders are found in prairies, open wooded hillsides, and thickets.

The Mesquakies used this plant for treating fevers (Smith, 1928, p. 250). The flower stalks, along with the leaves of the dotted bee-balm, *Monarda punctata* L., and daisy fleabane, *Erigeron philadel-*

phey, 1959, p. 42). The Paiutes, who live in the Great Basin, also made a wet dressing or poultice to be used on burns, rattlesnake bites, rheumatic pains, and various swellings (Train et al., 1941, p. 150). The Gosiutes, also Great Basin dwellers, used this poisonous plant as an emetic and to treat venereal disease (Burlage, 1968, p. 115).

In his 1901 "Preliminary List of Medicinal and Economic Kansas Plants," B. B. Smythe of the Kansas Medical College listed *Zigadenus elegans* and *Z. nuttallii* as cathartic, emetic, and narcotic. All parts of the plant are poisonous to humans and livestock. Humans have been poisoned by mistakenly eating the bulbs, believing they were a camass, *Camassia* species, or a wild onion, *Allium* species (Stephens, 1980, p. 143; Kindscher, 1987, pp. 74–75). All parts of the plant contain steroid alkaloids of the vertatrum group, including zygacine and vanilloyl-zygadenine (Sim, 1966, p. 151). It is believed

288

phicus L., were powdered and used as a snuff to alleviate headache.

Constantine Rafinesque reported in his 1830 *Medical Flora of the United States* that *Zizia* is "vulnerary, antisyphilitic, and sudorific" (Rafinesque, 1830, p. 267). Charles Millspaugh in his 1892 *Medicinal Plants* called it a nerve stimulant (Millspaugh, 1974, p. 260). Golden alexanders is potentially toxic and can cause vomiting (Foster and Duke, 1980, p. 110).

Glossary

Aboriginal. Indigenous or native; the first of its kind in a region

Abortifacient. A substance that causes abortion

Achene. A dry, indehiscent, one-seeded fruit

Alexiteric. A substance that is effective against infection or poison

Alicyclic. Organic chemical, essentially alphatic in behavior, but structured as a ring rather than a chain

Allelopathic. Substances that can harm or kill another plant

Alterative. A substance that gradually restores healthy bodily functions

Alternate. Growing at alternating intervals on either side of a stem

Amenorrhoea. Absence of menses

Analgesic. A remedy that relieves or allays pain

Anasarca. Fluid accumulation in the cellular tissue

Angina. Any disease in which spasmodic and painful suffocation or spasms occur; angina pectoris relates to chest pains

Anodyne. A medicine that relieves or allays pain

Anorexia. A lack of appetite or the inability to eat, usually from psychological causes

Anthelmintic. An agent that expels intestinal parasitic worms

Anthrax. An infectuous disease, usually fatal, characterized by malignant ulcers

Anticholinesterase. Any substance that inhibits the activity of the enzyme cholinesterase

Antifebrile. A substance that reduces fever

Antihydropic. A substance that relieves the excessive accumulation of serum-like fluid in a bodily cavity

Antipyretic. A substance that checks or reduces fever

Antiscorbutic. A substance that is effective in treating scurvy

Antispasmodic. Relieving or preventing spasms

Aperient. A medicine or food that acts as a mild laxative

Apothecary. A pharmacy or drugstore

Astringent. A substance that has a contracting or constrictive effect on bodily tissues

Atonic. Pertaining to, caused by, or characterized by insufficient muscular tone

Atopic. Ectopic; allergic

Bilaterally. Having two symmetrical sides

Bioregion. A geographical area defined by its unique life forms

Bolus. A small round mass

Bullae. A large vesicle containing serumlike fluid

Bursitis. Inflammation of a bursa, a serous sac in the shoulder, elbow, or knee joints

Calculous. Pertaining to or caused by stones in the kidney, gall bladder, or urinary tract

Carbuncle. A painful, circumscribed inflammation of the subcutaneous tissue

Carcinoma. A malignant tumor of the outermost bodily tissue

Carcinosarcoma. A malignant

tumor composed of both the outermost and inner bodily tissues

Cardialgy. Heartburn

Carminative. A substance that causes expulsion of gas from the stomach or bowel

Catarrh. Inflammation of the mucous membranes, especially of the nose and throat

Cathartic. A purgative; a substance that purges or cleanses, usually in reference to the bowels

Cauterization. The process of burning with a hot iron, fire, or caustic, especially for curative purposes

Cerate. A medicated substance used like an ointment but stiffer and nonmelting at room temperature; often made of lard, wax, or resin

Chilblain. A recurrent, localized, subcutaneous swelling caused by exposure to cold associated with dampness

Cholagogue. A substance that promotes the flow of bile

Chorea. Any of several diseases of the nervous system characterized by jerky, involuntary movements, chiefly of the face and extremities

Colic. A severe abdominal pain in the bowel or colon; often used in reference to infants

Conjunctivitis. Inflammation of the mucous membrane that lines the inner surface of the eyelid and exposed surface of the eyeball

Coprolite. Preserved or fossilized feces

Corroborant. Strengthening or invigorating

Counterirritant. An agent that induces local irritation to counteract general or deep irritation

Cutting. A twig or similar plant part removed to form roots and propagate a new plant

Cystic. Enclosed in a cyst

Cytotoxic. Toxic to cells

Debility. A state of abnormal bodily weakness

Decoction. A tea made by boiling a plant in water

Demulcent. A substance, often mucilaginous, used to smooth or mollify

Deobstruent. An agent that opens or removes obstructions

Depurative. A substance that cleans or purifies

Diaphoretic. A substance that produces perspiration

Discutient. An agent that causes the resolution of tumors and swellings

Diuretic. A substance that increases the volume of urine excreted

Division. The process of increasing the number of plants by dividing rhizomes, buds, or overwintering crown

Doctrine of Signatures. The belief that plants have a signature or sign that indicates for what ailment or part of the body they should be used

Dram. One-eighth ounce

Dropsy. An excessive accumulation of serumlike fluid in a serous cavity or in the subcutaneous cellular tissue

Dysentery. An infection of the lower intestinal tract that produces pain, fever, and severe diarrhea

Dysmenorrhea. Difficult or painful menstruation

Dyspepsia. Disturbed digestion, indigestion

Dyspnoea. Difficulty in breathing, often associated with lung or heart disease

Dysurea. Painful or difficult urination

Eclectic. A group of college-trained physicians from earlier in this century whose practices were based on a wide variety of techniques

Ecology. The relationship of an organism with its environment

Ecosystem. The complex of a community and its environment that forms a functioning whole in nature

Edema. An excessive accumulation of serumlike fluid in the tissue

Effusion. The seeping of serumlike or bloody fluid into a cavity

Emesis. Vomiting

Emetic. An agent that causes vomiting

Emeto-cathartic. An agent that causes both vomiting and emptying of the bowels

Emmenagogue. A substance that induces or increases menstrual flow

Emollient. An agent that softens or smooths the skin

Enteritis. Inflammation of the intestinal tract

Erysipelas. An acute infectious disease of the skin and subcutaneous tissue caused by bacteria

Escharotic. A caustic or corrosive substance

Ethnobotany. The study of the uses of plants by a culture

Ethnography. The systematic recording of human cultures

Expectorant. An agent that promotes or facilitates secretion or expulsion of mucus from the mucous membranes of the air passages

Felons. An acute or painful inflammation of the deeper tissues of a finger or toe, usually near a nail

Fibroblast. A cell that contributes to the formation of connective tissue fibers

Flatulent. Generating gas in the alimentary canal

Flix. Down; fur

Floret. A small flower, especially one of the disk or ray flowers of the Sunflower family

Flux. The discharge of large quantities of fluid material from a bodily surface or cavity

Fomentation. A medicinal compress or poultice

Forb. An herb other than a grass

Gangrene. Death or decay of tissue, usually in a limb, due to the failure of the blood supply, injury, or disease

Gastritis. Chronic or acute inflammation of the stomach

Gastroenteritis. Inflammation of the mucous membrane of the stomach and intestine

Gravel. Small concretions formed in the kidneys

Grippe. Influenza

Hemoptysis. The spitting or coughing of blood or bloody mucous

Hemostatic. A substance that arrests hemorrhage

Herb. A plant lacking persistent woody parts

Hydragogue. A substance causing the discharge of watery fluid, as from the bowels

Hydrophobia. Rabies

Hyperazotemia. An excess of nitrogenous matter, usually urea, in the blood

Hypotensive. Characterized by or causing low blood pressure

Immunostimulant. A stimulant of the immune system

Inflammatory. Pertaining to or attended with inflammation

Infusion. A tea made by pouring boiling water over a substance and letting it steep

Keratolytic. An agent that promotes the softening and dissolution or peeling of the horny layer of epidermis

Lachrymation. The process of producing tears

Lassitude. A state of exhaustion or torpor

Layering. The process of plant propagation where a shoot or twig is induced to root while still attached to the living stock, as by bending a twig and covering it with soil

Leucorrhea. A vaginal discharge containing mucous and pus cells

Liniment. A liquid preparation, usually oily, for rubbing on or applying to the skin for sprains and bruises

Lithontryptic. Having the quality of or used for dissolving or destroying stones in the bladder or kidney

Masticatory. A substance chewed to increase salivation

Melanoma. A dark-pigmented malignant tissue

Menstruum. A solvent

Moxa. A substance that is burned on the skin as a counterirritant

Nadir. A point on the celestial sphere diametrically opposite the zenith

Nasopharyngeal. Relating to the portion of the pharynx directly behind the nasal cavity and above the stiff palate

Naturalized. A plant that is not native, but has adapted to the region

Nephritic. Pertaining to the kidneys

Nervine. Affecting the nerves, calming nervous excitement

Neuralgia. A sharp and sudden pain along the course of a nerve

Offset. A short lateral shoot by which certain plants are propagated

Ophthalmia. Inflammation of the eye, especially of its membranes or external structures

Orchitis. Inflammation of the testes

Palliative. Serving to make less severe

Palpitation. Strong, rapid beating

Palsie. Condition marked by trembling or shaking

Panacea. A remedy for all diseases, a cure-all

Papescent. Having the consistency of soft food, like bread soaked in milk

Paralytic. Afflicted with or characterized by paralysis

Paroxysms. A severe attack or an increase in the violence of a disease or pain, usually recurring periodically

Parturition. Childbirth

Pectoral. Pertaining to the chest or breast

Pellant. A substance that cleanses or purifies

Peptic. Pertaining to digestion

Peripneumonia. Pneumonia or symptoms similar to it

Phagocytic. Pertaining to a blood cell that ingests and destroys foreign particles

Pharmacopoeia. A book, usually published under the jurisdiction of the government, which contains a list of drugs, methods of making medical preparations, and other information

Phthisis. A wasting away; tuberculosis

Pinnate. Having leaflets or other divisions in a featherlike arrangement on each side of a common axis

Piscicidal. Kills fish

Pomade. A scented ointment, especially one used for the scalp or hair

Postpartum. After giving birth

Prolapse. A falling down of an organ or part from its usual position; often refers to the uterus

Propagate. To increase by sexual or asexual methods

Prophylactic. A medicine or measure that protects or defends from disease

Psoriasis. A chronic skin disease characterized by scaly patches

Purgative. A substance that purges or cleanses, usually in reference to the bowels

Pyorrhoea. Inflammation of the gums and tooth sockets leading to loosening of the teeth

Quinsy. Acute inflammation of the tonsils and surrounding tissue, often leading to the formation of an abscess

Ray flower. Any of the flat, strap-shaped marginal flowers found in the Sunflower family

Renal. Pertaining to the kidneys

Resolvent. A medicine that reduces inflammation or swelling

Restoration. The act of revegetating land, such as returning a parcel of land to native prairie species

Restringent. An astringent or styptic

Rhinitis. Inflammation of the nasal mucous membrane

Rhizome. An underground stem, usually lateral and rooting at the nodes

Rubefacient. A substance that irritates the skin, producing redness

Scabies. A contagious skin disease caused by mites that burrow under the skin

Scarify. To cut or soften the wall of a hard seed to hasten germination; to make superficial cuts, as in surgery

Scleroderma. A disease in which all layers of the skin become hardened and rigid

Scorbutic. Pertaining or affected by scurvy

Scrofula. Tuberculosis of the lymph nodes characterized chiefly by swelling and degeneration of the lymphatic glands

Scurfy. Resembling or covered with scaly matter or encrustations

Scurvy. A disease caused by lack of vitamin C, marked by swollen and bleeding gums and prostration

Sedative. A substance that has a soothing, calming, or tranquilizing effect

Semipellucid. Semitranslucent; semitransparent

Sepal. One of the segments, usually green, that form the outer protective covering of a flower

Septicemia. Blood poisoning caused by pathogenic organisms or their toxins in the blood stream

Serous. Containing, secreting, or resembling serum

Sialogogue. A substance causing salivary flow

Spasmolytic. Relating to or bringing relief from a muscle spasm

Stamen. The pollen-producing reproduction organ of a flower

Sternutatory. Causing or tending to cause sneezing

Stomatitis. Inflammation of the mucous tissues of the mouth

Strangury. Slow painful urination with spasms of the urethra and bladder

Stratification. The process of storing seeds in a cold, moist environment to promote germination

Styptic. Tending to check bleeding; hemostatic, astringent

Sudorific. Causing or increasing sweat

Suture. Joining of the lips or edges of a wound by stitching or a similar process

Tenesmus. A painful, urgent, but ineffectual attempt to urinate or defecate

Trachoma. A contagious viral disease of the conjuctiva characterized by inflammations, hypertrophy, and granulations on the conjunctival surfaces

Treponema. Any of several anaerobic organisms, including syphilis

Typhoid. An infectious, often fatal disease, usually occurring in the summer, characterized by intestinal inflammation and ulceration

Typhus. An acute, infectious disease characterized by extreme prostration, severe nervous symptoms, and

eruption of reddish spots on
the body

Urethritis. Inflammation of the
urethra

Vermifuge. A substance that
serves to expel worms

Vertigo. A disordered state in
which a person or his or her
surroundings seems to be
whirling about

Vesicant. An agent that produces a
blister or blisters

Vesicle. A small, bladder-like
cavity, especially one filled
with fluid

Vulnerary. Used as a remedy for
wounds

Whorl. An arrangement of leaves,
petals, or other parts radiating
from a single node or organ

Literature Cited

Afifi, F. U., S. Al-Khalis, M. Aqel, M. H. Al-Muhteseb, M. Jaghabir, M. Saket, and A. Muheid. 1990. Antagonistic Effect of *Eryngium creticum* Extract on Scorpion Venom in Vitro. *Journal of Ethnopharmacology* 29: 43–49.

Albert-Puleo, Michael. 1978. Mythobotany, Pharmacology, and Chemistry of Thujone-containing Plants and Derivatives. *Economic Botany* 32: 65–74.

Ali, M. S., G. C. Sharma, R. S. Asplund, M. P. Nevins, and S. Garb. 1978. Isolation of Antitumor Polysaccharide Fractions from *Yucca glauca* Nutt. (Liliaceae). *Growth* 42(2): 213–23.

Andros, F. 1883. The Medicine and Surgery of the Winnebago and Dakota Indians. *American Medical Association Journal* 1: 116–18.

Arnason, Thor, Richard J. Herbda, and Timothy Johns. 1981. Use of Plants for Food and Medicine by Native Peoples of Eastern Canada. *Canadian Journal of Botany* 59 (11): 2189–2325.

Art, Henry W. 1986. *A Garden of Wildflowers*. Pownal, Vt.: Storey Communications.

Backer, R. C., E. Bianchi, and J. R. Cole. 1972. A Phytochemical Investigation of *Yucca schottii* (Liliaceae). *Journal of Pharmaceutical Science* 61: 1665–66.

Bailey, Liberty Hyde, and Ethel Zoe Bailey. 1976. *Hortus Third: A Concise Dictionary of Plants Cultivated in the United States and Canada*. Revision by L. H. Bailey Hortorium Staff. New York: Macmillan.

Bailey, Ralph. 1962. *The Self-pronouncing Dictionary of Plant Names*. Garden City, N.Y.: American Garden Guild.

Balandrin, Manuel F., James A. Klocke, Eve S. Wurtele, and Wm. Hugh Bollinger. 1985. Natural Plant Chemicals: Sources of Industrial and Medicinal Materials. *Science* 228: 1154–60.

Ballentine, Carol, Annabel Hecht, Herman Janiger, and Shelly Maifarth. 1985. Pretty but Poisonous. *FDA Consumer* 19 (May): 41.

Ballentine, Carol, and Shelly Maifarth. 1987. Luring Consumers down the Primrose Path. *FDA Consumer* 21 (November): 34–35.

Bard, Kathryn. 1982. The Archeology of Peppermint. *Early Man* (Autumn): 36–37.

Bare, Janét. 1979. *Wildflowers and Weeds of Kansas*. Lawrence: Regents Press of Kansas.

Barr, Claude A. 1983. *Jewels of the Plains—Wild Flowers of the Great Plains Grasslands and Hills*. Minneapolis: University of Minnesota Press.

Baurer, Von Rudolf, Ikhlas A. Khan, and Hildebert Wagner. 1987. Echinacea: Nachweis einer Verfalschung von *Echinacea purpurea* (L.) Moench mit *Parthenium integrifolium* L. *Deutsche Apotheker-Zeitung* 127: 1325–30.

Beal, James H. 1921. Comment on the Paper by Couch and Giltner on "An Experimental Study of Echinacea Therapy." *American Journal of Pharmacy* 93: 229–32.

Beardsley, G. 1941. Notes on Cree Medicines, Based on a Collection Made by I. Cowie in 1892. *Michigan Academy of Arts, Science, and Letters* 27: 483–96.

Beath, O. A. 1914. The Composition and Properties of the Yucca Plant. *Kansas Academy of Science* 27: 102–7.

Bemis, W. P., L. D. Curtis, C. W. Weber, and J. Berry. 1978. The Feral Buffalo Gourd, *Cucurbita foetidissima. Economic Botany*: 32: 87–95.

Beringer, G. M. 1911. Fluid Extract of Echinacea. *American Journal of Pharmacy*: 83: 324–25.

Berman, A. 1987. President's Column. *Missouri Prairie Journal* 8: 2.

Beuscher, Norbert, and Lothar Kopanski. 1985. Stimulation der Immunantwort durch Inhaltsstoffe aus *Baptisia tinctoria. Planta Medica* 51: 381–84.

Bigelow, Jacob. 1817. *American Medical Botany*. Vol. 1. Boston: Cummin and Hilliard.

Black, M. Jean. 1978. Plant Dispersal by Native North Americans in the Canadian Subarctic. In: *The Nature and Status of Ethnobotany*, edited by Richard I. Ford. Anthropological Papers of the Museum of Anthropology, University of Michigan, no. 67, pp. 255–62.

Blankenship, J. W. 1905. Native Economic Plants of Montana. Montana Agriculture Experiment Station, Bulletin 56.

Bodinet, C., N. Beuscher, and L. Kopanski. 1989. Purification of Immunologically Active Glycoproteins from *Baptisia tinctoria* Roots by Affinity Chromatography and Isolectric Focussing. *Planta Medica* 55: 659.

Bohlmann, F., M. Ahmed, M. Grenz, R. M. King, and H. Robinson. 1983. Bisabolene Derivatives and Other Constituents from *Coreopsis* Species. *Phytochemistry* 22: 2858–59.

Bolyard, Judith, W. Hardy Eshbaugh, Ronald D. Daley, and S. Michael Gaston. 1981. *Medicinal Plants and Home Remedies of Appalachia*. Springfield, Ill.: Charles C. Thomas.

Bonadeo, I., G. Bottazzi, and M. Lavazza. 1971. Echinacin B, an Active Polysaccharide from Echinacea. *Revista Italiana Essenze Profumi, Piante Officinali, Aromi, Saponi, Cosmetici, Aerosol* 53: 281–95.

Bray, Edmund C., and Martha Coleman Bray, editors and translators. 1976. *Joseph N. Nicollet on the Plains and Prairies—the Expeditions of 1838–39 with Journals, Letters, and Notes on the Dakota Indians*. St. Paul: Minnesota

Historical Society Press.
Briggs, Colin J. 1988. Senega
Snakeroot—A Traditional
Canadian Herbal Medicine.
*Canadian Pharmaceutical
Journal* 121: 199–200.
Brower, Lincoln P., Peter B.
McEvoy, Kenneth L. Williamson,
and Maureen A. Flannary. 1972.
Variation in Cardiac Glycoside
Content of Monarch Butterflies
from Natural Populations in
Eastern North America. *Science*
177: 426–29.
Brown, Lois Margaret. 1968.
Chemical Constituents of Some
Native Medicinal Plants.
Master's thesis, University of
Alberta.
Buechel, Eugene. 1983. *A
Dictionary of Teton Sioux
Lakota–English : English–
Lakota.* Pine Ridge, S. Dak.: Red
Cloud Indian School.
Burlage, Henry M. 1968. *Index of
Plants of Texas with Reputed
Medicinal and Poisonous
Properties.* Austin, Tex.: By the
author.
Bushnell, David, I., Jr. 1909. *The
Choctaw of Bayou Lacomb St.
Tammany Parish, Louisiana.*
Washington, D.C.: Smithsonian
Institution, Bureau of American
Ethnology, Bulletin 48.
Camazine, Scott, and Robert A.
Bye. 1980. A Study of the
Medical Ethnobotany of the
Zuni Indians of New Mexico.
Journal of Ethnopharmacology
2: 365–88.
Campbell, T. N. 1951. Medicinal
Plants Used by the Choctaw,

Chickasaw, and Creek Indians
in the Early Nineteenth
Century. *Journal of the
Washington Academy of
Science* 41 (9): 285–90.
Carlson, Gustav G., and Volney H.
Jones. 1939. Some Notes on
Uses of Plants by the Comanche
Indians. *Michigan Academy of
Science, Arts, and Letters* 25:
517–42.
Carpenter, Charles M, R. A. Boak,
L. A. Mucci, A. B. Warren, and
S. L. Warren. 1933. Studies on
the Physiologic Effects of Fever
Temperatures. *Journal of
Laboratory and Clinical
Medicine* 18 (10): 981–90.
Chamberlin, Ralph V. 1909. Some
Plant Names of the Ute Indians.
American Anthropologist 11:
27–40.
Chandler, R. F. 1985. Licorice,
More Than Just a Flavour.
*Canadian Pharmaceutical
Journal* 118: 421–24.
——— . 1989. Yarrow. *Canadian
Pharmaceutical Journal* 122:
41–43.
Chandler, R. F., S. N. Hooper, and
M. J. Harvey. 1982. Ethnobotany
and Phytochemistry of Yarrow,
Achillea millefolium,
Compositae. *Economic Botany*
36 (2): 203–23.
Chang, D. J., S. K. W. Khalil, and
L. J. Schermeister. 1970.
Separation of a Cardiac
Glycoside from *Penstemon
grandiflorus*. *Planta Medica* 19:
324–27.
Conn, Jerome W., David R. Rovner,
and Edwin L. Cohen. 1968.

Licorice-Induced Pseudoaldo-
steronism. *American Medical
Association Journal* 205:
492–96.
Costello, David F. 1981. *The
Prairie World*. Minneapolis:
University of Minnesota Press.
Couch, James F., and Leigh T.
Giltner. 1920. An Experimental
Study of Echinacea Therapy.
Journal of Agricultural Research
20 (1): 63–84.
Council on Pharmacy and
Chemistry. 1909. Echinacea
Considered Valueless. *American
Medical Association Journal*
53: 1836.
Croom, Edward M., Junior. 1983.
Documenting and Evaluating
Herbal Remedies. *Economic
Botany* 37 (1): 13–27.
Cunitz, Von G. 1968. Zur Wirkung
von Succus Liquirtiae auf die
Heilung experimenteller
Hautwunden. *Arzneimittel-
Forschung* 18: 434–35.
Curtin, Lenora Scott Muse. 1976.
*Healing Herbs of the Upper Rio
Grande*. New York: Arno Press.
Davis, N. S. 1949. Report of the
Committee on Indigenous
Medical Botany. *American
Medical Association
Transactions* 2: 663.
Declume, C. 1989. Anti-
inflammatory Evaluation of a
Hydroalcoholic Extract of Black
Current Leaves (*Ribes nigrum*).
Journal of Ethnopharmacology
27: 91–98.
De Laszlo, Henry, and Paul S.
Henshaw. 1954. Plant Materials
Used by Primitive Peoples to

Affect Fertility. *Science* 119:
626–31.
Denig, Edwin Thompson. 1855.
An Account of Medicine and
Surgery as It Exists among
the Cree Indians. *St. Louis
Medical and Surgical Journal*
13: 312–18.
———. 1930. *Indian Tribes of the
Upper Missouri*. Edited by
J. N. B. Hewitt. Washington,
D.C.: Smithsonian Institution,
Bureau of American Ethnology,
Bulletin 44.
Densmore, Frances. 1974 (1928).
*How Indians Use Wild Plants
for Food, Medicine, and Crafts*
(formerly titled *Uses of Plants
by the Chippewa Indians*). New
York: Dover Publications.
———. 1936. *Teton Sioux Music*.
Washington, D.C.: Smithsonian
Institution, Bureau of American
Ethnology, Bulletin 61.
Dittmer, Howard J., and Burney P.
Talley, 1964. Gross Morphology
of Tap Roots of Desert
Cucurbits. *Botanical Gazette*
125 (2): 121–26.
Dominguez, X. A., E. Gomez,
A. Gomez, N. Villarreal, and
C. Rombold. 1970. Physical Data
on the Essential Oils of Five
Compositae Plants. *Planta
Medica* 19: 52–54.
Duke, James A. 1985. *CRC
Handbook of Medicinal Herbs*.
Boca Raton, Fla.: CRC Press.
———. 1986. *Handbook of
Northeastern Indian Medicinal
Plants*. Lincoln, Mass.:
Quarterman Publications.
———. 1987. *Psoralea*

corylifolia L. (Fabaceae).
Economic Botany 41: 524–26.
Dunbar, John D. 1880. The Pawnee
Indians. *Magazine of American
History* 5 (5): 321–42.
Ellingwood, Finley. 1902. *A
Systematic Treatise on Materia
Medica and Therapeutics*.
Chicago: Chicago Medical
Press Co.
Elmore, Francis H. 1944.
Ethnobotany of the Navajo.
University of New Mexico,
Monographs of the School of
American Research. Number 8.
El-Olemy, M. M., J. J. Sabatka, and
S. J. Stohs. 1974. Sapogenins of
Yucca glauca Seeds.
Phytochemistry 13: 489–92.
Elvin-Lewis, Memory. 1979.
Empirical Rationale for Teeth
Cleaning Plant Selection.
Medical Anthropology. Fall
1979: 431–56.
Embroden, William. 1979.
Narcotic Plants. New York:
Macmillan.
Erichsen-Brown, Charlotte. 1979.
*Use of Plants for the Past 500
Years*. Aurora, Ontario: Breezy
Creeks Press.
Farnsworth, Norman R., A. S.
Bingel, G. A. Cordell, F. A.
Crane, and H. H. S. Fong. 1975.
Potential Value of Plants as
Sources of New Antifertility
Agents I. *Journal of
Pharmaceutical Sciences* 64 (4):
535–91.
Felger, Richard S. 1979. Ancient
Crops for the Twenty-first
Century. In: *New Agricultural
Crops*. Edited by Gary Richie.

AAAS Selected Symposium
No. 38. Boulder, Colo.:
Westview Press.
Felter, H.W. 1898. The Newer
Materia Medica. I. Echinacea.
Eclectic Medical Journal 58:
79–89.
Fish, F., A. I. Gray, P. G. Waterman,
and F. Donachie. 1975.
Alkaloids and Coumarins from
North American *Zanthoxylum*
species. *Lloydia* 38: 268–70.
Fletcher, Alice C., and Francis
La Flesche. 1911. The Omaha
Tribe. Washington, D.C.: Smith-
sonian Institution, Bureau of
American Ethnology, *27th
Annual Report*.
Fluck, H. 1955. The Influence of
Climate on the Active
Principles in Medicinal Plants.
*Journal of Pharmacy and
Pharmacology* 7: 361–85.
Fong, H. H. S., W. Bhatti, and N. R.
Farnsworth. 1972. Antitumor
Activity of Certain Plants Due
to Tannins. *Journal of
Pharmaceutical Sciences*
61: 1818.
Foster, Steven. 1984. *Herbal
Bounty! The Gentle Art of Herb
Culture*. Salt Lake City:
Peregrine Smith Books.
———. 1985. Echinacea.
American Horticulturist
August: 14–17.
———. 1991. *Echinacea—
Nature's Immune Enhancer*.
Rochester, Vt.: Healing
Arts Press.
Foster, Steven, and James A. Duke.
1990. *A Field Guide to
Medicinal Plants: Eastern and*

Central North America. Boston: Houghton Mifflin.

Frohne, Dietrich, and Hans Jurgen Pfander. 1984. *A Colour Atlas of Poisonous Plants*. London: Wolfe Publishing.

Gaertner, Erika E. 1979. The History and Use of Milkweed (*Asclepias syriaca L.*). *Economic Botany* 33 (2): 119–23.

Galinat, W.C. 1959. Plant Remains from the Lodaiska Site in the Denver, Colorado Area. *Denver Museum of Natural History Proceedings* 8: 104–118.

Gassinger, Bon C. A., G. Winstel, and P. Netter. 1981. Klinische Prufung zum Nachweis der therapeutischen Wirksamkeit des homopathischen Arzneimittels Eupatorium perfoliatum D 2 (Wasserhanf composite) bei der Diagnose. *Arzneimittel Forschung* 31 (1): 732–33.

Gerarde, John. 1636. *The Herball, or General Historie of Plantes*. London: Iliffe, Norton, and Whittaker.

Gershenzon, Jonathan, and Tom J. Mabry. 1984. Sesquiterpene Lactones from a Texas Population of *Helianthus maximiliani*. *Phytochemistry* 23: 1959–66.

Gibson, Melvin R. 1978. Glycyrhiza in Old and New Perspectives. *Lloydia* 41 (4): 348–54.

Gill, S., M.W. Dembinska, and S.M. Zielinska. 1981. Investigation of Chemistry and Biological Activity of Lactones of *Gaillardia aristata* Pursh. Herb. Part 1. Isolation of Sesquiterpene Lactones. *Herba Polish* 27: 213–19.

Gilmore, Melvin. 1913a. A Study in the Ethnobotany of the Omaha Indians. *Nebraska State Historical Society* 17: 314–57.

———. 1913b. Some Native Nebraska Plants with Their Uses by the Dakota. *Nebraska State Historical Society* 17: 358–70.

———. 1914. Trip with White Eagle Determining Pawnee Sites." Unpublished Manuscript No. 231, Nebraska State Historical Society Archives.

———. 1930. Notes on Gynecology and Obstetrics of the Arikara Tribe. *Michigan Academy of Science, Arts, and Letters* 14:71–81.

———. 1977 (1919). *Uses of Plants by the Indians of the Missouri River Region*. Lincoln: University of Nebraska Press. Reprint of a work first published as the 33rd Annual Report of the Bureau of American Ethnology. Washington, D.C., 1919.

Giordano, O. S., E. Guerreiro, M. J. Pestchanker, J. Guzman, D. Pastor, and T. Guardia. 1990. The Gastric Cytoprotective Effect of Several Sesquiterpene Lactones. *Journal of Natural Products* 53: 803–09.

Great Plains Flora Association. 1977. *Atlas of the Flora of the Great Plains*. Ames: Iowa State University Press.

———. 1986. *Flora of the Great*

Plains. Lawrence: University Press of Kansas.

Grinnell, George Bird. 1905. Some Cheyenne Plant Medicines. *American Anthropologist* 7 (new series): 37–43.

———. 1962. *The Cheyenne Indians*. 2 vols. New York: Cooper Square Publishers.

Hart, Jeffrey A. 1976. *Montana: Native Plants and Early Peoples*. Helena: Montana Historical Society.

———. 1981. The Ethnobotany of the Northern Cheyenne Indians of Montana. *Journal of Ethnopharmacology* 4: 1–55.

Hartzell, A. 1947. Plant Products for Insecticidal Properties and Summary of Results to Date. *Contributions of the Boyce Thompson Institute* 15: 21–34.

Havard, V. 1877. Botanical Outlines of the Country Marched over by the Seventh United States Cavalry during the Summer of 1877. *Annual Report Chief of Engineers, U.S.A.*, Appendix QQ: 1681–87.

Havenhill, L. D. 1919. The Cultivation of Medicinal Plants. *Kansas Academy of Science Transactions* 38: 33–39.

Hayden, F. V. 1859. Botany: in "Report of the Secretary of War," 35th Congress, 2nd Session, 1858–1859, Senate Executive Document, Vol. 3, No. 1, Part 3, pp. 726–47.

Hellson, John C. 1974. Ethnobotany of the Blackfoot Indians. National Museum of Man, Mercury Series, *Canadian*

Ethnology Service Paper No. 19.

Henkel, Alice. 1906. Wild Medicinal Plants of the United States. *USDA Bureau of Plant Industry Bulletin* No. 89.

———. 1907. American Root Drugs. *USDA Bureau of Plant Industry Bulletin* No. 107.

———. 1911. American Medicinal Leaves and Herbs. *USDA Bureau of Plant Industry Bulletin* No. 219.

Herz, Werner, Palaiyur S. Kalyanaraman, Ganapathy Ramakrishnan, and John F. Blount. 1977. Sesquiterpene Lactones of *Eupatorium perfoliatum*. *Journal of Organic Chemistry* 42: 2264–71.

Heyl, F. W., and M. C. Hart. 1915. Some Constituents of *Brauneria angustifolia*. *Journal of the American Chemical Society* 37 (7): 1769–78.

Hinman, C. Wiley. 1984. New Crops for Arid Lands. *Science* 225: 1445–48.

Hobbs, Christopher. 1989. *The Echinacea Handbook*. Portland, Ore.: Eclectic Medical Publications.

Hocking, G. M. 1956. Some Plant Material Used Medicinally and Otherwise by the Navaho Indians in the Chaco Canyon, New Mexico. *El Palacio* 63: 161.

———. 1965. *Echinacea angustifolia* as a Crude Drug. *Quarterly Journal of Crude Drug Research* 5 (1): 679–82.

Horrobin, D. F. 1984. Placebo-controlled Trials of Evening Primrose Oil. *Swedish Journal* of *Biological Medicine* 3: 13–17.

Hrdlicka, Ales. 1932. Disease, Medicine and Surgery among the American Aborigines. *Journal of the American Medical Association* 99: 1661–66.

Hunter, John D. 1957. *Manners and Customs of Several Indian Tribes*. Minneapolis: Ross and Haines.

Itoigawa, M., N. Kumagai, H. Sekiya, K. Ito, and H. Furukawa. 1981. Isolation and Structures of Sesquiterpene Lactones from North Carolina. *Yakugaku Zasshi* 101: 605–13.

Jackson, Donald, and Mary Lee Spence, editors. 1970. *The Expeditions of John Charles Frémont*, Vol. 1. Urbana: University of Illinois Press.

Jackson, Wes. 1985. *New Roots for Agriculture*. Lincoln: University of Nebraska Press.

Jacobson, Martin. 1954. Occurrence of a Pungent Insecticidal Principle in American Coneflower Roots. *Science* 120: 125–29.

Johnston, A. 1970. Blackfoot Indian Utilization of the Flora of the Northwestern Great Plains. *Economic Botany* 24: 301–24.

Jordan, Julia Anne. 1965. *Ethnobotany of the Kiowa-Apache*. Master's thesis, University of Oklahoma.

Kearney, Thomas H., and Robert H. Peebles, 1951. *Arizona Flora*. Berkeley: University of California Press.

Keller, Konstantin, and Egon Stahl.

1983. Composition of the Essential Oil from Beta-Asarone Free Calamus. *Planta Medica* 47: 71–74.

Keller, Konstantin, Karl P. Odenthal, and Elke Leng-Peschlow. 1985. Spasmolytische Wirkung des Isoasaronfreien Kalmus. *Planta Medica* 47: 6–9.

Kemal, M., S. K. W. Khalis, and N. G. S. Rao. 1979. Isolation and Identification of a Cannabinoid-like Compound from *Amorpha* species. *Journal of Natural Products* 42: 463–68.

Kindscher, K. 1987. *Edible Wild Plants of the Prairie: An Ethnobotanical Guide*. Lawrence: University Press of Kansas.

Kinghorn, A. D., and F. J. Evans. 1975. A Biological Screen of Selected Species of the Genus *Euphorbia* for Skin Irritant Effects. *Planta Medica* 28: 325–35.

Kingsbury, John M. 1964. *Poisonous Plants of the United States and Canada*. Englewood Cliffs, N. J.: Prentice Hall.

Koch, William E. 1980. *Folklore from Kansas—Customs, Beliefs, and Superstitions*. Lawrence: Regents Press of Kansas.

Krochmal, A., and S. Paur. 1951. Canaigre—A Desert Source of Tannin. *Economic Botany* 5: 367–77.

Krochmal, Arnold, Leon Wilken, and Millie Chien. 1972. Plant and Lobeline Harvest of *Lobelia inflata* L. *Economic Botany* 26: 216–20.

Krochmal, A., and Connie Krochmal. 1973. *A Guide to the Medicinal Plants of the United States.* New York: New York Times Book Co.

Kroeber, A. L. 1908. The Ethnology of the Gros Ventre. *American Museum of Natural History, Anthropological Papers* 1: 145–281.

Kupchan, S. Morris, Richard J. Hemingway, and Raymond W. Doskotch. 1964. Tumor Inhibitors. IV. Apocannoside and Cymarin, the Cytotoxic Principles of *Apocynum cannabinum* L. *Journal of Medicinal Chemistry* 7: 803–4.

Kuyantseva A. M., and E. S. Davidyants. 1988. Regenerative Activity of *Silphium perfoliatum* Extract. *Farmatsiya Moscow* 37: 36–38.

La Flesche, Francis. 1932. *A Dictionary of the Osage Language.* Washington, D.C.: Smithsonian Institution, Bureau of American Ethnology, Bulletin 109.

Lampe, Kenneth F., and Mary Ann McCann. 1985. *AMA Handbook of Poisonous and Injurious Plants.* Chicago: American Medical Association.

Lee, P. K., D. P. Carew, and J. Rosazza. 1972. *Apocynum cannabinum* Tissue Culture. Growth and Chemical Analysis. *Lloydia* 35: 150–56.

Leung, A. Y. 1980. *Encyclopedia of Common Natural Ingredients Used in Food, Drugs, and Cosmetics.* New York: John Wiley and Sons.

Lewis, John R. 1974. Carbenoxolone Sodium in the Treatment of Peptic Ulcer. *American Medical Association Journal* 229: 460–62.

Lewis, Walter H., and Memory Elvin-Lewis. 1977. *Medical Botany.* New York: Wiley.

Linard, A., P. Delaveau, and R. R. Paris. 1978. Sur les Flavonoides du *Lespedeza capitata* Michaux. *Plantes Medicinales et Phytotherapie* 12: 144–47.

Lloyd, John Uri. 1904. History of *Echinacea angustifolia. American Journal of Pharmacy* 76 (1): 15–19.

———. 1917. A Treatise on Echinacea. *Drug Treatise* No. 30.

———. 1918. A Treatise on Eupatorium Perfoliatum. *Drug Treatise* No. 32.

———. 1921a. Echinacea. *American Journal of Pharmacy* 93: 229.

———. 1921b. *Origin and History of All the Pharmacopeial Vegetable Drugs, Chemicals, and Preparations.* Cincinnati: Caxton Press.

Lloyd, John Uri, and Curtis Gates Lloyd. 1886. *Drugs and Medicines of North America.* Cincinnati: Robert Clarke.

Locock, R. A. 1987. Acorus Calamus. *Canadian Pharmaceutical Journal* 120:341–44.

McClintock, Walter. 1909. Materia Medica of the Blackfeet. *Zeitschrift fur Ethnologie*: 273–79.

————. 1923. *Old Indian Trails.* Boston: Houghton Mifflin Company.

McGregor, Ronald L. 1968. The Taxonomy of the Genus *Echinacea* (Compositae). *University of Kansas Science Bulletin* 48 (4): 113–42.

Marshall, H. H., and R. W. Scora. 1972. A New Chemical Race of *Monarda fistulosa* (Labiatae). *Canadian Journal of Botany* 50:1845–49.

Martin, Craig E. 1988. Want Directions? Look at the Compassplant. *Grassland Heritage Foundation* 4 (1): 1–2.

Menichini, F., F. D. Monache, and G. B. Marini Bettolo. 1982. Flavonoids and Rotenoids from Tephrosieae and Related Tribes of Leguminosae. *Planta Medica* 45:243–44.

Meyer, H. C. F. 1887. Echinacea Angustifolia. *Eclectic Medical Journal* 83: 315–24.

Millspaugh, Charles F. 1974 (1892). *American Medicinal Plants.* New York: Dover.

Mitchell, John, and Arthur Rook. 1979. *Botanical Dermatology—Plants and Plant Products Injurious to the Skin.* Vancouver, B.C.: Greengrass Press.

Moerman, Daniel E. 1982. *Geraniums for the Iroquois: A Field Guide to American Indian Medicinal Plants.* Algonac, Mich.: Reference Publications.

Mooney, J. 1891. The Sacred Formulas of the Cherokees. Washington, D.C.: Smithsonian Institution, Bureau of American Ethnology, 7th Annual Report, 1885–1886, pp. 301–98.

Moore, Michael. 1979. *Medicinal Plants of the Mountain West.* Santa Fe: Museum of New Mexico Press.

Munson, Patrick J. 1981. Contributions to Osage and Lakota Ethnobotany. *Plains Anthropology* 26: 229–40.

Murphey, Edith Van Allen. 1959. *Indian Uses of Native Plants.* Ft. Bragg, Calif.: Mendocino County Historical Society.

Nebraska Statewide Arboretum. (No date.) *Common & Scientific Names of Nebraska Plants: Native and Introduced.* Lincoln: University of Nebraska, Forestry Sciences Laboratory, Publication Number 101.

Nickel, Robert K. 1974. *Plant Resource Utilization at a Late Prehistoric Site in North-central South Dakota.* Master's thesis, University of Nebraska.

Nickerson, Gifford S. 1966. Some Data on Plains and Great Basin Indian Uses of Certain Native Plants. *Tebiwa* 9.1: 45–47.

Nicollier, G., and A. C. Thompson. 1983. Flavonoids of *Desmanthus illinoensis. Journal of Natural Products* 46: 112–17.

Nikol'skaya, B. S. 1954. The Blood-clotting and Wound-healing Properties of Preparations of Plant Origin. *Trudy Vsesoyuz. Obshchesiva Fiziologov, Biokhimikov i Farmakologov, Akad. Nauk S.S.S.R.* 2: 194–197.

Ognyanov, I., and T. Somleva.

1980. Rotenoids and 7,2′,4′,5′-Tetramethoxyisoflavone in *Amorpha fruticosa* L. Fruits. *Planta Medica* 38: 278–80.

Olch, Peter D. 1985. Treading the Elephant's Tail: Medical Problems on the Overland Trails. *Bulletin of the History of Medicine* 59: 196–212.

Parsons, J. J. 1985. On "Bioregionalism" and "Watershed Consciousness." *Professional Geographer* 37 (1): 1–6.

The Pharmacopoeia of the United States of America. 1882. New York: William Wood.

The Pharmacopoeia of the United States of America. 1905. Philadelphia: Blakiston's Son.

The Pharmacopoeia of the United States of America. 1926. Tenth Decennial Revision. 1920. Philadelphia: J. B. Lippincott.

The Pharmacopoeia of the United States of America. 1965. Seventeenth Revision. Easton, Pa.: Mack Publishing Co.

Phillips, Jan. 1979. *Wild Edibles of Missouri*. Jefferson City: Conservation Commission of the State of Missouri.

Phillips Petroleum Company. 1959. *Pasture and Range Plants*. 6 sections. Bartlesville, Okla.

Piatak, David M., J. Patel, C. E. Totten, and R. P. Swenson. 1985. Cell Growth Inhibitory Glycosides from *Asclepias amplexicaulis*. *Journal of Natural Products* 48: 470–71.

Pichon, P. N., J. Raynaud, and C. Mure. 1985. O-Glycosyl Flavonols of *Ceanothus americanus* L. (Rhamnaceae). *Annuals of Pharmaceutical Franceise* 43: 27–30.

Pinkas, M., N. Didry, M. Torck, L. Bezanger, and J. C. Cazin. 1978. Phenolic Components from Some Species of *Grindelia*. *Annuals of Pharmaceutical Franceise* 36: 97–104.

Pitts, Olin M., Hugh S. Thompson, and J. H. Hoch. 1969. Antibacterial Activity of *Solanum carolinense* L. *Journal of Pharmaceutical Science* 58: 379–80.

Rafinesque, Constantine S. 1828, 1830. *Medical Flora or Manual of Medical Botany of the United States*. 2 vols. Philadelphia: Samuel C. Atkinson.

Reichling, J., and U. Thron. 1989. Comparative Study on the Production and Accumulation of Unusual Phenylpropanoids in Plants and In Vitro Cultures of *Coreopsis tinctoria* and *C. lanceolata*. *Pharmaceutisch Weekblad* 11: 83–86.

Rimpler, H. 1970. Hastatoside, a New Iridoid from *Verbena hastata*. *Lloydia* 33(4): 491.

Rizk, A. M. 1986. *The Phytochemistry of the Flora of Qatar*. Doha: University of Qatar.

Robbins, Wilfred, John P. Harrington, and Barbara Freire-Marreco. 1916. *Ethnobotany of the Tewa*. Washington, D.C.: Smithsonian Institution, Bureau of American Ethnology, Bulletin 55.

Rock, Harold W. 1977. *Prairie Propagation Handbook.* Milwaukee: Milwaukee County Park System, Wehr Nature Center.

Rogers, D. J. 1980. *Lakota Names and Traditional Uses of Native Plants by Sicangu (Brule) People in the Rosebud Area, South Dakota.* St. Francis, S.Dak.: Rosebud Educational Society.

Salac, S. S., P. N. Jensen, J. A. Dickerson, and R. W. Gray, Jr. 1978. Wildflowers for Nebraska Landscapes. Nebraska Agricultural Experiment Station, MP 35.

Sale, Kirkpatrick. 1985. *Dwellers in the Land: The Bioregional Vision.* San Francisco: Sierra Club Books.

Sayre, L. E. 1895. Cucurbita Foetidissima and Ipomea Leptophylla. *American Pharmacy Association Proceedings* 43: 297–302.

———. 1897. Therapeutical Notes and Descriptions of Parts of Medicinal Plants Growing in Kansas. *Kansas Academy of Science Transactions* 16: 85–89.

———. 1903. Echinacea Roots. *Kansas Academy of Science Transactions* 19: 209–13.

Schroeder, Daniel R., and Frank R. Stermitz. 1984. Hordenine and N-methyl-4-methoxyphen-ethylamine from *Eriogonum* species. *Journal of Natural Products* 47: 555–56.

Schulte, K. E., G. Ruecher, and J. Perlick. 1967. Polyacetylene Compounds in *Echinacea*

purpurea and *E. angustifolia. Arzneimittel Forschung* 17 (7): 825–29.

Segal, R., S. Pisanty, R. Wormser, E. Azaz, and M. N. Sela. 1985. Anticariogenic Activity of Licorice and Glycyrrhizine I: Inhibition of In Vitro Plaque Formation by *Streptococcus mutans. Journal of Pharmaceutical Sciences* 74: 79–81.

Shemluck, Melvin. 1982. Medicinal and Other Uses of the Compositae by Indians in the United States and Canada. *Journal of Ethnopharmacology* 5: 303–58.

Sim, Stephen K. 1966. *Medicinal Plant Alkaloids.* Toronto: University of Toronto Press.

Simon, David Z., and Jacques Beliveau. 1986. Extraction by Hydrodiffusion of the Essential Oil of *Monarda fistulosa* Grown in the Province of Quebec: Assay of Geraniol in the Hydrodiffused Oil. *International Journal of Crude Drug Research* 24: 120–22.

Smith, Huron H. 1923. Ethnobotany of the Menomini Indians. *Bulletin of the Public Museum of the City of Milwaukee* 4 (1): 1–174.

———. 1928. Ethnobotany of the Meskwaki Indians. *Bulletin of the Public Museum of the City of Milwaukee* 4 (2): 175–326.

———. 1928. Ethnobotany of the Ojibwa Indians. *Bulletin of the Public Museum of the City of Milwaukee* 4 (3): 327–525.

———. 1933. Ethnobotany of the Forest Potawatomi Indians. *Bulletin of the Public Museum of the City of Milwaukee* 7 (1): 105–127.

Smith, J. Robert, and Beatrice S. Smith. 1980. *The Prairie Garden.* Madison: University of Wisconsin Press.

Smith, L.W., and C. C. J. Culvenor. 1981. Plant Sources of Hepatotoxic Pyrrolizidine Alkaloids. *Journal of Natural Products* 44: 129–149.

Smythe, B. B. 1901. Preliminary List of Medicinal and Economic Kansas Plants. *Kansas Academy of Science Transactions* 18: 191–209.

Snegirev, D. P. 1959. Antibiotic and Chemical Properties of Phytocides. *Trudy Gosudarst. Nikistsk. Botan. Sada* 30: 36–40.

Stephens, Homer A. 1980. *Poisonous Plants of the Central United States.* Lawrence: Regents Press of Kansas.

Stevens, William Chase. 1961. *Kansas Wild Flowers.* Lawrence: University Press of Kansas.

Stevenson, Matilda. 1915. Ethnobotany of the Zuni. Washington, D.C.: Smithsonian Institution, Bureau of American Ethnology, *30th Annual Report.*

Steyermark, Julian A. 1981 (1963). *Flora of Missouri.* Ames: Iowa State University Press.

Stimson, Anna Katherine. 1946. *Contributions towards a Bibliography of the Medicinal Use of Plants by the Indians of the United States of America.* Master's thesis, University of Pennsylvania.

Stockberger, W.W. 1915. Drug Plants under Cultivation. USDA *Farmers' Bulletin* No. 663.

Stohs, S. J., H. Rosenberg, and S. Billets. 1975. Sterols of *Yucca glauca* Tissue Cultures and Seeds. *Planta Medica* 27: 257–61.

Stoll, A., J. Renz, and A. Brack. 1950. Antibacterial Substances II. Isolation and Constitution of Echinacoside, Glycoside from the Roots of *Echinacea angustifolia. Helvetical Chim. Acta* 33: 1877–93.

Stone, Abraham. 1954. The Control of Fertility. *Scientific American* 190 (4): 31–33.

Swanton, John R. 1928. Religious Beliefs and Medical Practices of the Creek Indians. Washington, D.C.: Smithsonian Institution, Bureau of American Ethnology, *42nd Annual Report (1924–1925),* pp. 473–900.

Teborg, Dirk, and Peter Junior. 1989. Martynoside and the Novel Dimeric Open-chain Monoterpene Glucoside Digipenstroside from *Penstemon digitalis. Planta Medica* 55: 474–76.

———. 1991. Iridoid Glucosides from *Penstemon nitidus. Planta Medica* 57: 184–86.

Tehon, Leo R. 1951. The Drug Plants of Illinois. *Illinois Natural History Survey* Circular 44, 1–124.

Thwaites, Reuben Gold, editor. 1904. 6 vols. *Original Journals of the Lewis and Clark Expedition.* New York: Dodd, Mead, and Company.
———— 1905, 1906. 32 vols. *Early Western Travels.* Cleveland: Arthur Clark Company.
Vol. 5. Bradbury's Travels in the Interior of America, 1809–1811.
Vol. 10. Woods, John. Two Years Residence in the Settlement on the English Prairie (1821–1822).
Vol. 13. Nuttall's Travels into the Arkansa Territory, 1819.
Vols. 14, 15. Edwin James Account of the Steven H. Long Expedition, 1819–1820.
Vol. 23. Prince Maximilian of Wied's Travels, 1832–1834.
Tin-Wa, N., N. R. Farnsworth, and H. H. S. Fong. 1969. Biological and Phytochemical Evaluation of Plants. VI. Isolation of Kampferitrin from *Lespedeza capitata. Lloydia* 32: 509–11.
Train, Percy, James R. Henrichs, and W. Andrew Archer. 1941. Medicinal Uses of Plants by Indian Tribes of Nevada. In *American Indian Ethnohistory, California and Basin-Plateau Indians, Paiute Indians.* 1974. Vol. 4. Edited by David Agee Horr. New York: Garland Publishing.
Trease, George Edward, and William Charles Evans. 1973. *Pharmacognosy.* London: Bailliere Tindall.
Tyler, Varro E. 1981. *The Honest Herbal.* Philadelphia: George Stickley Co.

————. 1986. Plant Drugs in the Twenty-first Century. *Economic Botany* 40 (3): 279–88.
Vestal, Paul A., and Richard Evans Schultes. 1939. *The Economic Botany of the Kiowa Indians.* Cambridge, Mass.: Botanical Museum.
Voaden, D. J., and M. Jacobson. 1972. Tumor Inhibitors 3. Identification and Synthesis of an Oncolytic Hydrocarbon from American Coneflower Roots. *Journal of Medicinal Chemistry* 15 (6): 619–23.
Vogel, Virgil J. 1970. *American Indian Medicine.* Norman: University of Oklahoma Press.
Wacker, A., and A. Hilbig. 1978. Virus Inhibition by *Echinacea purpurea. Planta Medica* 33: 89–102.
Wagner, H., and A. Proksch. 1985. Immunostimulatory Drugs of Fungi and Higher Plants." Pages 113–53 in *Economic and Medicinal Plant Research.* Vol. 1. Edited by H. Wagner et al. New York: Academic Press.
Wagner, H., A. Proksche, I. Riess-Mauere, A. Vollmar, S. Odenthal, H. Stuppner, K. Jurcie, M. Le Turdu, and J. N. Fang. 1985. Immunstimulierend wirkende Polysaccharide (Heteroglykane) aus hoheren Pflanzen. *Arzneimittel-Forschung* 35(8): 1069–75.
Wakefield, E. G., and Samuel C. Dellinger. 1936. Diet of Bluff Dwellers of the Ozark Mountains and Its Skeletal Effects." *Annals of Internal*

Medicine 9: 1412–18.
Warm, J. S., W. N. Dember, and R. Parasuraman. 1990. Effects of Fragrances on Vigilance Performance and Stress. *Perfume Flavor* 15: 17–18.
Watt, Bernice K., and Annabel L. Merrill. 1963. *Composition of Foods*. USDA Agricultural Handbook no. 8.
Weaver, John Ernest, and T. J. Fitzpatrick. 1934. The Prairie. *Ecological Monographs* 4: 109–295 (reprinted by the Prairie-Plains Resource Institute, 1980, Aurora, Nebr.).
Wedel, Waldo R. 1936. *An Introduction to Pawnee Archeology*. Smithsonian Institution, Bureau of American Ethnology, Bulletin 112.
————. 1955. *Archaeological Materials from the Vicinity of Mobridge, South Dakota*. Washington, D.C.: Smithsonian Institution, Bureau of Ethnology, Bulletin 157 (Anthropology Paper 45), pp. 144–46.
Wells, Philip V. 1970. Postglacial Vegetational History of the Great Plains. *Science* 167: 1574–82.
Westbrooks, Randy G., and James W. Preacher. 1986. *Poisonous Plants of Eastern North America*. Columbia: University of South Carolina Press.
Whiting, Alfred, E. 1939. The Ethnobotany of the Hopi. Museum of Northern Arizona,

Bulletin 15, Flagstaff.
Will, Drake W. 1959. The Medical and Surgical Practice of the Lewis and Clark Expedition. *Journal of the History of Medicine* 14 (3): 273–97.
Wink, M., L. Witte, T. Hartmann, C. Theuring, and V. Volz. 1983. Accumulation of Quinolizidine Alkaloids in Plants and Cell Suspension Cultures: Genera Lupinus, Cytisus, Baptisia, Genista, Laburnum, and Sophora. *Planta Medica* 48: 253–57.
Woods, Esli Longworth. 1930. The Chemical Constitution of the Hydrocarbons of Echinacea Angustifolia. *American Journal of Pharmacy* 102: 611–30.
Wyman, Leland C., and Stewart K. Harris. 1951. *Ethnobotany of the Kayenta Navaho*. Albuquerque: University of New Mexico Press.
Youngken, Heber W. 1924. The Drugs of the North American Indian. *American Journal of Pharmacy* 96: 485–502.
————. 1925. The Drugs of the North American Indian (II). *American Journal of Pharmacy* 97: 158–185, 257–271.
Yun-choi, Hye Sook, and Jae Hoon Kim. 1990. Potential Inhibitors of Platelet Aggregation from Plant Sources, V. Anthraquinones from Seeds of *Cassia obtusifolia* and Related Compounds. *Journal of Natural Products* 53: 630–33.

Index

Astragalus canadensis, 64–67, 115
Astragalus crassicarpus, 66,
  69, 166
Astragalus gracilis, 65, 66
Astragalus mollissimus, 66–67
Astragalus racemosus, 65, 66
Astragalus species, 66, 245, 265
Astringents: alum root, 124;
  avens, 250; evening primrose,
  162; field thistle, 235; fleabane,
  97; horseweed, 237; leadplant,
  226; New Jersey tea, 232;
  smooth sumac, 187; wild indigo,
  70; wild plum, 274; wild rose,
  192; wild strawberry, 246;
  willow, 197, 198
Athlete's foot treatment: mint,
  154; snakeweed, 251
Aurones, 238
Avens, 249–50
Azulene, 20, 21

Backache treatment: beardtongue,
  267; fleabane, 97; red cedar, 132
Baldness, prevention of: dogbane,
  43; goat's rue, 285
Baneberry, 48, 266
Bannocks, use of American
  licorice, 115
Baptisia australis, 70
Baptisia bracteata, 68–71
Baptisia lactea, 69, 70
Baptisia tinctoria, 70
Bartram, William: on morning
  glory, 128; on Silphium, 201
Bearberry, 185
Beardtongue, 267–68
Beaver, 254, 275
Beebalm, 8, 29, 87, 97, 155–59,
  252, 275, 288
Beer ingredients: raspberry, 277;
  yarrow, 19
Beta-asarone, 25

Big bluestem, 3, 226–27
Bigelow, Jacob, on red cedar, 134
Birth control. See Contraceptives
Black ash, 282
Blackberry, 277, 278
Blackfeet: names for plants, 28, 37,
  42, 47, 61, 65, 119, 123, 137, 142,
  152, 156, 161, 170, 190, 195, 204,
  220, 241, 249, 261, 266, 267,
  279, 281, 287; plant use: alkali
  lily, 162; alum root, 124;
  American licorice, 115;
  aromatic sumac, 186; aster, 61;
  beardtongue, 267; beebalm, 157;
  blanket flower, 246; buffalo
  berry, 281; Canada milkvetch,
  64; chokecherry, 171;
  cottonwood, 270; cow parsnip,
  255; curly-top gumweed, 120;
  cut-leaved nightshade, 204;
  death camass, 287; dock, 279;
  gayfeather, 138; green
  milkweed, 56; horsetail, 241–
  42; locoweed, 266; mint, 153;
  prairie turnip, 177; puccoon,
  142; Rocky Mountain juniper,
  132; silverweed, 272; skeleton
  weed, 261–62; snakeweed, 251;
  soapweed, 221; sweetgrass, 256;
  torch flower, 249; white sage,
  50; wild onion, 29; wild parsley,
  260; wild rose, 191–92; wild
  strawberry, 245; willow, 196;
  windflower, 39; yarrow, 18
Black-footed ferret, 109
Black raspberry, 276
Bladder problems, treatment of:
  gayfeather, 138; rattlesnake
  master, 100; wild strawberry,
  246; willow, 197
Blankenship, J. W., on calamus, 24
Blanket flower, 246–47
Blazing star, 87, 136–40

Bleeding, plants used to arrest:
beebalm, 157; Canada
milkvetch, 66; chokecherry,
171; red cedar, 133; smooth
sumac, 185; soapweed, 221;
spikenard, 282; yarrow, 18
Blindness, treatment of with
showy milkweed, 56
Blood platelet aggregation, use of
senna for, 231
Bluebell, 266
Blue flax, 259–60
Blue grama grass, 5
Boils, treatment of: blue flax, 259;
cow parsnip, 254; white sage, 50
Boneset, 103–7, 212, 216
Botulism, treatment of with
purple coneflower, 91
Bouteloua gracilis, 5
Bouteloua hirsuta, 5
Bowel problems, treatment of:
black raspberry, 276; fragrant
everlasting, 250; horseweed,
326; New Jersey tea, 232; sweet
sand verbena, 224; western
ragweed, 34; wild
strawberry, 246
Bradbury, John: on milkvetch, 66;
on western wallflower, 244
Breast milk. *See* Lactation
British Pharmacopoeia, 116
Bronchitis treatment: curly-top
gumweed, 120; dogbane, 44;
horseweed, 237; rattlesnake
master, 101
Buchloë dactyloides, 5
Buffalo, 49, 77, 97, 119, 132, 201,
225, 236, 257, 269
Buffalo berry, 281
Buffalo bur, 205
Buffalo currant, 276
Buffalo gourd, 75–79, 128
Buffalo grass, 5

Burns, treatment of: compass
plant, 202; death camass, 288;
sawtooth sunflower, 254;
velvety gaura, 248; western
snowberry, 284; wild rose, 191;
yellow-spined thistle, 234
Bur oak, 110
Bursitis, treatment of with
dogbane, 44
Bush morning glory, 126–29
Buttercup, 252
Butterflies, 58–59
Butterfly milkweed, 53–59

Calamus, 22–26, 55, 241, 282
Callirhoe involucrata, 229–30
Camass, 288
Camassia species, 288
Camphor, 20
Canada milkvetch, 64–67, 115
Canada plum, 274
Cancer treatment: alum root, 124;
curly-top gumweed, 120; goat's
rue, 285; milkweed, 58; purple
coneflower, 90, 92
Carbenoxolone, 116
Carbuncle, 29
Cardiac glycosides, 44, 58
Cardinal flower, 146, 148
Carminative. *See* Flatulence
Carver, J., on prickly ash, 286
Cassia angustifolia, 231
Cassia marilandica, 230–31
Cassia obtusifolia, 231
Cataracts, 39, 191
Cathartic. *See* Purgative
Cattail, 244
Ceanothus americanus, 231–32
Ceanothus herbaceous, 232
Ceanothus velutinous, 232
Ceremony, plants used in:
butterfly milkweed, 55; lobelia,
147, 148; puccoon, 142; prairie

Diabetes, treatment of: fleabane, 97; yellow-spined thistle, 235
Diaphoresis, plants used for: beebalm, 158, 159; boneset, 105, 106; butterfly milkweed, 57; compass plant, 202; flowering spurge, 111; goat's rue, 285; horseweed, 237; prickly poppy, 229; rattlesnake master, 101; sage, 51; Texas croton, 74; vervain, 212, 213; wild onion, 30; yarrow, 20
Diarrhea, treatment of: alum root, 124; American licorice, 114; beebalm, 158; blackberry, 277; butterfly milkweed, 57; chokecherry, 171; cinquefoil, 272; cottonwood, 270; cow parsnip, 255; cut-leaved nightshade, 204; dock, 278, 279; dwarf milkweed, 56; fetid marigold, 241; flowering spurge, 111; fragrant everlasting, 250; gayfeather, 138; horsetail, 242; horseweed, 236; puccoon, 143; purple prairie clover, 82; ragweed, 34; skeleton weed, 261; smooth sumac, 184, 186, 187; wild cranesbill, 82; wild plum, 274; wild rose, 191; wild strawberry, 245; willow, 196
Diuretics: aromatic sumac, 185; beardtongue, 267; beebalm, 158; compass plant, 202; dogbane, 43; evening primrose, 162; false gromwell, 265; field thistle, 235; fleabane, 97; gayfeather, 139; horsetail, 241, 242; horseweed, 237; milkweed, 57; morning glory, 128; mountain mint, 275; prickly poppy, 229; rattlesnake master, 101; rattlesnake root, 273; red cedar, 134; round-head

lespedeza, 257; sage, 51; Texas croton, 73; vervain, 212; wild currant, 276; wild onion, 30; wild rose, 192; yarrow, 18
Dock, 278–79
Doctrine of Signatures, 8, 56, 77, 110, 262, 273
Dogbane, 41–45, 283
Dogwood, 187
Downy gentian, 248–49
Drums, 195
Dugaldia hoopesii, 177
Dunbar, John: on prickly poppy, 229; on yarrow, 18
Dwarf juniper, 133–34
Dyes: prickly poppy, 229; puccoon, 142–43; smooth sumac, 184, 186; wild begonia, 278; willow, 195
Dysentery, treatment of: blackberry, 277; buffalo berry, 282; chokecherry, 171; cinquefoil, 272; fragrant everlasting, 250; nine-anther prairie clover, 82; ragweed, 34; spurge, 110, 111; sumac, 186, 187; white wild indigo, 70; wild rose, 192; willow, 196, 197
Dyssodia pappaosa, 120, 240–41

Eagle, 261, 267
Ear problems, treatment of: American licorice, 115; aster, 62; locoweed, 8, 266; prairie turnip, 177; sand lily, 263; Seneca snakeroot, 166; wild onion, 29; yarrow, 18
Eastern red cedar, 130–35
Echinacea angustifolia, 8, 84–94, 245, 263, 264
Echinacea pallida, 86, 87, 91, 92, 93, 110, 283
Echinacea paradoxa, 93

cottonwood, 270–71; on lobelia, 148; on pasque flower, 38–39; on prairie clovers, 82; on prickly ash, 286; on purple coneflower, 86, 88; on scarlet globe mallow, 208; on smooth sumac, 184; on thyme-leafed spurge, 110; on wild rhubarb, 279

Ginseng, 55, 148, 248, 279

Glucosides, 129, 173, 213, 228, 231, 235, 240

Glycosides, 40, 44, 51, 58, 78, 106, 116, 193, 197, 239, 243, 249, 250, 253, 259, 268

Glycyrrhiza glabra, 115–17

Glycyrrhiza lepidota, 66, 113–17

Glycyrrhizin, 115, 116

Gnapthalium obtusifolium, 250–51

Golden alexanders, 97, 288–89

Golden aster, 233

Goldenrod, 286

Gold thread, 277

Gonorrhea, treatment of: blackberry, 277; boneset, 105; curly-top gumweed, 120; gayfeather, 138; lobelia, 148; prickly ash, 286, 287; ragweed, 34; rattlesnake master, 101; smooth sumac, 187; Texas croton, 74; wavy-leafed thistle, 234

Gooseberry, 275, 276

Gosiutes, 288

Grindelia robusta, 120–21

Grindelia squarrosa, 118–21, 241

Grinnell, George Bird, on wild buckwheat, 243

Grizzly bear, 174

Ground cherry, 7, 268–70

Groundplum milkvetch, 66, 69, 166

Gros Ventres: names for plants,

54, 152; plant use: chokecherry, 171; curly-top gumweed, 120; mint, 153; red cedar, 133; sage, 50; yarrow, 18

Gum inflammation and disease, treatment of: cinquefoil, 272; willow, 197

Gutierrezia sarothrae, 251–52

Gymnocladus dioica, 77

Hair loss preventative, soapweed as, 221

Hairy grama grass, 5

Harmalol, 44

Harmol, 282

Hart, Jeffrey: on Rocky Mountain juniper, 133; on white sage, 48–49; on willow, 196

Havard, Valery, on cottonwood, 270

Hayden, Dr. Ferdinand V.: on lobelia, 147; on purple coneflower, 88

Hay fever treatment with willow, 197

Headache, treatment of: aster, 62; beebalm, 158; cow parsnip, 255; dogbane, 44; false solomon's seal, 283; fetid marigold, 240, 241; fleabane, 97; gayfeather, 139; golden alexanders, 289; ground cherry, 269; lemon scurfpea, 177; mint, 153; nineanther prairie clover, 82; prairie coneflower, 181; sneezeweed, 252; western wallflower, 245; white sage, 49; wild onion, 29; willow, 196, 197

Heartburn, treatment of: cottonwood, 270; sage, 50; skeleton weed, 262

Heart problems, treatment of: buffalo berry, 282; dogbane, 44;

Lakotas, *continued*
240–41; gayfeather, 138; green
milkweed, 56; ground cherry,
269; horseweed, 236; lead plant,
7, 226; milkvetch, 66; mint,
153; mountain mint, 275;
narrow-leafed milkweed, 56;
false gromwell, 265; fleabane,
97; Plains coreopsis, 237–38;
prairie clover, 82; prairie
coneflower, 180–81; puccoon,
143; purple coneflower, 86, 88;
purple poppy mallow, 230;
ragweed, 34; red cedar, 132; sage
brush, 48; scarlet gaura, 248;
skeletonweed, 261; snakeweed,
251; snow-on-the-mountain,
110; soapweed, 221; swamp
milkweed, 55–56; sweetgrass,
256; Texas croton, 73; western
wallflower, 244; white sage, 48;
whorled milkweed, 56; wild
alfalfa, 177–78; wild buckwheat,
243; wild four-o'clock, 264;
wild rhubarb, 278
Lameness, treatment with
fleabane, 97
Large beardtongue, 267
Larkspur, 238–39
Laryngitis, treatment of:
gayfeather, 138; rattlesnake
master, 101
Lavender hyssop, 224–25
Laxatives: buffalo berry, 281;
buffalo gourd, 78; cinquefoil,
272; Culver's root, 162, 217;
dogbane, 43; dock, 279; evening
primrose, 162; blue flax, 259;
flowering spurge, 110; goat's rue,
285; sage, 51; soapweed, 221;
sweet sand verbena, 224; wild
currant, 275; wild onion, 30;
wild rose, 192

Leadplant, 7, 225–26, 236, 257
Leptandrin, 217
Lespedeza capitata, 7, 225, 257–58
Leukemia, treatment of: goat's
rue, 285; purple coneflower, 92;
scurfpea, 178
Lewis and Clark Expedition, 148,
172, 177
Liatris aspera, 77, 137, 138
Liatris punctata, 136–40
Liatris pycnostachya, 138, 140
Liatris spicata, 139
Licorice, 113–17
Lilium canadense, 258
Lilium philadelphicum, 258–59
Limonene, 35, 159
Linoleic acid, 163
Linum perenne, 259–60
Linum usitatissimum, 259
Lithospermum arvense, 145
Lithospermum carolinense, 142
Lithospermum incisum, 141–45
Lithospermum ruderale, 143–44
Lithospermum species, 8, 143
Little bluestem, 5, 227
Liver problems, treatment of:
curly-top gumweed, 120;
morning glory, 128; pussy-
toes, 228
Lloyd, Curtis Gates, on purple
coneflower, 88–89
Lloyd, John Uri, on dogbane, 43
Lobelia, 146–50, 212, 260
Lobelia cardinalis, 147, 148,
150, 260
Lobelia inflata, 146–50
Lobelia siphilitica, 147, 148
Lobeline, 149
Locoweed, 8, 65–67, 265–67
Lomatium dissectum, 260
Lomatium foeniculaceum, 148,
260–61
Lomatium triteratum, 261

Puffball spores, 87
Purgatives: beardtongue, 267;
   boneset, 106; buffalo gourd, 78;
   chokecherry, 171; Culver's root,
   216, 217; death camass, 288;
   dogbane, 43; lobelia, 149;
   morning glory, 128; prairie
   clover, 82; prickly poppy, 229;
   scurfpea, 178; senna, 231;
   spurge, 110, 111; Texas croton,
   73, 74; wild indigo, 70
Purple coneflower, 8, 84–94, 110,
   245, 263, 264, 283
Purple poppy mallow, 229–30
Pursh, Frederick, on boneset,
   105–6
Pussy-toes, 227–28
Pycnanthemum virginianum,
   274–75
Pyrrolizidine alkaloids, 107, 144

Quercus alba, 82
Quercus macrocarpa, 110
Querticin, 121
Quincula lobata, 269
Quinine, 197, 217

Rabies, treatment of: nightshade,
   205; prickly poppy, 229; purple
   coneflower, 86; scarlet globe
   mallow, 209; skullcap, 280; wild
   currant, 276; rabbit brush,
   233–34
Rafinesque, Constantine: on aster,
   63; on beebalm, 158; on
   blackberry, 277; on chokecherry,
   172–73; on Culver's root, 216;
   on dogbane, 43; on evening
   primrose, 162; on golden
   alexanders, 289; on lobelia, 148;
   on prickly ash, 286–87; on
   raspberry, 277; on sage, 51; on

skullcap, 280; on sneezeweed,
   253; on sumac, 186–87; on
   vervain, 212; on wild currant,
   276; on wild onion, 30; on wild
   rose, 192; on wild strawberry,
   246; on willow, 197; on
   yarrow, 19
Ragweed, 11, 32–35
Ranunculus flabellaris, 252
Rashes, treatment with green
   milkweed, 56
Raspberry, 191
Ratibida columnifera, 179–81
Rattlesnake master, 99–102
Rattlesnake root, 272–73
Red cedar, 11, 130–35
Red Cloud, 132
Red false mallow, 171
Red willow dogwood, 184, 185
Respiratory problems, treatment
   of: beebalm, 158; white sage, 50
Revival of consciousness, plants
   used for: aster, 62; beebalm,
   158; bush morning glory, 127;
   Culver's root, 216; false
   solomon's seal, 283; fragrant
   everlasting, 250
Rheumatism, treatment of: alum
   root, 124; boneset, 105; buffalo
   gourd, 78; cup plant, 201; death
   camass, 288; dogbane, 44;
   fleabane, 97; flowering spurge,
   110; leadplant, 226; nine-anther
   prairie clover, 82; pasque flower,
   38, 39; prickly ash, 287;
   puccoon, 143; purple
   coneflower, 87; Rocky Mountain
   juniper, 132; round-head
   lespedeza, 7, 257; sand lily, 263;
   scarlet gaura, 248; snakeroot,
   252; sumac, 186, 187;
   willow, 196
Rhus aromatica, 183, 184, 185, 186

335

Shoshones, plant use: blue flax, 259; curly-top gumweed, 120; death camass, 287; mountain balm, 232; wild currant, 275
Shrubby cinquefoil, 271–72
Silphium laciniatum, 199–202
Silphium perfoliatum, 201–2
Silver-leafed scurfpea, 176, 177
Silverweed, 272
Sioux, 157, 166, 171, 226. *See also* Dakotas; Lakotas
Skeleton weed, 261–62
Skin afflictions, treatment of: beardtongue, 268; beebalm, 157; blanket flower, 246; butterfly milkweed, 57; curly-top gumweed, 120; dock, 279; evening primrose, 163; scarlet globe mallow, 209; snakeweed, 251; willow, 197
Skullcap, 279–81
Skunk oil, 87
Smallpox, treatment of: aromatic sumac, 186; purple coneflower, 87; rabbit brush, 233; sand lily, 263
Small soapweed, 219–23
Smilacina racemosa, 282
Smilacina stellata, 282–83
Smith, Huron: on beebalm, 158; on butterfly milkweed, 55; on horseweed, 237; on white wild indigo, 70
Smoke treatment, plants used in: aster, 62; bush morning glory, 127; cup plant, 201; false solomon's seal, 282; fragrant everlasting, 250; gayfeather, 138; purple poppy mallow, 230; rabbit brush, 234; red cedar, 131; soapweed, 221; wild onion, 29
Smoking, plants used for:

aromatic sumac, 185; leadplant, 226; pussy-toes, 228; smooth sumac, 182, 184, 185, 187
Smooth sumac, 182–88
Snakebite, treatment of: beardtongue, 267; boneset, 105; Culver's root, 216; death camass, 288; gayfeather, 139; gentian, 248; New Jersey tea, 232; prairie coneflower, 181; purple coneflower, 86, 87, 88, 89, 90, 91; pussy-toes, 228; rattlesnake master, 101; Seneca snakeroot, 165, 167; snakeroot, 242; sunflower, 254; tarweed, 262; Texas croton, 73; whorled milkweed, 56–57
Snakeweed, 251–52
Sneezeweed, 97, 177, 252–53
Snowblindness, treatment of: showy milkweed, 56; wild rose, 191
Snow-on-the-mountain, 8, 109, 110
Soapweed, 219–23
Solanine, 205, 269
Solanum carolinense, 205
Solanum elaeagnifolium, 205
Solanum nigrum, 204, 205
Solanum rostratum, 205
Solanum triflorum, 203–6
Solidago canadensis, 286
Solomon's seal, 282
Sore throat, treatment of: blackberry, 277; blue flax, 259; boneset, 105; chokecherry, 171; cinquefoil, 272; false solomon's seal, 283; gayfeather, 139; green milkweed, 56; locoweed, 266; prairie turnip, 177; prairie clover, 82; prickly ash, 286; purple coneflower, 88; scarlet globe mallow, 209; Seneca

Vomiting, plants used to arrest: beardtongue, 267; beebalm, 158; buffalo bur, 205; cup plant, 201; fetid marigold, 241; mint, 152, 153, 154; ragweed, 34; Rocky Mountain juniper, 132; vervain, 212; wild onion, 29; wild plum, 274. *See also* Emesis

Wart removal, 187, 255
Wavy-leafed thistle, 234–35
Western ragweed, 33, 34
Western snowberry, 283–84
Western wallflower, 243–45
White milkwort, 165
White oak, 82
White sage, 7, 46–52
Whooping cough, treatment of with snakeweed, 251
Wichitas, 279
Wild alfalfa, 7, 175–78
Wild anise, 269
Wild begonia, 278–79
Wild black cherry, 171–72
Wild black currant, 275–76
Wild buckwheat, 242–43
Wild columbine, 148
Wild cranesbill, 82
Wild four-o'clock, 263–64
Wild ginger, 87
Wild indigo, 68–71
Wild licorice, 66
Wild lily, 258–59
Wild onion, 27–31, 288
Wild parsley, 148, 260–61
Wild plum, 273–74
Wild rhubarb, 279
Wild rose, 166, 189–93, 284
Willow, 171, 194–98

Windflower, 37, 39, 41
Winnebagos: names for plants, 17, 23, 28, 47, 194; plant use: beebalm, 157; Culver's root, 216; cup plant, 201; downy gentian, 248; prickly ash, 286; purple coneflower, 87; Seneca snakeroot, 165; wild currant, 275; wild onion, 29; wormwood, 51; yarrow, 18
Woods, John: on gentian, 248; on sumac, 248
Worms. *See* Anthelmintics
Wounds. *See* Sores

Xanthyletin, 287

Yarrow, 8, 17–21
Yellow wild indigo, 68–71
Yellow-spined thistle, 74, 234
Yucca glauca, 8, 219–23
Yucca schottii, 222

Zanthoxylum americanum, 285–87
Zigadenus elegans, 288
Zigadenus nuttallii, 288
Zigadenus venenosus, 287–88
Zizia aurea, 97, 288–89
Zunis, plant use: American licorice, 115; annual bursage, 34; aster, 62; buffalo bur, 205; buffalo gourd, 78; curly-top gumweed, 120; sand lily, 263; snakeroot, 252; sunflower, 254; Texas croton, 73–74; western wallflower, 245; wild buckwheat, 242, 243; yellow-spined thistle, 234